Playing for Their Lives

PLAYING FOR THEIR LIVES

Helping Troubled Children Through Play Therapy

Dorothy G. Singer

THE FREE PRESS
A Division of Macmillan, Inc.
New York

Maxwell Macmillan Canada
Toronto

The Free Press
A Division of Macmillan, Inc.
866 Third Avenue, New York, N.Y. 10022

Maxwell Macmillan Canada, Inc.
1200 Eglinton Avenue East
Suite 200
Don Mills, Ontario M3C 3N1

Macmillan, Inc. is part of the Maxwell Communication
Group of Companies.

Printed in the United States of America

printing number
1   2   3   4   5   6   7   8   9   10

Library of Congress Cataloging-in-Publication Data

Singer, Dorothy G.
    Playing for their lives : helping troubled children through play
therapy / Dorothy G. Singer.
        p.   cm.
    Includes bibliographical references and index.
    ISBN 0-02-928903-3
    1. Play therapy.   2. Problem children—Behavior modification.
I. Title.
RJ505.P6S55   1993
618.92'891653—dc20   92-38390
                                                                CIP

TO JERRY
WITH RESPECT, APPRECIATION, AND LOVE

CONTENTS

CONTENTS

PREFACE

Children, even in the best of homes, must struggle with all the tasks of childhood: there are so many things to learn about the large, confusing world of grown-ups. The children who have come to see me for help over the years have been those who not only had to deal with the normal growth processes involved in cognitive, social, and emotional development but also had pressures imposed on them by forces they could not control: parental illness; family financial stresses; the emotional disturbances of adults; adults' inadequate parenting skills; and neglect that was psychological and sometimes even physical.

In this book, I wanted to share with readers my attempts to help troubled children to find some solace and to gain some competencies and inner strengths. I suffered with them as they faced unbearable problems. Sometimes, I felt as angry as they did about their circumstances, but I could not let this anger to immobilize me. Instead, I had to use it as a motivation to think more diligently about how I could help alleviate these children's distress.

In this book, I hoped to show how, through the work of play therapy, the process of healing can take place and what are the limitations of therapy with children, who are truly pawns in the hands of their adult caregivers. I hope, too, that the reader will recognize my silent screams when a parent thwarted a child's progress and will also share in the sweetness of the mending process and the beginnings of individuality and autonomy.

Many parents ask, "What is play therapy?" "How is it different

from just playing?" "How can children become better by playing?"
Jean Piaget, the noted Swiss psychologist, believed that play could
heal through its compensating and cathartic characteristics. For example, through play, a preschooler can compensate for the loss of a
pet by "curing" the animal and restoring it to life. The child plays
this game many times in trying to understand the meaning of death.
Each time she reenacts the event, her anxiety lessens and the pet
becomes increasingly a memory in a broader context subject to the
child's own control. A child may feel better after expressing anger
at a doll and even spanking it or sending it off to bed with no supper;
in this way, the child may be able to handle anger that he or she
cannot express openly to a sibling or even to a parent. Piaget believed
that through the use of symbols, children could "liquidate a disa-
greeable situation by reliving it in make-believe." Thus, forbidden
actions may be carried out in make-believe games and fears may
be neutralized by doing "in play what one would not dare do in
reality."

Over the years, children have labeled my playroom a "safe
room," "the smiling room," the "happy-sad room," and even "Pee
Wee's Playhouse." In the playroom, a child's "sacred space," I have
tried to offer troubled children an opportunity to heal; to become
more integrated, more self-actualizing, and more positive in their
self-images; and to play with joyful abandon. To do this, I listen
carefully to the children's fears, complaints, and sorrows and to
their shouts of triumph, their expressions of excitement about
new accomplishments and their emerging proclamations of love of
themselves, their siblings, and their parents. I respond empathically
and reflect, when appropriate, on the children's behavior and emotions as they converse with me or play, paint, draw, and build. I
offer limits, structure, and information when necessary, to help children learn how to control negative behavior that has been damaging
to themselves and to others. I try to help them learn new approaches
so they can adapt to home and school demands more constructively.

In general, I draw on a variety of therapeutic methods, depending
on the age, the intelligence, the capacity for insight, and the respon-
siveness of the child. The playroom is carefully planned to house a
variety of materials, but not all are on display because I don't want
the children distracted by too much stimulation. My methods
include:

Traditional play techniques, using the dollhouse, dress-up clothes, puppets, water play, arts-and-crafts materials, board games, and music
Modeling behavior through role playing, in which the child and I take turns becoming, for example, a sibling, a parent, or a teacher so that the child can learn more appropriate responses to conflict
Imagery techniques without the use of props that encourage the child to picture people, events, moods, conflicts, and resolutions
Behavior modification, which reinforces a child's positive behavior with external symbols, such as a star or a sticker, and which ultimately leads to self-reward and intrinsic satisfaction.

The key elements that distinguish play therapy from "playing around" are the therapist's interpretations of symbolic play in words the child is ready to accept and understand; the offering of new ways to control and handle fears, anxieties, and negative emotions; and the teaching and modeling of adaptive skills that will enable a child to cope with an ego-threatening home or school situation and to increase his or her capacity for daily problem solving. Through symbolic play, children cast their conflicts, fears, unresolved wishes, and concern about their parents or siblings into miniaturized form in order to confront their own anger, distress, sadness, shame, guilt, and humiliation.

The skilled therapist is, in effect, a substitute for the absent, inadequate, or troubled parent. This key figure, however, must be careful not to usurp the role of parent and, instead, to help the child identify those features in a complex, confusing world that need special attention. The therapist provides approval of a child's play efforts to assimilate material that is disturbing, teaches imaginative skills to help solve problems, makes major life issues more concrete, and uncovers significant people and conflicts in the child's life. New ideas and scripts or plans are developed to help reduce anxiety, ambiguity, confusion, fear, and terrors. For example, a four-year-old I worked with had a fear of airplanes and airports in addition to other fears. He was unable to sleep after a flight with his parents and had regressed in his behavior. He had been bewildered by the enormity of the buildings, the hustle and bustle of the crowds through the corridors, and the roar of the airplanes' engines as they took off and landed. His play consisted of a continuous reenactment of the airport scene, in which he used miniature airplanes, plastic people, and blocks to create his airport. By playing this game repeatedly, he was able to master his confusion and anxiety about his frightening experience.

Through play, a child becomes more flexible, more empathic, and more capable of sharing, taking turns, and delaying gratification of needs; the child also learns to express feelings in words, increasing her or his vocabulary in the process: think of all the new words a child needs to play "knights," or the words that may enrich a game of "space"!

As it is essential that the child's parents be involved in the therapeutic process, I have monthly sessions with them and keep in touch with them by telephone, when necessary. One of my major frustrations, however, is my inability to engage some of the parents in the process of healing their child. Sometimes, parents are unresponsive to my suggestions, defensive about their treatment of their children, or guarded in revealing their own personality or emotional makeup. In some cases, a parent is simply unavailable because of divorce and residence in another state; in others, marital problems keep a couple from viewing their child objectively, as a separate person with her or his own needs for love and support.

Often, I feel like a detective, trying to put the pieces of an emotional puzzle together. I may find gaps in information and wonder why the parents aren't more informative, or they may even distort facts in order to present themselves in a more favorable light. In addition, a child's perception of the events that transpire in a household is often quite different from a parent's perception of those same events. Nevertheless, I work with each child as best I can. Generally, the children are willing partners in the therapeutic process. Even when a child resists help initially, trust develops and as time passes, the child gradually becomes more receptive to the possibility of change and growth.

The school is another partner in the healing process, and I visit the schools to observe the children in this milieu. Conferences with teachers and principals give me further insight into the children's cognitive processes and social adjustment. I have found teachers open to my suggestions, and I see them as important adjuncts in my work.

The therapist, I must stress, acts *not* as a parent but as a role model for the child, by offering structure, support, and a willingness to share thoughts through play. As a therapist, I try to be more objective than usually is possible for a parent. I also interpret children's comments in order to help them feel comfortable about saying things that they fear would lead to distress or to reprisal on the part of the parents. The children can reconsider their own remarks in the context of my interpretations and gradually reshape them without the expected recrimination from parents. If, for example, a child is pounding a mother doll and says "I hate you," I can help the child explore these feelings, try to find the basis for such anger, and offer different ways in which the issue may be resolved. I can also work with parents to help them understand their child's point of view. The therapist maintains a curiosity, a lively imagination, and a sense of wonder and humor and opens the way for troubled children to see possibilities other than those that confront them.

The cases I chose for this book are drawn from my files and illustrate the various methods that I have used to foster change and growth in troubled children. These six cases are, I believe, typical of the referrals to child therapists in our society; a child experiencing bereavement; an aggressive child of drug-addicted parents; a child who has been sexually abused; a child with an attention-deficit hyperactivity disorder; a depressed child in the midst of a parental divorce; and an enuretic child involved in a fierce sibling rivalry. The actual cases have of course been disguised in this text.

Writing this book has been rather disquieting. It revived in me memories of these six children: my own joys at their triumphs, my own frustrations when I could not alter events in their lives at home, my many self-searching thoughts about the steps I took in each child's treatment, and those exhilarating times when I knew I had made a difference in their lives.

I hope this book will be enlightening to parents, child therapists, students, and teachers. I learn much from my small patients, and to all of them I offer my thanks. I dare to hope that, as they grow up, somewhere in the corners of their memory they, too, may recall and appreciate the time they spent with the "play lady."

ACKNOWLEDGMENTS

I want first of all to thank the children who were my clients. I feel privileged that they trusted and confided in me; I feel that my life has been enriched by the opportunity to play a part in their psychological growth.

I also want to thank Susan Arellano of The Free Press for her astute comments, and for her conversations with me about the issues raised in each chapter. Her editorial input helped me considerably, as did the careful attention of editing supervisor Edith Lewis and copy editor Margaret Ritchie. Finally, I appreciate, as I have so many times in the past, the excellent word processing skills of Virginia Hurd. She ensured that the mechanics of the preparation of the manuscript could be smooth and comfortable for me.

CHAPTER ONE

~~~~~~~~~~~~~~~~~~~~~~~~~~~~~~~~~~~~

LOIS, THE PRINCESS IN THE TOWER

The Effect of a Parent's Death on a Child

The Mother

The mother came for her first visit on December 2. She died on October 5 of the following year. Although it was early December and an icy-cold day, on her first visit she wore no coat, but a heavy black sweater, a long gray skirt, and a black jersey turban hiding her thin wisps of hair. She reminded me of old Gloria Swanson photos taken when this kind of headgear was fashionable.

Jean Melton had called the week before, referred by a colleague of mine. She was forty-one years old, slim and of medium height, with piercing gray eyes. She examined my face and in a tormented voice asked, "Can I entrust my child to you? Will you help her handle her fears, her worries? How will we cope?" A flood of tears followed.

When Jean appeared calmer, I asked her to give me some facts.

She had a rare form of leukemia and the prognosis was not good, but Jean was determined to live: " 'Do not go gentle into that good night.' I say these words by Dylan Thomas over and over—my private prayer. Do you know the poem?" I nodded. "I read these words and I rage and rage. I'm prepared to undergo all kinds of treatment. I can't leave Lois. She's too young to be without a mother—it's unfair."

Gradually, the story unfolded. Jean seemed to be reciting from memory, as if she had rehearsed her personal history in advance so that nothing would be omitted. From time to time as she spoke, she would hesitate, turn away, and stare at the floor or at the wall, trying to recall some detail. It was important to her that I understand her background and the urgency of her situation and of her child's need for therapy.

Jean had divorced her husband, Ron, four years before, when Lois, the only child of that marriage, was four. Jean had been awarded physical custody of Lois, but both parents had been granted legal custody. Ron Melton had holiday visitations at Easter, Thanksgiving, and Christmas, and each parent had Lois for one month of the summer vacation. It was clear that Jean resented any contact between father and daughter, and during the initial session with me, she spoke of Ron in completely negative terms. He had recently remarried and was now the stepfather of two daughters, aged eleven and nine, his second wife's children from a previous marriage.

Jean continued, "After Lois was born, things seemed all right—at least until she was two. Then Ron started to drink, and life was hell. He had been an alcoholic years ago, but when we married, he had been abstinent, and I had no reason to believe that he would give up his sobriety. Lois witnessed terrible fights between us, was harshly disciplined by her father, and often saw him push me, strike me, and abuse me verbally.

"I remember one vivid scene when Lois was almost three. We were in the kitchen about to have dinner. Lois was at the table seated on her booster, and I was at the kitchen sink preparing the salad. When Ron came in, he spotted the soup on the stove bubbling. Before he or I could get to it, it boiled over, making a green pea trail on the stove, running down the oven door, and ending in a mess on the floor. Ron exploded: "Can't you get anything right?" He grabbed my arm and hurled me against the tile wall. Lois was now screaming, and I was terrified. Ron was like a madman, completely out of control, because I had simply forgotten to turn the burner down. Sometimes I do daydream, and I'm not thoroughly efficient. Things like that upset Ron—meticulous, exacting, practical Ron. No wonder he's an accountant! I think he had been drinking. He was under a lot of pressure at work, and since I had stopped working when Lois was born, we had always seemed pressed for money. I often wanted to leave but didn't have the courage or the resources. I also suspected that Ron was involved with Susan, the woman he later married, but Ron denied this whenever I mentioned it.

"Eventually we separated, and soon after the separation, I decided to go back to school. I had been a paralegal before our marriage and had continued doing this work until Lois was born. We had thought we could manage on one salary, and until the drinking and Susan, we seemed to. Later, with financial help and encouragement from my sister, I was able to begin divorce proceedings. At the same time, I applied to law school and decided to fulfill a dream of mine."

Jean paused and stood up. She asked for some water and, gulping it, asked for more. Because her voice had become hoarse, and it was clear that she was getting tired, I suggested that we take a break. But Jean wanted to continue—we could not afford the luxury of wasting time:

"We had lived in Pennsylvania during our marriage, but after the divorce—it took almost a year—I took Lois to Connecticut where we lived with my sister and I took courses and later attended law school. Last June, I completed my degree, and in July, my world caved in: the cancer was discovered. There had been moments of extreme fatigue, dizzy spells, and feelings of nausea, but I had thought all these symptoms were related to the stress of the divorce, law school, and trying to raise my child alone, so I put off going for a checkup until my days and nights had become unbearable. I've undergone treatment of every variety. I'm almost completely bald. I'm tired all the time. And yet I'm determined to fight. I've heard of a new treatment at a hospital in Texas and plan to explore my options."

Jean was a highly intelligent, strong woman, but facing tremendous difficulties, physical, financial, and most pressing now, psychological. She was consumed with worry about her daughter's future, adamant about wanting Lois to remain with her sister if she should die, and yet aware that Ron would be granted custody of Lois because he was her biological parent and, in the eyes of the law, her rightful guardian. Jean was also filled with guilt about her "mothering role" during the past three years while she had attended law school.

As Jean told me all of this, I made notes, listened, and observed her closely. Her hands never stopped moving, accenting her words, expressing her pain, her anger, and her bewilderment. Her weeping under control, she spoke quickly, as if there would not be enough time to tell me everything about her experiences over the years. I tried to get her to focus on Lois, to tell me about the child: what she thought Lois knew about the illness, whether Lois was aware of Jean's negative feelings toward Ron, and what Lois's feelings were about him.

Jean was forthright: "I've told Lois I hate her father. I know that's wrong, and I try not to express it, but why should he live and have her and why—why—should I die? It's not fair! I know I sound bitter. I try not to be but I am, I am." Jean looked at me imploringly. "How can I tell my child that I might die? How can I tell her that she will live with Ron and his new family? How do I do this? It will shatter both of us. Is there a right way to tell her?"

I told Jean that I would try to help Lois deal with her feelings through our play, but that, at some point, if her death was inevitable, Jean must tell Lois herself. Jean nodded assent and went on to express concern about leaving a more favorable memory of herself. She felt that her time in law school had robbed Lois of a positive image of her as a mother and that she now had too little time to make up for the past three years of Lois's life.

During our first session. I obtained a history of Lois from Jean. Lois had been a full-term baby with a normal delivery. She had walked and talked within the usual period and had been a "good" baby until the marriage became more disruptive and fragile. Jean told me that Lois was a bright eight-year-old who was not happy at school, although she adored her teacher. She had no close friends, was teased at school constantly, was called a crybaby and was now "worrying" about her mother. Although Lois said she "hated her father," she spent summers with him and, during the year, saw him on the prescribed holidays for extended visits. According to Jean,

Lois was now an A student and loved to read, write, and play imaginative games. She was in third grade and seemed to be getting along with some of the children, but others still teased her. One child, teasing her about Jean's baldness, had told Lois that it was contagious and that Lois and everyone who played with her would get bald. After Jean had met with the school principal and the third-grade teachers concerning that incident, Lois's teacher had carried on a discussion in class about various diseases, including cancer and the fact that it's not contagious. With materials from the American Cancer Society, the teacher was able to handle this issue in an informed and intelligent manner.

Jean went on: "Lois is clingy lately and wants to stay in my bed at night. She seems babyish at times and often says to me, 'Don't go bye-bye.' I know she senses that I'm quite ill—I have given her *some* information. I haven't had the courage to tell her exactly what the circumstances are. Look, she must know 'bye-bye' means 'die,' doesn't she? Help me—help me—help me to tell her."

Our first meeting ended with some suggestions concerning how Jean might prepare Lois for her visit with me. I told Jean to tell Lois that I was a person who listened to children and who tried to help them with their problems. We would play games; we would talk; we would share feelings. Jean left, and I felt somewhat relieved that she had taken the first step in coming to grips with her possible death. She was willing to entrust Lois to another adult and to allow Lois to express her deepest fears, and I knew that one goal was to enable Jean and Lois to share their feelings and accept the reality of Jean's illness and fate.

I felt humbled by Jean's request. She was demanding a great deal of me and I could not disappoint her. But how does anyone prepare a child for the death of a parent? This lovely woman was seriously ill just at a point in life when she was ready to launch a career in law. I tried to put myself in her place, but it was too frightening for me to contemplate. It was important for me to focus my energies on helping Lois. I was eager to meet her and apprehensive as well.

After Jean's first session with me, she telephoned and expressed concern about Lois's Thanksgiving visit with her father: Lois had come home rather mournful, and Jean could not get Lois to share her feelings. My first meeting with Lois would take place in mid-

December, and Jean hoped I would be able to find out what was troubling Lois, who seemed clingy, depressed, and anxious. Jean was also apprehensive about the coming Christmas holidays and wondered whether she should send Lois to Pennsylvania to visit Ron. After our first session, Jean had called Ron to tell him about the seriousness of her illness and had begged him not to discuss it with Lois over Christmas.

During my second session with Jean, approximately one month later (and after my first contact with Lois), she described her law school years in Connecticut: "They were good and bad—good because I was using my brain at full speed. I thought it had atrophied during my seven years of marriage. I found the professors, students, and readings stimulating, but I was consumed by my eagerness to do well. Lois was so young when I started school; she was in kindergarten and miserable. If I had classes or library work, a sitter picked her up. My sister worked full time as an architect, and eventually, I had to get my own small apartment; there was just too much tension between us. I was in debt to her and to the bank. Ron's support checks for Lois were always late. I struggled with finances continuously and hated this aspect of myself. I became a Class A worrier. I was a physical wreck: no sleep, no time for vacation or recreation, no sex! I was short-tempered with Lois—she'll tell you herself; she called me 'picky-picky.' Lois became even more clingy, demanding every minute of my time at home, and I finally decided to study after she went to sleep, but even then it was difficult. She awoke nearly every night with bad dreams and sobbed until I brought her into my bed. It was obvious to me that just as I did, she felt the strain of the divorce and the added demands that law school was putting on me. Through signals that I wasn't even aware of, I was communicating all of my distress to her. I'm afraid I was not a very good mother. Now, almost too late, I've started to see a therapist.

"My brother, who is quite well off, is now helping me out with finances. We've never been close, but I know he cares for me, and since the divorce, he's rallied to my cause. I felt humiliated at first, having two siblings support me, but now I'll accept everything if it means a chance to survive for Lois's sake. I thought that when I finished school, I'd have a good job in a prestigious law firm. Look at me now! No job, in my family's debt, no future, no more Lois. Oh God, what am I saying?"

Jean broke down again; she was in torment and desperately needed help. I was relieved to learn that she had started psychotherapy for herself, and that she and I could concentrate on Lois's problems.

What was I to make of this account? Jean was obviously distressed, facing death, weakened by her long illness, and facing bouts of nausea, exhaustion, and depression following chemotherapy. She was consumed by anger—anger because of her husband's treatment during their stormy marriage, anger because he had made a new life for himself, anger because he was the survivor, anger because he would become Lois's custodian, and anger because she would not see Lois grow into womanhood. This anger surged up and gave her the courage to continue fighting her illness and searching for remedies that unfortunately did not exist.

I tried to sort out the details in the long history that Jean had presented. How much was true? Was Ron the villain described by Jean? Did Lois really dislike her father as much as Jean insisted she did? Would I be able to help Lois deal with the inevitable loss of her mother? Jean and I agreed that we would meet once a month to discuss Lois's progress, and that Jean would telephone me with questions and concerns about Lois as the therapy proceeded.

I felt the urgency of Jean's request. Although I did not know then that the cancer was terminal, I was about to engage in a battle against the passage of time: I needed time to help Lois, and I didn't know how much time there would be before Jean died. Jean was hopeful that she could be cured, and for Lois's sake, I wanted to believe in a cure as much as Jean did. If only I could play a trick on death as Gramps does in Paul Osborn's play *On Borrowed Time*. Gramps, like Jean, is near death, but he does not want to die until he can find a proper home for Pud, his grandson, just as Jean wanted someone other than Ron to take care of Lois. When Death, in the guise of a Mr. Brink, comes for Gramps, Gramps persuades him to climb up a tree to pick "one last apple before I go." Once up the tree, Brink is trapped by the branches, and for a short time, Gramps has a reprieve. I, too, was searching for a reprieve for Lois. But of course, death does triumph in the end.

Between my first two monthly sessions with Jean, I met Lois, and our play therapy began.

The Intellectual: Codes and Words

Our first play therapy session took place approximately two weeks after Jean's initial meeting with me. My plan was to meet with Lois twice a week if possible. Thinking about her as often as I did, I found myself confronting my own mortality. Just as Jean raged against death, I raged. But while Jean suffered physically and mentally, I needed to find a way to help Lois with the possibility of her mother's death and with what this loss would mean to her. I had to remain a constant and a supportive figure for her in a crumbling world. First, I wanted Lois to trust me. As our relationship deepened, I planned to become more active in directing our sessions. Although at first, Lois would choose her own toys and games, later I would guide her, to help her express the pain and mourning that she would eventually experience.

Lois came willingly into the playroom, obviously well prepared for our session by Jean. Lois told me that I was going to be her "helper" and then sat down at the table and announced, "I'm a mover." She explained, "I'm always on the move. I never sit still. I really like to do things. I'm even a monitor in school."

> ▶ You like being a mover?
> ▶ Yes, I do. It keeps me busy.
> ▶ When you're busy, you don't have to think.

Lois became quiet, and I could sense she was pulling back. I had probed too quickly. After we had sat awhile in silence, I asked Lois if she knew why she was coming to see me.

> ▶ Yes. I get sad, that's all. I'm thinking of Mommy and my dad, that's all.
> ▶ Can you tell me what you're thinking about?

Again, she resisted. She was guarded, refusing to expand on this topic, and I decided that for all her bravado and characterization of herself as a "mover" and of me as a "helper," she needed more time to become truly comfortable with me.

Producing a small notebook, Lois proceeded to tell me that it was her "code book" and that, if I wanted to, I could try to figure out her "codes." While she made one up for me, I had an opportunity to note her features. Lois was of about average height for an eight-year-old, but somewhat chubby. She had long blond hair, blue eyes, and a sweet smile, very much like Jean's, but dimples gave her an impish expression. She wore sneakers and was dressed in a two-piece exercise outfit, pink and gray with designs of small balloons floating across the top of the shirt. Her hair was long and loose and kept falling into her eyes as she worked. She brushed it back with her hand or chewed on a strand, frowning as she intently devised a coded phrase for me to solve.

When she finished, she challenged me but generously offered me some hints. When I successfully deciphered her message—"School is fun"—Lois seemed pleased that I took this game seriously. When I asked her to tell me more about school, Lois again retreated. It was clear that she was not ready to share her feelings with me, and that she would try to control our discussions through secret "codes" and messages that I would have to decipher.

We had more time left in this session, and Lois found some *Highlights* magazines on the bookshelf. She wanted to do the puzzles, again using her intellectual strengths to relate to me while keeping me at a distance, and clearly wanting to impress me with her cognitive skills. Lois finished the puzzles in the magazine and further explored the bookshelf, avoiding the games, toys, and other play equipment in the room. She felt safe with her word games and resisted my attempts to probe about school or her friends and family. This was all right. We would go slowly until Lois felt comfortable enough to share her concerns about her mother.

At the beginning of the session, I had explained the rules of the playroom to Lois: what she could and could not do, the fact that the toys must remain in the room, and the length of time we would spend. I also explained that what she told me would be confidential. I told her she could call me Dr. Singer or Dorothy. Lois chose Dr. Singer. It suggested to me her need to be formal. Now, as we had only five minutes left, I told her that our session was drawing to a close, and Lois immediately blurted out, "I go to visit my dad in Pennsylvania. He has a house on a lake and it's OK."

▸ You like to go there?
▸ Yes! Well—No.
▸ You're not sure?
(*Silence on Lois's part.*)
▸ Can you tell me more about the house or your visists?
▸ No, I don't want to.

I had touched a sore spot and Lois resisted.

Our time was up. She gathered up her notebook and pencils and said, "Thank you for the visit. I'll be happy to come again and do more puzzles." Lois's speech was formal, controlled, and very much like Jean's.

When we entered the waiting room, Lois and Jean hugged. Jean buttoned Lois's coat, tied her sneaker laces, and spoke to her in a babyish way. When Lois told Jean she would come back and it was "fun," Jean seemed relieved, and they left holding hands. The intellectual "mover" and "coder" became the helpless "baby" in the presence of her mother. I reflected on Jean's need to baby Lois. Was she trying to make up for all those years when she had been in law school and had spent very little time mothering Lois? Or was Jean trying to move the clock back, to hold onto Lois as a baby, to revive those years before the diagnosis of leukemia? Jean needed to be "Mama," to cling to this mother–daughter relationship, to suspend time, to refuse to acknowledge Lois's growth—Lois growing up without Jean. The future was too painful for Jean to contemplate.

Lois had given me clues about her worries, just as she had given me clues to the secret code she had devised for me. I wondered, had Lois tested me to see if I were worthy of solving her problems—her fears of her mother's illness and perhaps her death and her concerns about her father and the family in Pennsylvania? Lois, the "mover," was using codes and puzzles to communicate with me. Our first session had been filled with intellectual defenses and also with hints to me of her distress. She had been resistant to my probes but had not shut me out completely, and I looked forward to my next session with this articulate, intelligent, complicated child.

The following week Lois brought some of her test papers for me to see, to admire her A pluses and 100 percents. She wanted to play tick-tack-toe, and while we played, I tried to engage her in conversation about her family. As before, Lois avoided my questions and wanted to focus only on the game, expressing great pleasure that she could beat me.

> ► You like to win.
> ► Yes, I sure do. I feel awful whenever I lose a game.
> ► Why?
> ► I don't know. It's like I'm no good or dumb.
> ► Do you think you always have to win?
> ► Well, no, but losing is bad, or scary.
> ► Scary?
> ► Yes. "Don't lose anything," that's my rule.
> ► Grown-ups lose games, and even very smart people lose games. We can't always win.
> ► Well, you have to. That's all.
> ► Why?
> ► I don't know. Anyway, I don't want to talk about this.

Here was another topic that was taboo: winning and losing. Lois was afraid of loss: the loss of her mother and the loss of her security. It was important for her to hold on tightly to whatever she had, and her games were symbols for her family.

Lois shifted away from our tick-tack-toe contest and to the doctor's kit. She took the teddy bear and proceeded to examine it, using the toy instruments. While doing this, she told me about an incident in her life when she was about four years old:

> ► I swallowed Tylenol—a whole bunch—and I went to the hospital, where they pumped me out.
> ► That must have been scary for you.
> ► Yes, I remember it. I don't like to be sick, and I don't like anyone to be sick.
> ► Who's sick, Lois?
> ► No one. Let's play "house."

Lois took the bear and the dolls to the couch, cuddled them, fed them, and put them on the slide. She play-acted "mother" for about ten minutes. I felt she was reassuring herself that her mother was well and doing her job of tending her "baby." I made some comments about Lois as the "mother," such as "You are really taking good care of the doll and teddy," but it was clear that Lois was not inviting me to join this game. She was not ready to explore its significance for her in terms of the mothering she had missed during Jean's law student years and the mothering she was afraid of losing now.

She soon tired of the game and asked me to help her to write a letter to *Highlights*. She drew a house and wanted to send it to the magazine editors, who chose readers' submissions each month for reproduction in a special section. Again, I could be her "helper" in an intellectual task. Her drawing was of a house, perhaps the house and home she wished she could have, a complete family, all well and together under one roof, but it was too soon for me to say this and too soon for Lois to tell me what her drawing meant.

Our session ended. I gave Lois a Christmas present, a book she had mentioned to me that dealt with science experiments that could be done in one's own kitchen. Lois was excited, telling me that she planned to share the book with her father over the Christmas holidays, and that she would see me "next year."

Our next meeting was indeed in the New Year—in January. I wondered how the visit in Pennsylvania with her father had gone and was eager to see Lois. Jean had communicated with me regularly since Lois had begun therapy. She called at least once a week, had had the second session with me, and kept me informed about her medical condition, which was gradually worsening. She seemed pleased that Lois wanted to come to the sessions and felt that at some level, Lois was aware of how serious the illness was. Lois wanted to sleep with a light on in the hallway, and many times, when Jean awoke, Lois was in her bed. Time was growing short for Jean. She was not responding satisfactorily to treatment.

I also felt the pressure of time. It would be important for me to take a more aggressive role early in play therapy and try to get Lois to open up. Her codes and word games were strong defenses against the reality of her mother's illness. They were challenges that Lois could easily tackle. All the fragments became whole, solved, and deciphered—unlike Jean's illness. But I was caught in a dilemma. I did not know how much time I would have to work with Lois to uncover her feelings about her mother's illness. Lois needed time to adjust to the possibility of Jean's death—and time to begin the grieving process for Jean and the healing process for herself.

I decided to try some tests with Lois. During our next two sessions after the Christmas vacation, I gave Lois the Blacky Test, which consists of pictures of a dog and his family in various encounters. The scenes are constructed to evoke children's spontaneous feelings about their relationships with their siblings and their parents. Themes emerge such as contentment, friendliness, and playfulness, or preoccupations with food, toileting, and hostility. A child's self-concept and defenses can be determined from his or her responses as well as from an avoidance or denial of certain aspects of the scenes.

Lois made up stories about each card and answered some structured questions. She described Blacky as always seeking attention, getting his own way, and threatening to "break something" if he did not. Her responses also revealed her worries about separation and loss, as well as her view of her mother as "good" and her father as "bad." Blacky (like Lois) had "secret passwords" and "secret clubs" and clearly liked his mother better than his father.

In addition, Lois drew her family and gave me her Three Wishes, another test. Her wishes were for (1) a family that was normal because no divorce had ever taken place; (2) a club with lots of people in it; and (3) lots of toys.

We were able to talk about these two tests and what they meant. Lois's responses to the cards and my gentle probing had had an extraordinary effect: she was able to talk with me more openly than before. I also picked up on her first wish for a "normal" family. Lois talked at length about how "awful" it was when "Mommy was at law school. She never read me a story." Lois remembered this period as one of tension, during which there had been no time for games, stories, and play with her mother. She also remembered the arguments between her parents over custody and visitation rights. Lois described her family members as "picky": "Everyone was picky-picky-fighting. I was two when it started and five when it stopped."

The tests were crucial in allowing Lois to reveal some of her feelings to me and in letting me gain insight into her current situation. The Blacky Test was the catalyst that helped bring Lois's thoughts to the surface, and yet I was still wary. Lois spoke about the past, but she still avoided talking about Jean's illness and the possibility of her death.

During that session, Lois wanted to tell me about a dream she often had. She was in a forest and seemed to become a unicorn, but lately, new elements had appeared in this recurring dream: "I changed my shape and became a monkey. A flood came and then snow. Then I went up to the North Pole in the flood. I put two parts of my body above the surface of the water. I was then a horse again. Pegasus, up on all fours. I escaped. But then a person caught me around the neck. I awoke."

The person, she told me, was an "animal catcher." The catcher put her in the stable and made her a racehorse. This horse won all the races.

The dream seemed to be one of flight and transformation: Lois was almost drowning but was saved, was put in a stable (where she could be taken care of), and became a racehorse. Lois told me she often daydreamed about being Pegasus, the mythological winged horse, or the racehorse and "winning." Lois called this her "adventure dream." In this recurrent dream, she left the earth as a unicorn, was transformed into a monkey, almost drowned, became a horse again, and was rescued from cold, icy waters or won a race by running "so fast."

Lois had shared her feelings with me for the first time: her memories of her unhappy household, her desire to escape from the world around her, her fear of drowning, and her rescue. The dream made me think of Lois as the lonely unicorn, a mythical creature who is odd, unusual. It reminded me of a cartoon I had seen years ago in the *New Yorker* in which Noah's ark sails off, leaving a unicorn alone on the shore, a misfit, left behind, as perhaps Lois would be left. But the unicorn in Lois's dream changed shape and became a racehorse, an animal that is real—one that survives and wins.

Could I help Lois? Was I going to be the "animal catcher" and keep her in a safe stable? Would Lois win? Could I rescue her from her unspoken fears about her mother's death, from her future with her father? These sessions, although only our second and third, were critical. Lois was able to express her anxieties about the divorce and her own fear of being alone and "drowning" or losing safety and control.

The Circus and the Horses

Our fourth session took place two weeks later, in February. Jean was quite ill and could no longer drive. This information unnerved me. I felt the pressure of time and realized that I would have to be more direct in my work with Lois. I no longer had the luxury of waiting for Lois to reveal her feelings about her father and her future living arrangements. I would have to take a chance and interpret her remarks even if I caused Lois some temporary discomfort. Arrangements were being made for a full-time housekeeper, and in the interim, Lois was supposed to go to her father in Pennsylvania. At the last moment, Ron had canceled the visit, and Lois was spending the time with her aunt. According to Jean, Lois was furious and felt rejected by her father, but she had taken the stance that "It didn't really matter," and that Ron was "mean" and "selfish." When Lois came for her session, she looked morose and troubled. Nonetheless, she did seem relieved to enter the playroom and asked if we could play "circus."

Lois took some miniature horses from the shelf, made a tightrope out of pipe cleaners, and proceeded to construct some cages out of blocks for the various toy animals. Two small horses became a "father" and a "mother," which she made walk along the tightrope. The father horse kept falling off the rope, and Lois became rather rough with him, knocking him down, picking him up to kiss him, and knocking him down again.

I commented about this ambivalent behavior:

- ► You seem angry at the father horse.
- ► Yes, I am. He's not good, he's not fair.
- ► Why isn't he good or fair?
- ► He can't keep a promise—so down he goes!
- ► Sometimes things happen that prevent us from keeping promises.
- ► Well, this father is mean.
- ► But you kissed him, too.
- ► Well, so I did, but he's mean.

▸ Do you want to tell me more about why he's mean?
▸ No, he's mean, mean, mean!

With that outburst, Lois tossed the father horse down, broke up the circus arrangement, and then, of her own accord, proceeded to tell me that her father had canceled her visit with him. Instead of going to Pennsylvania, she had spent the past two weeks with her aunt and was very unhappy. Through her play, Lois was able to express her feelings and then transfer them to words and tell me about disappointment.

▸ When your Dad cancels a visit with you, it makes you angry.
▸ Yes. He does that a lot. Maybe he doesn't really care about me.
▸ Do you think that's really true? Sometimes we love someone, but something happens and we have to disappoint that person.
▸ But he does it a lot!
▸ It seems like a lot when you want something so much. Do you know why you are so disappointed this time?
▸ No. Well, yes, maybe . . .
▸ Can you tell me the maybe?
▸ No!

Lois carefully avoided discussing Jean's illness and the reasons she had been supposed to visit her father. When I tried to broach the subject of Jean's treatment and illness, Lois withdrew, became sullen, sat on the couch, and just stared ahead, her signal to me to stop probing. Despite my need to move more aggressively, it was still too soon in our relationship for Lois to express her fears about Jean's cancer.

I talked with Lois about the new housekeeper, Diane, who was helping out and would be driving Lois to our sessions. Cheering up, Lois told me that they had stopped at McDonald's on the way for hamburgers and that it had been fun. We ended the session by cleaning up the circus mess, and as Lois put the toys away, she kissed the father horse once again.

The following week, a bubbly Lois came with great news to share: "My Mom cut herself—and guess what, the cut clotted! That's good. It means she's getting better."

This was Lois's first mention of her mother's illness since she had started therapy, giving me an opportunity to explore what Lois knew about the cancer and how much she really understood about its consequences.

> ► You've been worried about your mother, but you didn't want to tell me about this worry.
> ► No, I didn't. I feel OK about it today. Mommy seems OK lately. I'm making her a heart. Look!

Taking a large white piece of cloth out of her book bag, Lois showed me the design of a heart stenciled on the material. She was almost through with the stitching and was quite proud of her design and embroidery: "It says, 'I love you' in the middle, see? I only have that much left to do. All the heart around it is finished. It's a surprise. Don't you tell her! It will be for a pillowcase."

Reassuring Lois that I would keep this secret and that I thought her work was excellent, I tried to help her to talk more about her mother, but she only gave me her good news about the clot and would go no further. At least the door was opening a bit more. Perhaps this was the beginning. Despite my own desire to make faster progress because of my awareness of Jean's condition, I had to be patient and could not rush the process.

During this session, Lois again played circus. She placed the horses in the stable and again hit the father horse. One horse fell and broke a leg, and Lois called the "doctor." The baby dolls were used in her game, too; one doll also became ill and needed a shot but hid from the doctor. Putting five baby dolls on a Big Bird scooter, Lois took them for a ride to the doctor. She spent a considerable part of the hour between the two games—"circus" and "doctor"—injuring the horse and one baby doll. My comments to her concerned healing:

▶ Doctors help people get well. Is that what you're doing to the horse and the baby doll?

▶ Well, yes, but, see, this horse just keeps breaking his leg—and then he's saved.

▶ He's like the horse in your dream. I think.

▶ You mean Pegasus? Yes, he gets saved, but that's an "adventure dream." Remember, I drown and get saved. I don't need a doctor.

▶ But you were saved by the animal catcher weren't you?

▶ Yes, but this is not a dream. This horse needs a doctor.

▶ Your mom needs a doctor, too, doesn't she?

▶ My Mom has lots of doctors and may even have a special kind of medicine put in her when she goes to Texas.

▶ Do you think about that a lot?

▶ Yes, Dr. Singer, a lot—and today it's OK. I told you, her blood made a clot.

▶ So today you feel better. Can you tell me, Lois, when you feel worried? Can you share that with me? You said I was your helper.

▶ You're my helper—but you can't help Mommy.

This was true. I could only remark to myself that this child knew that I was powerless as far as Jean's illness was concerned. But could I help Lois deal with her feelings about this tragic event? For the first time, Lois had used my name (I was *her* doctor), a signal to me that she was comfortable with me and perhaps ready to confide.

As Lois was leaving the room, she gave me a present, a postcard with a reproduction of Picasso's painting *First Steps*. It is of a mother holding onto a child's hands at it tries to keep its balance and walk. Lois had chosen this card herself during a class outing to the local art gallery. She had no way of knowing that this was one of my favorite paintings, a copy of which is on my office wall at the university. *First Steps*—what did this mean to Lois? I liked to think it was her first attempt to separate from her mother, her first attempt to go by herself into the world. Perhaps I was reading more into her selection than was there, but it was significant to me that Lois had now reached out for me with this little gift. It told me that a relationship was developing. She had written "To Dr. Singer from Lois" on the back and seemed delighted that I was so enthusiastic about the card. Time was up, and I hoped that during the next session, we could talk more about *First Steps*.

Babies and Dr. Butterscotch

Lois was pale and sleepy. Her nose was stuffed up; she was whiny and out of sorts. She had fallen asleep in the car on her way to my office and was trying to wake up. She lay down on the couch for a while and refused all suggestions about play. Finally, I asked if she would like to draw.

> ► Okay, but what?
> ► Well, how about three drawings for me?

I decided to give her the House-Tree-Person and Kinetic Family Drawings tests to see if they would help to release some emotions. These tests are based on the premise that patients' drawings symbolize feelings about their families and themselves. Seeming to cheer up, Lois came to the table and proceeded to draw a house:

> ► This is my house, way up on a hill. I'd like to live in it. It would have an attic, my room, a bathroom, a living room, and a dining room. In this house I have a gerbil, a dog, a rabbit, and a gerbil's girlfriend. My tree is an apple tree in the yard of the house. It's a happy tree. It never gets chopped. I'm going to erase its roots. I don't want it to have roots. I don't like trees—it's a grumpy old tree—it feels happy but always is grumpy. Yes, it's grumpy. It hates everything, rabbits, cats, everything, grumpy old tree.
> ► Why is it so grumpy?
> ► Because it is! And this is my person—my teacher. I like this person. She's usually happy.

Lois asked if she could draw another person. When I agreed, she drew a tiny person and then shaded it in until it was completely black except for the face.

> ▸ Who is this?
> ▸ I don't know. Well, yes, this is a person with three wishes.

Lois remembered our Three Wishes exercise from a few weeks before and became a little intellectual:

> ▸ She wants a room to be quiet, all of us to behave, and to work more on computers.
> ▸ Lois, can you tell me who that person is?
> ▸ It's the teacher!
> ▸ Can you draw your family and have each one doing something?
> ▸ Yes.

Lois began to draw. The first figure was "Daddy," drawn far apart from her two females. He was holding a book. The mother was "combing her hair. This is a picture of her when she had hair."

We talked about the drawings for a little while. The house was a "dream house" on a hill, because "I don't live on a hill now. That 'grumpy tree' could be me."

> ▸ Sometimes you feel that way, grumpy?
> ▸ Yes, a lot of times.
> ▸ Your tree had roots. Why did you draw over them and hide them?
> ▸ I don't know.
> ▸ You said it was an apple tree, but you didn't draw any apples. Why?
> ▸ I told you, no roots now—it's grumpy.

It seemed clear to me that Lois felt like her tree, empty and rootless: her tree—her self-image. She was no longer happy, feeling less secure. Perhaps, too, the drawing of the tree, the mention of apples, and the tree never to be "chopped" down or die were expressions of her need for her mother to remain vital and blooming. However, Lois felt that her yearnings were being denied, and the tree became grumpy, with no roots, dead. Was the tree her mother?

The desire for her mother's restoration was powerful and was conveyed in her family picture, where her mother held a comb, stood close to Lois, and her long and flowing hair. The father was there, slightly apart from Lois and her mother, holding his book—reading, withdrawn, and passive, similar to Lois, who was portrayed as sleeping and helpless.

I put the drawing aside, and Lois discovered a new toy, a bright yellow "talking" teddy bear. She loved it, picked it up, and named it "Dr. Butterscotch." She seemed to perk up, and started a game: "This doll is Peter. He has a splinter in his belly button. This doll has a sore arm and must go to the hospital for an operation."

Lois gave "shots" and "pills" to each of the dolls and used Dr. Butterscotch as her healer.

This session revealed Lois's concern about her mother in a vivid way. The transformation of the healthy, happy apple tree to a grumpy, rootless tree signified her preoccupation with Jean's illness and dying. The doctor play then enabled her to gain some control. As Dr. Butterscotch, Lois could administer medicine, repair broken limbs, remove splinters, and be in control. She needed to be the "mover," but at a deeper level she was aware of her inability to change circumstances. Of course, the tree had become grumpy. It had lost its life-giving roots—its support system—and it would die.

For the next few sessions, the Dr. Butterscotch game continued, alternating with displays of babyish behavior. Lois would suck her thumb, act sleepy, whine, and ask to sit on my lap. I felt that Lois was worried about Jean and had even suspected that Jean was more fragile than ever. At my monthly session with Jean in March, I had found out that she was now quite weak and spent much time in bed; the cancer was not responding to treatment.

A week before this visit, I had actually spotted Jean as she was leaving a building near my office at the university. I had just parked my car, and I watched while Jean seemed to float down the street like an ethereal creature in a Chagall painting. As usual, she was dressed in black: a long, gored skirt; her familiar woolen sweater, now hanging loosely over thin hips; and a wide-brimmed hat that shielded her pale face from the strong spring light. I had never seen Jean in daylight, only in the soft light of my office. Now as I watched her, I suddenly saw that the cancer had transformed this once vital woman into a gaunt, fragile person. A tremor passed through my body as if I had seen a phantom, and a fleeting image of death personified passed through my mind—a figure I associated with an old Ingmar Bergman film, *The Seventh Seal*. I restrained an impulse to call out to her, not wanting her to see the distress that I was sure my face would convey. Jean waited on the corner until Diane came to drive her home. When I got out of my car, my hands trembled as I put a coin in the meter.

Jean came to the March session worried about Ron's gaining custody of Lois and again expressed her conviction that he was not a good father. I must admit that I, too, was concerned about Ron. I knew very little about him other than what Jean had told me and what Lois had conveyed to me through her play. I wondered if Ron truly understood the seriousness of Jean's illness. I wondered, too, how he could disappoint Lois so often and deny her the attention that she craved. Was he so unfeeling, or was Jean purposely distorting her portrayal of him in order to win my sympathy?

Jean admitted that she was still putting Ron down in her conversations with Lois. As a result, Lois was becoming more and more angry at Ron, and even when her visits with her father were pleasant, she denied it. I explained to Jean that Lois felt that she would betray Jean if she enjoyed Ron's attention. It was a question of allegiance. If she admitted that her time with Ron was good, Lois felt that Jean would be jealous, and Lois could not hurt her mother. As a result, she denied her own feelings in order to keep Jean happy. She was afraid of losing Jean and wanted to give what Jean asked of her: total devotion. This was a burden and too much to ask of Lois.

"I understand what you're telling me," Jean said, "but I'm in terrible conflict about my feelings toward Ron. I know that Lois will need a parent. It's just too bad that Ron has to be that parent. I haven't the time to work through my feelings about him, and I can't continue my therapy. It's too exhausting to analyze my feelings— to dig down and relive all the memories. It's all too painful, too debilitating. I'm so tired now; I sleep a lot. I can't even read. I feel so weak, and I'm losing ground."

We could not talk further; the visit was becoming too taxing. Diane came to drive Jean home. As we parted, Jean said, "I'll try not to denigrate Ron. But I can't help it—I resent him so."

Before Lois came to her session during the last week in March, Jean was finally able to tell Lois that she might die. Up to this point, there had been hints, but the facts had never been clearly stated. Jean had talked about cancer before, but always with the possibility of a cure. Now, Jean told Lois, there was no longer any hope. This was difficult for Jean to do, but I gave her support in her decision to tell Lois, as did her sister and brother. It seemed apparent to me that Lois had figured out this change in the course of the cancer, but now that she knew, I wondered what the next session would bring.

Lois Begins to Confront Her Mother's Approaching Death

At the end of March, Lois came into the playroom ready to talk about her father. She listed the "bad" things first and then the "good." The bad things included his choosing her clothes, preventing her from using a night-light ("He wants me to grow up"), and preventing her from petting his wife's cats. The good things included watching cartoons on Saturday morning and staying up until 9:00 P.M. Together, Ron's family usually shopped, ran errands, cooked, and had "great desserts like chocolate chip cookies, but I can't hum at the table or tap my feet."

Lois then told me about Jean: "She's basically just nice unless I treat her meanly, like if I'm in a bad mood. Usually I'm very co-operative." Lois's mood then changed. She became quiet and con-fided her worries: "I worry a lot when the cancer goes on. I'm just scared. It's hard to explain. When I'm in school, I get nervous. It's like the time when Mommy was going to law school. I was nervous then. I bit my nails. I threw up. I was afraid she wouldn't ever finish. It was not good then. It's not good now."

Lois stopped talking abruptly and I felt she needed relief. I watched as she went over to get out the doctor's kit and Dr. Butterscotch. She began to get wild and silly: "Take that, you—and you, too!"

Lois picked up another doll: "You get this shot, too. See how you like it. Here's one for you, too!"

Lois was jabbing at all the dolls, giggling and shouting at them. Each doll received a needle and was hurled onto the couch.

Lois was out of control, and I intervened. I took the toys from Lois and guided her to the armchair, sitting nearby and urging her to relax. She gradually regained control and soon began to breathe more evenly. I knew that this was a time not to talk, but just to feel. Lois knew that I was there, closeby. She reached for my hand and held it tightly. When I felt that she was composed, I walked with her to greet Diane. Lois smiled a sad smile, waved, and said, "I'll see you."

Lois found relief in playing doctor, but today she had been almost hysterical. I think she knew that "doctoring" was useless for her mother's illness.

Spring was approaching, and Lois and I had been together since early December. April 2 would be exactly four months since Lois's treatment had begun. In that time, Lois had dropped her defenses and resistances and had gradually communicated her feelings to me. I was still concerned about whether she truly understood what death meant. Her play conveyed her anger and her helplessness.

I wanted to cry out and attack, too—but whom and where? How could I ventilate my feelings of impotence in this struggle with Jean's impending death? Death, Jean's own Mr. Brink, was climbing slowly down from those tree branches.

Jean needed to go to the hospital for observation and for a new treatment, and I knew that this next session would be a difficult one for Lois. She came into the waiting room that lovely early spring day looking pale, as she had a few weeks previously. She was sleepy, was sucking her thumb, appeared depressed and listless, and leaned against me as we walked into the playroom. Lois had told me previously that she would like to write a book, *The Magical Voyage*, and I had agreed to find all sorts of pictures for her to put together in her story. I felt that Lois needed a concrete task to do that day, and that perhaps, through the story, she could work out her feelings. Lois wrote her story about a trip through the sky in a balloon that floated all over the world. The heroine was a ballerina, who found lots of food to eat, a magical fish that gave her everything she wanted, and three horses to take on her journey back home. This book would be a gift for Jean, but claiming that she was too dizzy and too tired, Lois refused go to the hospital to give it to her. Lois enjoyed making the book and said she would give it to Jean when she was discharged from the hospital. We talked about Lois's dizziness:

> ► When did this start?
> ► Way before Mommy went to the hospital.
> ► Did you tell her about it?
> ► No. I didn't tell you either.
> ► I know that, but why not?
> ► I'm telling you now.
> ► Yes, I'm glad you can share this with me. Can you tell me how you feel about Mommy's being in the hospital.
> ► I'm scared she won't come home.
> ► Does that make you dizzy? Thinking about her?
> ► Yes. When I think of her, I worry, and I feel sick, and I can't do my homework.
> ► Lois, tell me what you think might happen in the hospital?
> ► She might die. I found a dead caterpillar. I buried him.

Lois started to cry. Our session was drawing to a close, and I felt that she needed to leave on a more upbeat note.

"Well, look, you made this book for your mother," I said. "You told me it's for Mother's Day. Perhaps you will want to visit her then. It would cheer her up. It's a beautiful book, and she'll feel better knowing you were thinking about her."

Seeming somewhat comforted, Lois took the book and put it in her book bag. She then asked if we had time to play "space." She took the miniature plastic space people and made a "space house" on a "distant planet where everyone lived happily ever after."

Lois was attempting to come to grips with her mother's dying, yet still retained her fantasies about a possible happy outcome: about the planet where everyone was safe, about Dr. Butterscotch and his cures, about the animal catcher who saved Pegasus, about the house on the hill where everyone was happy, and about her mother combing her flowing hair. All of these images passed through my mind—

pictures conjured up by watching a child mourning before her mother's death occurred.

Lois then left, and I pondered her need to bury the caterpillar. It reminded me of a haunting French film about World War II, *Forbidden Games*, in which a child sees her parents gunned down by enemy planes flying low over the heads of a long line of refugees fleeing from besieged Paris. The little girl tries to "awaken" her parents as they lie on the road and cannot understand why they won't respond to her voice and touch. As I watched the film, I had felt as devastated as that little girl. Now, as I watched Lois suffer, once again the pain returned. The child in the film tries to master her confusion and fears by repeatedly playing a ritual game of cemetery. She digs small graves for dead animals and places crosses to mark the sites. Like that child, Lois had been trying to understand death as she buried her caterpillar.

A few days later, Jean called to tell me that her bone marrow transplant, scheduled for April, had been postponed. She would not be going to Texas after all. She was too weak for the procedure, and it would be too dangerous to try it at this time.

Ron had telephoned and asked if he could see me. This was the first time he had expressed interest in Lois's progress, and I felt it would be useful to meet him and help him understand her distress. It seemed inevitable that he would soon have physical custody of Lois, and I needed to know more about him as a father. My previous attempts to meet with him had failed. There had always been a reason why he could not get away: his job, family illnesses, vacation plans. But now Ron seemed eager to come, and I was curious about him, given the history of the family and Jean's resentment toward him. I wondered, too, if Lois had expressed any thoughts to Ron about her future with him and his new family.

Ron came during the same week of the session during which Lois had put together her *Magical Voyage* book. He was a tall, slender, handsome man but seemed cold, distant, and reserved. In a very matter-of-fact way, he described his marriage to Jean as a "big mistake" and saw Jean as a "poor housewife" and an "incompetent mother." He felt some guilt about his past actions, but it was clear that he did not find Jean blameless in their marriage, as she saw herself. Ron admitted that he used to say "nasty things" about Jean to Lois but had stopped. He had explained to Lois that "grown-ups get angry, but it's between Mommy and me, not anything to do with you."

Ron described Lois as "affectionate and responsive" to him, but as wary of revealing her feelings about Jean's illness. He told me that Lois spent time sitting on his lap, sucking her thumb, and playing with his hair, loving the physical contact with him, and he said, "I do, too!" He felt that Lois tried to keep her two worlds apart—his new family and Jean's relations and friends. She had a secret place where she hid his letters.

Ron had had limited conversations with Jean in the past few months and was dismayed to learn of her setback. He felt that he needed to know more about Jean's condition so that he could share in what would be appropriate steps in helping Lois. Expressing both "anger" and "sadness" that Jean would not share information with him, he found it extremely difficult not to know what Lois was dealing with: "I feel shut out of Jean's life. I don't know what to say to Lois about Jean's dying. It's hard for me to find the proper words. I know Jean resents the fact that Lois will come to live with me and that it must bother Jean more than dying does."

Ron continued in a low voice and was tearful as he spoke: "I desperately want my daughter to trust me, to confide in me. I want her to reach out to me for support. I want to ease her burden. Jean is cheating me of my right to be a father."

As he left, he said, "Will I have to be an active parent? If this is terminal, I have to make plans." He asked if he could see me again in a month or so, and I agreed.

I now had a better sense of Ron as a person. I would never have accurate details of the relationship before the divorce, but at least I now saw a man who truly wanted to be helpful, and who was ready to accept his daughter into his new household.

The Princess in the Tower

Lois had expressed her fears about her mother's death through her drawings, through burying the caterpillar, and only partially through words. My first session with Lois in May was a key one in her the therapy. She came into the playroom, sat down, and blurted out, "I'm scared. I can't put it in words—my brain says I'm scared. I have mixed feelings. I don't know what will happen. If my mom is still in the hospital on Mother's Day, I will visit her. On Mother's Day, I'll give her my book."

Lois was revealing her feelings but still could not say the words *dying* and *death*. She seemed very tense, anxious, and depressed. After this outburst, she picked up the blocks and constructed what looked like a closed box.

▶ What are you making?
▶ It's a tower. I'm playing princess. Here she is—inside. There are no windows, no doors. No one can come in. No one can go out.
▶ Why is that?
▶ She's safe here. She's protected. This is a palace all around here. Here is a mother, a father, one brother, a husband, a maid. People can come into the palace—but only four at a time. The jewels are locked up. There are four horses—two boy horses and two girl horses. This horse will always save the princess. He gets apples for a reward.
▶ Doesn't the princess ever leave the tower?
▶ No, never. She needs to stay in there always.
▶ When will she come out?
▶ She might go out but in disguise—maybe on a picnic.
▶ When will that be?
▶ I don't know. Everyone is in the palace—all the people are there to protect her, to keep her safe. She is afraid to go out.
▶ What will happen to her?
▶ It's dangerous. She just has to stay in the tower.

Lois then carefully put all the toys and blocks away and told me we would play this game again.

And we did. The princess in the tower was Lois's game throughout the month of May. Many events took place during that month. Jean was able to come home from the hospital. To her dismay, she learned that the bone marrow transplant had been canceled for good, and that it would be best for her to continue the current treatment. The news shocked her, and she asked to see me again.

Jean and Ron came together to this session, which was devoted to making plans for Lois's future. Both parents were trying to control their emotions. Jean was filled with resentment because she, the "good parent," was dying and Ron, the "bad parent," would win out after all. He would have Lois. Meanwhile, Lois saw herself as the princess surrounded by people she loved but isolated from them in her tower. Her play theme was one of security, protection, and safety. Only in her tower, where there were no windows and no doors, was she safe. She did not have to face her mother's death or leave her. She did not have to cope with Ron's new family. If she remained in the tower, no one could harm her. Lois played this game while her mother fought valiantly to recover, reading about all kinds of medications and various procedures, and taking more drastic forms of therapy. Lois had retreated symbolically from the illness that engulfed the family. My task was to help her deal with this crisis and to help her begin now to plan for the future—to help her emerge from the tower.

I picked up on her idea of "disguise" and asked if she could become another one of the dolls and come out. I promised that the "horse" would be there to protect her, and that we could pretend that the horse had special powers. Was there anything the princess needed or wanted that would induce her to come out? Lois was willing to open a window and look around. Perhaps the princess could visit a family in the dollhouse, where it was safe, and see if she liked it there? Lois sucked her thumb, sat on my lap, and seemed to be giving this suggestion some thought.

▸ Well, I could try that game, but I'm thinking and wishing now.
▸ Do you want to tell me your wishes?
▸ I wish my mom would get better. I wish my family would be happy. Mom has not been feeling good for such a long time.

► Is that why you shut the princess away, so she won't
have to think about the future?

Lois looked at me and didn't reply, but I felt that she had recognized
what she was doing in her princess game. She became very quiet
and then told me we could play "house." She went over to the tower
and removed more blocks, leaving an opening for a door and for
more windows, but the princess doll remained inside. Lois took one
doll, her favorite "mama doll," and had her put six tiny dolls to
bed. She pretended to turn on a night-light and then said, "I wish I
had a lot of kids in my family. I'm going to Pennsylvania this whole
summer. I'll have more kids there in my family. When I go there,
I can cook and clean and play."
　　"Sounds as if you're looking forward to the summer and your
visit with your dad," I said.
　　Lois didn't answer but took the toy dog and made it bite the
father doll's ankle.

► Well, that dog seems angry at the daddy. Why?
► Look at this.

And Lois proceeded to make the dog climb all over the "daddy,"
knocking him down.
　　It was clear to me that Lois was still working out her ambivalent
feelings toward her father, and the possibility that she would be with
him for more than just vacations was beginning to penetrate. At
least, in this session, we had made some progress: the princess could
look out her window, the door was open, and Lois had now begun
to play "family." She was beginning to think of other possibilities
for her after her mother's death, and the fear of being alone and abandoned was lessening. She needed a big family, a loving mother, and
the night-light for security, and "daddy" was there, but still not fully
accepted. Accepting him completely could signify the finality of
Jean's death and, in Lois's mind, would be a betrayal of Jean's love.

Playing House

At the end of May and throughout June, Lois's play themes were mainly "house" and "doctor." The princess was still in the tower and remained there as an observer. Lois did not want to play with her or talk about her. She was not quite ready to emerge into the reality of the new family and the new life in Pennsylvania.

The "house" games suggested a tremendous need for a family. Lois usually had two sets of parents living in the dollhouse. My interpretation was that they were her own parents as they had been at one time, and now her father and Susan, his second wife, and eventually Lois' stepmother.

The game of house was restorative for Lois. She was able to play-act a family life with the routines of meals, bedtime stories, playful antics among the toy dolls, shopping, school, and all of the activities that signified a normal life to her. These miniaturized versions of "house" and "family" enabled Lois to envision herself in a new house with a new family. The repetitiveness of the games created opportunities for her to rehearse and master the emotions that her new life with Ron and Susan might engender. In mid-June, Lois was ready to talk at length about her feelings, and I report them here from my detailed notes. It was a long monologue that I didn't interrupt. The "house" game had stimulated these thoughts:

> I have kind of mixed-up feelings—some go one way, some go another. These are crammed in my head. I don't know how many there are. I'm just estimating—confused, scared, happy. Scared of not going on time to Daddy. I'll miss Susan's children. Sort of confused about my feelings. I want to stay with my mom. Also I like my dad. It feels like they want you to say who I like better. I have no idea. So I'm confused about what to do. I spent time with my gerbil. When I'm angry at Mom, I shut down. I listen to music. I talk to my animals. Little Bear is all worn out. Little Bear and I snuggle—since I was a baby I snuggle next to Little Bear. Sometimes kids tease me about my Mom—call me

"cancer kid" or "AIDS patient." I get emotional about my feelings. When someone teases, I get agitated or fussy. I try to hide it inside. I've been crying lately in school. I hurt myself in gym so they call me sissy or baby. That annoys me. I have no particular friend. My best friend moved away. And now I'm looking forward to my birthday party—but who will come?

When Lois finished this outpouring, we talked about her stream of associations, and I tried to make connections for her. She was in conflict about her desire to go to Pennsylvania. She had been exposed to sickness for so long that she needed a joyful household. Yet she was afraid that if she went away, something might happen to Jean while she was gone. She also felt torn between these two parents, each of whom wanted her solely and had fought so bitterly in the past. We talked about how like the princess Lois was, hiding inside the tower, hiding her feelings and not wanting to come out and face reality. We talked about her need to play and to reconstitute a family. We talked about the children who teased her, about how they did not understand cancer and how they confused illnesses. Jean and Lois had now had many discussions about cancer, using the booklets from the American Cancer Society that I had given them. As I have mentioned, the school principal and Lois's teacher had tried to help, but some children remained cruel and unsympathetic.

Lois seemed to feel relief after airing her feelings. She went over to the tower and, one by one, removed the blocks. At last, the princess came out.

Family

At the end of May, and until mid-June, Lois played house, now her favorite game. Sometimes, at the beginning of our session, she would try out tongue twisters or revert to making codes again, but the intellectual defenses she had used in our early sessions were sharply reduced. Lois needed to engage in family play with a mother doll clearly in charge. All the children (six small dolls) and the mother slept in the same bed so "she could take care of them." The rooms were arranged and then rearranged repeatedly, as if Lois could not find a satisfactory plan for her "house." I think she was playing out the uncertainty and chaos in her life. Where would she live? Where would she sleep? Mother would not be there to love and protect her as the mother doll did the six small dolls. The father doll was left outside the house. Lois did not want him "inside." This meant that if he became a more permanent part of her life, the mother would be gone.

Our last session for the summer took place at the end of June. Lois told me about her "comfy blanket," which she took with her on "sleepovers" and to Pennsylvania:

▸ This blanket is monster-proof. I need it to protect me from slimy monsters—one-eyed or two-eyed monsters.
▸ Lois, do you dream of monsters?
▸ Only sometimes, when my dad won't let me have my night-light.
▸ Can you tell him that you need it?
▸ I can't. I'm scared to.
▸ Well, we could play-act "Daddy and Lois." Would you like to try that?
▸ OK, but you be Lois first.

We role-played, taking turns as Lois asked her father for the night-light several times, until she felt she could now "ask for my rights."

As our session drew to a close, Lois told me she would spend the summer in Pennsylvania. She felt guilty leaving her mother, but she was also looking forward to the change. Jean wanted Lois to go away for the summer because her health was failing and her reactions to the drugs necessitated periodic hospitalization.

Before Lois left for Pennsylvania, she called me to say that she had planted a small peach tree in front of her house. I remembered her drawing of the apple tree and her comments. She had relabeled the originally happy tree as a "grumpy tree." Now, I think, she was trying to plant a tree that might bear fruit. Lois wanted her mother to live, and the tree was her way of handling death: it was a substitute, a living memory of her mother. She knew death was near, and this gentle, sensitive child who was trying to understand life and death felt a need to try actively to control some aspect of nature. Lois had planted the tree next to the caterpillar's "grave."

Death and Mourning

According to the researchers in this area, children do not truly understand the meaning of death until they are about ten years old. Jean Piaget, the eminent Swiss psychologist, was fascinated by the thinking processes of children, and one of his interests was the child's conception of living and nonliving objects. Just as Piaget believed that other concepts, such as language, mathematics, and a knowledge of science, develop through various stages, he also believed that there are definite stages in a child's understanding of death.

Until age three, children's cognitive and language development is too immature for them to have any accurate concept of death. If they are asked to define death, they usually say, "Someone went to sleep," "Someone went away," or "Someone does not move anymore." Death is also conceptualized as reversible (the new puppy takes the place of the dead dog, and the sleeping person wakes up). This conceptualization is analogous to how children interpret animated characters on television, who after disastrous falls, knockouts, or shootings and stabbings are miraculously revived to go on to the next "death" scene—all accompanied by music and special effects.

Children aged five to nine begin to have some understanding that death is final, but they cannot quite believe that it will happen to them. They have some preoccupation with death during this period, and some children express fears about going to sleep, afraid that they will not awaken. They may also have dreams about dead people or animals and may fear that their parents will die.

Until ages eight and nine, it is difficult for children to understand that death is a biological process. Eight-year-old Lois was curious about what would happen to the caterpilllar after she buried it. Through this symbolic burial, she was trying to understand what would happen to her mother's body after death. She was beginning to accept her own mortality as well, but only tentatively. Her magical games of "rescue" were part of her inability to completely assimilate the notion of death as final.

After age ten, children begin to accept the various causes of death, to perceive it as inevitable and final, and to acknowledge the cessation of all biological functions: respiration, circulation, brain function, and body movement. Just as other developmental concepts may be absorbed by different children at different ages, children show considerable variation in their conception of death, and when emotionally threatened, they may regress, denying their intellectual understanding of this natural occurrence.

Lois, who was a little past her eighth birthday at the beginning of her therapy, expressed many of the same ideas about death that are outlined above. Her preoccupation with and handling of Jean's impending death was manifested in *denial* at first and then, later, in acceptance, through the *symbolic caterpillar burial* and her planting of the fruit tree (her desire to find life in another form). Lois also coped with her grief and fears by *regressing* (in her thumb-sucking and her baby talk about Jean's going bye-bye) despite her intellectual understanding of death.

Throughout the summer, I kept in touch with Lois's parents, mainly by telephone. During an interval between hospital stays, Jean and I met. That day in mid-July was the last time we would talk. Jean was extremely weak and coughing up blood, and could barely walk or talk, but she told me that Lois "was doing great" but that she "missed her [Lois]." Jean told me, too, that Lois had "announced her rights" about shopping for clothes for Pennsylvania and had told Jean that she would "tell Daddy to keep the light on at night in the hall." Jean seemed more relaxed despite the severity of her illness, feeling that she had been able to talk more openly with Lois about the cancer and her approaching death. She agonized over the possibility that she might not "hold out" until September: "I promised Lois I would still be around when she came home. It was important for her to go away knowing I would be here. I call her twice a week, and I've told her to call me whenever she wants to."

We talked about Ron. Jean felt somewhat better about him and knew that she had no choice but to help Lois think more positively about Ron and Susan: "That's where Lois's future lies now, so I have to help her to accept them as her parents."

We spent two hours together while Jean poured out her feelings about death: "It's not myself I think about, but Lois—growing up and not seeing me—and I guess I will never know what beauty she will have or what she will do with her life. Will she remember me with love? Will she only think about our difficult, miserable days? Will Susan be a good mother to her? Will you help Lois after I die? Promise you will."

I promised Jean that I would see Lois as much as possible before she left Connecticut. I also reminded Jean that Lois would return in September and that we had already scheduled our session for the first week of that month. We shook hands and hugged. Clinging to me, Jean kissed my cheek and said good-bye.

The "Princess" Says Good-Bye

Lois came back from Pennsylvania and resumed her therapy. Our first meeting was a mixture of excitement and sadness. She gave me a hug and kiss and then spotted some new dress-up clothes. Immediately she put on a long skirt, a crown, two boas, and a frilly collar: "Look, I'm a princess."

Lois danced around the room in her costume, gravitated toward the playhouse, and, as she arranged the dolls, blurted out, "I'm afraid my mom will die—I don't want to go to my dad's house—he bothers me—I can't put it into words why he bothers me."

▸ I thought your summer was a good one.
▸ Yes and no.
▸ Why "no"?
▸ "No" because I thought of my mom a lot.
▸ You missed her.
▸ Yes, and I shouldn't have left her.
▸ You feel bad because you left her and maybe because you had fun?
▸ Yes—no—yes.
▸ Sometimes we feel guilty when we have fun and a person we love isn't there to share the fun.

▶ Yes.
▶ Is that what's bothering you?
▶ Yes.
▶ Why does your dad bother you?
▶ 'Cause—he's there.
▶ 'Cause he's there and Mommy isn't, is that it?
▶ Yes, I guess so.

Lois felt that her happiness that summer had not been deserved, that if she enjoyed her father's household and cared for her father, something might happen to her mother: living with her father would mean that Jean was gone. Many times, through her play and through her words, Lois conveyed these confused feelings to me. It was as if she had no right to be happy or to have her father if her mother died.

Lois continued to play house, still in her princess outfit—no longer in her tower but outside, active, trying out her role in her new family. She picked up a toy swan.

▶ Look a newborn bird will come out of this shell. We will have a magic potion and make a baby mouse, too.
▶ You want some babies around, I see.
▶ This will be a game where a witch comes to all these dolls—Lulu, Doo-doo, Pooh-Pooh—and makes all new babies.
▶ Why so many babies?
▶ Well—it's new—beginning.

Lois then picked up the two sets of parent dolls and placed them in the dollhouse. She told me both families could live there now. The father was "allowed inside." She took off the costume and put everyone "to sleep."

During September, Lois continued to play with the dollhouse. She was aware of Jean's weakened condition, and she now acted it out in her play:

▸ The mother is in bed. Sh, sh—no noise please!
▸ Where is everybody?
▸ Well, baby is in the crib, and this doll is the big sister.
She's reading a book. She's sad.
▸ Why is she so sad?
▸ 'Cause nothing is the same, that's why.
▸ Tell me about what's changing.
▸ Everyone will leave the house.
▸ Is the father still inside the house?
▸ No, he's in a new house, and the moving truck is com-
ing to take everyone away.
▸ Everyone?
▸ No, they'll leave the mother sleeping in her room.

Lois told me everything in this vignette. It was as if she had a
premonition.

Two days later, Jean's sister called to say that Jean was in a coma.
Would I come to the house to see Lois? I spent most of the afternoon
with her in the garden. Lois was angry. She took me to see her tree:
"Look, no peaches on the tree! My mother is dying, and my father
is a crumb."

After this outburst Lois refused at first to talk about her mother
or father, but lay down on a blanket, curled up in a fetal position,
and sucked her thumb:

▸ I wish I were a baby. It was better when I was a baby.
See? Now I look like a baby!
▸ Yes, you look like a baby. When you were a baby, you
had your mom. Now you're afraid.
▸ It's scary. She's dying. She's all white and doesn't open
her eyes. I sleep on the couch in the living room where she
is. Do you want to come in with me and we can sit near her?
▸ Yes, I'd like that.
▸ Let's do that, but let's look at my caterpillar. Remember?
I buried him. He's near my peach tree. *Lois stopped short
and shook her head.*) No, I won't dig it up. It's probably
disintegrated by now.

What happens after you die? Lois had buried the caterpillar as one way of dealing with death, and now that death was so close, she was curious but afraid to see the caterpillar—afraid that nothing would be left of it in the earth. She was more realistic now about her mother's inevitable death. She posed questions typical of children her age: "What is a pulse?" "How does one stop breathing?" "What does it mean to be not living?" "What happens to the body?" Curious as she was, the caterpillar was going to remain in its grave.

We went inside to visit Jean. Lois held her mother's hand. Jean was attached to various tubes and looked pale and puffy, breathing with the help of oxygen tubes inserted in her nose. Lois sat quietly and then took my hand and led me outside. We spent the afternoon together talking about babies and her future, and about how "spooky" she felt seeing her mother like that. We talked about some of the things that Lois could look forward to doing in Pennsylvania and about how memories can help us keep a person we love close to us. I left Lois when I felt she seemed more in control, and I told her that we could talk again tomorrow. Her aunt and uncle were staying with her and trying to be of comfort.

The next day Jean died. Lois was out with the housekeeper running errands, and when she came back, her aunt told her the news. Lois called me later in the day and asked if she could come to see me. She came with her aunt, burst into tears, and said, "I wished I had been there when Mommy died."

Lois told me that now she just wanted "to sleep on the couch in the same room where Mommy died, so I can be near where Mommy was." She asked me many questions about the funeral: what would happen and when it would take place. I told her I would go with her to the funeral home (I did so the next day).

She then talked about Ron and Pennsylvania: "It's confusing. I don't want to go away. It's confusing. I don't want to hurt Daddy's feelings. I want to stay here a week or two. Then I'll go. Is that all right?"

I assured Lois that it would be all right to stay in Connecticut until she was ready to go and that I would talk to her father about it. Lois then felt better and played house. She set up the doll family in various rooms, engaging them in different activities: "Today will be school—a new school—and Teddy will no longer be Dr. Butterscotch. He's the teacher."

Lois had no need for the "doctor" anymore. Now she was able to use Teddy in a new role. She was beginning to think about her new school. Lois would have many events to deal with in Pennsylvania, and I wished that I could have more time to work with her, but that was not to be. Time was still my enemy.

Ron called me after the funeral to tell me that he was bringing Lois to me for our last session. He would wait while we talked, and then they would be off to Pennsylvania. He said that Lois had seemed to be all right during the funeral and had handled the day with "appropriate behavior."

Lois came for our last visit. She thanked me for having gone to the funeral parlor and said that it had not been too scary after all: "Mommy looked beautiful and like asleep and not in pain."

Lois knew that this was our last time together. She wanted to play house with me as the "mother" doll, and "I'll be father doll":

> ▸ Father goes to work. The children build a hideout. Father can't come in. Now this hideout is a hole in the closet—no one can get in.
> ▸ Why do you need a hideout?
> ▸ Well, if I need to go in there, I can.
> ▸ What will you hide from?
> ▸ I don't know.

Lois wanted to be sure that she had a place to retreat to if she became troubled. She played quietly with the dolls, directing me (the "mother") to "cook," take care of the baby dolls, and tell the children to "love Father and respect him." She was working out her feelings about her new family. She then gave me a photograph of herself and wrote down her new address, asking if she could take the "baby doll" with her to Pennsylvania. I reminded her that toys were to remain in the playroom. We continued to play, and Lois put the doll in her pocket.

"Remind me to give it to you when our time is up," Lois said.

We continued our house game, repeating daily routines with all the family dolls involved.

Our last session was soon over. Lois returned the "baby doll," kissed me, and said, "It's hard to go away. I can't be that baby, and you can't be my mother—only in our play—isn't that the way?"

Lois left with her father and continued treatment with a therapist in Pennsylvania. I shared my notes with this woman and felt that Lois would be in good hands. A Christmas card came from Lois with a new photograph. She was smiling, and I saw the alert look of Jean shining through her expression. There was much work left to be done by her new therapist: children may express feelings of sadness, rage, fear, shame, and guilt after the death of a parent. The questions that I had tried to deal with revolved around Lois's concern about her future, her fears about whether she would get cancer, and her fears about her surviving parent. The nine months of treatment had given us time to focus on her perception of her mother's illness, the changes in Lois's home situation and having a housekeeper as a helper, and Lois's adjustment to Ron's new wife and children.

It had been crucial for Lois to attend the funeral and to be able to express her grief. She still needed to deal with her conflict concerning her pleasure in Ron's home while her mother was ill. She would also have to deal with her guilt about her absence at the moment of her mother's death. Many of these issues were discussed with Ron before he left, and with Lois's new therapist. I could only hope that Lois would continue to make a satisfactory adjustment in her new school, would accept her new family, and would continue to work with her therapist on these areas of concern, but I do believe that Lois's native intelligence, her capacity for insight, and her gift of imagination will free the princess from the tower forever.

~~~~~~~~~~

PERRY, THE
VOLCANO MAKER

The Child of Chemical-
Abusing Parents

Perry Begins Psychotherapy

A few days after his fifth birthday, Perry bounded into the playroom announcing proudly, "I can count to five—but I don't go to school anymore. I kicked a kid. I was bad." He then smiled at me, wiggled a loose tooth with his tongue, inspected the room, and donned a toy helmet and a blue jacket, pretending he was a "spaceman." Unfortunately, Perry was unable to sustain a story line. Within a couple of minutes, he took off the play clothes and, examining the cupboard where the art supplies are kept, sought a new activity.

I had met Perry's parents, Bill and Patty Donne, the week before in order to get a history of Perry and some sense of his problem. The parents were particularly concerned about his aggressive behavior at school.

Perry was a sturdy-looking boy, with sandy-colored hair, large blue eyes, an engaging smile, and a dimple in his chin. His angelic looks contrasted with his rambunctious behavior and energy level. His speech was clear, punctuated by a slight lisp, and his body movements suggested good large-motor coordination.

▶ Would you like to hear me count?
▶ Sure.

Perry did so, counting to five repeatedly, insisting that he could count to twenty, but only "if I want to."

▶ I guess you don't want to now.
▶ No, I don't, but I can.
▶ Perry, do you know why you are here and who I am?
▶ Sure, you're a nurse.
▶ No, I'm not a nurse, but I am someone who will listen to your problems, and I'll try to help you.

A long period of silence followed, and then Perry said softly, "I have a problem."
This unexpected statement was followed by another long silence. Perry then moved closer to me, kept his eyes averted, and again in a voice barely audible said, "I really have a problem."

▶ Do you want to tell me what your problem is?
▶ Well, my dad took a beer yesterday. He's not supposed to, you know. Maybe it was a soda with a beer label on the bottle. Do you think so?
▶ I don't know, Perry, but it seems you wanted it to be a soda, not beer.
▶ Yeah, I don't like him to drink beer. He gets real mad, grrr, grrr, grrr, like that!

I was surprised that Perry was so direct at this first meeting, but when I tried to pursue the subject, gently encouraging Perry to talk more about his feelings, he just made an angry face. He kept "growl-ing" and then refused to expand on "his problem" for the remainder of our time. He continued to explore the playroom, however, more like his energetic self, and he talked more about school, avoiding any attempt on my part to return to his concern about his father and the beer episode.

▶ I'll go to kindergarten in September. No more nursery school for me.
▶ You sound eager to go to regular school.
▶ Yep. How far away is September?
▶ Not very far. You have four months to go. You said you were bad in nursery school. Do you want to tell me about it?
▶ No. Next time—or maybe never!
▶ Talking about things that bother you make you feel uncomfortable.
▶ It's none of your business!

With that retort, Perry took some Play-Doh cans from the cabinet and went to the table. He chose yellow and blue clay and proceeded to mix the colors with red while building a "volcano": "Fire comes out the middle, and brown rocks run down the sides. I saw an oil truck on fire on my way over here. I bet the TV news doesn't even know that yet."

Perry continued building his volcano, pounding the sides, adding small pieces of red clay for the "rocks." He was excited about his volcano project and kept making noises imitating loud eruptions as he added the rocks: "This explodes all over—just watch it go!"

I watched quietly. Perry had revealed all that he wanted to. It was too soon to press him. It was important for him to feel com-fortable with me, and to understand that he could set the pace in sharing emotions and expressing anxieties. Perry's play with the volcano was his way of allowing some pent-up anger to emerge and, for the moment, was a good substitute for his usual outbursts of aggression at home and at school. I let Perry continue to play with the clay until clean-up time, my only comments referring to the mechanics of making the volcano, rather than to the feelings behind his intense behavior.

Time was up. Perry put the clay away, washed up, and seemed more relaxed and pleased with himself. He ran to his father, who was in the waiting room and, as he left, smiled and said, "Next time we'll play again."

Perry's Parents

"Our problems are Perry's problems, and I guess there have been a lot of problems in our marriage—starting way back when." Bill Donne took the initiative, blurting this out even before he sat down. It was obvious that he was eager to talk about his relationship with Patty, his wife, and about Perry.

The Donnes had been referred to me by a local pediatrician who was disturbed by Perry's disruptive behavior in the waiting room and during the frequent examinations necessitated by chronic ear infections. Perry's nursery school teacher had also suggested that the Donnes seek help for Perry because of his uncontrollable behavior at school. She could no longer manage Perry in her nursery group, citing his aggressiveness, his destruction of toys, and his "sassy" attitude. Robert, Perry's three-year-old brother, attended the same school, and the rivalry was "intense" according to the school staff.

Bill and Patty gave details of Perry's negative behavior, focusing on his temper tantrums, his taunting of Robert, his lack of respect for rules, his willful destruction of their things as well as his own, and his failure to show them any affection. The list of his antisocial, aggressive characteristics seemed interminable.

When I inquired about Perry's good points, Patty told me that he was "bright," "creative," and fascinated by anything scientific or related to nature, "especially dinosaurs." "Perry is good at artwork, and loves to do things with his hands," she added. Bill explained that Perry was sensitive, and that what looked like "coldness" and "toughness" was really "Perry's way of hiding his craving for love. He's actually a good kid underneath, whose feelings are easily hurt. He doesn't want anyone to help him—being helped makes him feel as if he's not so tough." Bill was right. As I found out through my experiences with Perry, he needed to hide his vulnerability by acting independent and bossy.

The Donnes characterized their marriage as "shaky." Perry had not been a planned baby, and the Donnes had decided to get married because of the pregnancy. Bill currently worked as a telephone repairman. He had succeeded in getting his first-ever steady job a year before. Until Perry was three, the family had lived in a rundown trailer, traveling all around the country while Bill worked at odd jobs.

Bill said, "We used all kinds of drugs for maybe four years or so, but only for recreational purposes. I guess we tried everything: coke, heroin, marijuana—coke only a half dozen times." Both parents admitted to drinking heavily in the evenings and on weekends, insisting that they had always been in control of their use of drugs and alcohol.

Patty claimed that she had tried to stay off drugs when she discovered she was pregnant with Robert but admitted that after he was born, she had begun abusing both drugs and alcohol again. When they came to see me, both parents were in counseling: Bill was attending Alcoholics Anonomous (AA); Patty, Narcotics Anonymous (NA). The Donnes were a tall, attractive, blond-haired couple in their early thirties. Patty was a licensed hairdresser and worked part time. When I met her for the first time, she was extremely thin and mousy-looking, but as the year progressed, she became quite heavy and increasingly sloppy in dress and physical appearance. (Later, during the course of Perry's treatment, Patty hid the fact from Bill and from me that she had been skipping counseling sessions, and that she was again abusing drugs.)

I was sure that Perry perceived that something was amiss between his parents, but I believe he did not know it was rooted in Patty's abuse of drugs. Perry's destructive behavior in the playroom reflected his anxiety about his parents. In a way, Patty's distancing from Bill and from the children was more tragic than the physical punishment she had inflicted during Perry's early years as he was growing up in the trailer camps. Strange as it may seem, then there had at least been physical contact, and Perry had known, if only through pain, that Patty was aware of him.

Perry was further described by his parents as an unhappy, strong-willed child who "talked back" to the nursery school teacher, to them, to his uncle, and to adults in general. Bill said, "Perry is impatient and restless and likes to punch kids for no reason. He is very jealous of Robert, but he's protective of him, too."

"Perry often teases and provokes Robert," Patty added, "but he can be affectionate with Robert—and *only* with him."

Patty reluctantly told me some of her history: "I've had a lot of counseling—years of it—never regular—on and off. My own childhood was lousy. My parents were alcoholics. I saw my dad beat my mother, and he beat me, too. I never had a real childhood. I was always sad, unhappy. My folks divorced when I was a kid. I really don't want to talk about those days."

The Donnes admitted that they, too, frequently fought in front of their children, and that Bill had often "shoved" Patty, had hit her, and, when drunk, was sometimes violent toward her and the children.

In general, Bill appeared to be the more talkative parent, more open, more warm, and more involved with the children than his wife.

During our initial contact, and during many subsequent visits, Patty spoke very little, remained guarded, was strongly defensive, rarely looked at me, and wore a surly expression, projecting hostility toward both Bill and me.

"Perry has seen violence in our house," Bill said. "We've had real fights, and ever since Perry was born, it's been a big problem. Perry's first three years were a bummer.

"Perry was lonely, I guess. He was practically isolated, had no friends, didn't know how to play, and even today is a kind of loner. He can't play in a nice way with other kids.

"I'm good with my hands (Perry gets that from me), so I took any job I could whenever we camped. Patty did ladies' haircuts and sets in the camps for a few dollars each. We drank up the money or spent it on drugs. A guy I met in one of the camps taught me about telephone wire repair, but I couldn't find work doing that until I got to Connecticut last year. My counselor helped me get more training and my job here. I'm good at it now. With Patty's part-time job in a beauty parlor, we're doing OK financially.

"We came to Connecticut because I have a brother who lives here. He's a decent guy. He's been helpful to both of us, and he loves the kids. Patty's family lives in Colorado, and she's cut off all ties with them. My family stinks. The only good person is my brother, Ed."

Patty listened to this, nodding her head on occasion to agree with Bill. She constantly plucked at her skirt, removing invisible lint it seemed, and dropped small pieces of wool on the floor when she actually found a tangle. She described Perry's early months as "difficult": "He was ill often and even now has constant nose and ear infections. Winters were and still are especially bad—Perry's sick a lot from November to February. He's solid-looking, but he always seems to have a runny nose."

Both parents continued to add to my picture of Perry: "He wants his own way" and "won't listen" to them but "gets mad and runs out of the room" when they try to reason with him. Bill and Patty admitted that their main method of discipline was a "spanking with a hairbrush" and "once in the camps, Bill fractured Perry's arm." Since they had been in counseling, they had been trying to control their tempers and were trying to use "time-out" techniques with Perry and Robert: When the boys were naughty, they sat in a chair until they calmed down, then Patty or Bill talked about the problem and tried to resolve it.

Perry was a good eater. He slept through the night and was an early riser, watching television as soon as he got up. Because Patty slept late, Bill supervised breakfast and dressed the children, then drove Perry and Robert to school, at least until Perry was dismissed for his aggressive behavior.

Robert was described as the "quiet" child, although he sometimes got into mischief to get attention. He "worshipped" Perry, copied everything that Perry did, and followed him everywhere. According to the Donnes, Perry would try to get Robert into trouble by encouraging him to do "bad things" like "turning on the hose to soak the flowers, cutting his hair, spilling milk, and other things like that," but "like we said, Perry will also hug and kiss him." Perry loved to watch television with Robert. Because of Perry's obsession with television, the Donnes, acting on my advice, began to control the number of hours that the children were permitted to watch, as well as to monitor the kinds of programs the children selected.

"Perry likes our house and yard, and is always trying to plant things," commented Bill. "I feel good that we're in one place now. We have better food. I remember when we ate peanut butter sandwiches every lunch and suppertime, or spaghetti, or just lots of white bread. We never ate fruit or vegetables even when we had some money; the money bought us booze. We were kicked out of some trailer camps because we would fight, yell, throw things, make a racket. Robert's first year was hell, too. Maybe that's why we decided to settle down, because he was fretting and whining so much. Perry began to break things just the way we did, yell for no reason, and try to hit Robert and even us. One time when Patty and I had a fight, he got in the middle and just pounded me and pounded, pounded, until I broke down and cried and picked him up and hugged him. It was enough, enough. We both knew we had to settle down or we would lose the kids."

It was clear to me after my first meeting with Perry that he was reacting to his family's stressful history and to their current attempts to reconstitute their lives. Perry was a victim of chronic domestic violence and instability. His year-long therapy was like a roller-coaster ride. Sometimes, when Bill and Patty were responding to their own treatment and were abstaining from drugs and alcohol, Perry was calmer, smiled more, did well in school, and teased Robert less frequently, and his play was more sustained and constructive. When his parents fought or lapsed into chemical abuse, Perry's play reflected this chaos through anger, turmoil, feelings of helplessness, and moments of withdrawal. Like other victims of violence, children who had experienced physical or sexual abuse, Perry showed difficulty with trust and self-control, concern about his personal safety, and a fear of authority figures, and he was unable to develop appropriate relationships with children his own age. In the playroom, I attempted to teach Perry some skills that I hoped would enable him to survive in his fragile and confusing home environment.

A Question of Trust

In the first stage of therapy, a stage that would last for many meetings, Perry tested whether he could trust me. Within ten minutes of our first encounter, Perry had shared with me his anxiety about his father's alcoholism and the possibility that he might be drinking again after a long period of abstinence. But could Perry trust me with such an important disclosure? He wasn't sure. He felt more at ease when he used his hands and made clay volcanoes, expressing his own feelings through its eruptions and falling rocks.

During the many months of play therapy, Perry continued to test his trust in me. He needed reassurance that he could be angry, sad, even scared, and that I would listen, comfort him, and "keep" his secrets. His father's sobriety was of paramount importance to Perry. Although he was aware that both his parents attended "meetings" with their counselors, he felt burdened by a need to be his parents' watchdog.

Two major issues had emerged during our first session: Perry's concern about his father's drinking, along with the violent temper that accompanied a drunken episode, and Perry's own aggressive behavior or, as he put it, "I'm bad." The theme of aggression and its symbolic erupting volcano was repeated on numerous occasions and became an integral metaphor for Perry's emotions all during therapy. Later, Perry would express rage, helplessness, and guilt as his real world began to fall apart, just as the "rocks" came tumbling down in his imaginative play. Omens for Perry of possible catastrophe in his life came now, first in his dismissal from school, then in the beer episode suggesting that his father was breaking his pledge to stop drinking.

Later, as the weeks went by, Perry's play themes were filled with alien spaceships, "bad guys who killed the good guys," drawings, papier-mâché or Play-Doh volcanoes, and block buildings that were erected as tall towers, only to be knocked down in a whirlwind of fury. Perry made numerous attempts to test my loyalty and caring by hitting me, by throwing objects, or by refusing to speak to me and hiding in a little place that became a safe "nest" for him.

I was a person who set limits and boundaries for Perry. Once, for example, Perry threw a block at a lamp before I could stop him. I told him that he must not throw objects: blocks were for building, or for any kind of play he chose, but not for throwing. Looking straight at me, Perry hurled the block again. I took him by the hand, and just as I had warned him, I led him to the waiting room: "Time is up, Perry. We end our play whenever you break a rule." Perry cried, asking for a second chance, and I agreed. He came back, settled down, and played constructively.

Perry needed to learn that he could vent his anger through words, play, or art forms, but that if he tried to hurt me or destroy property, our time would end for that day. My goal was to encourage Perry to express his needs in more appropriate ways than attacking objects or other people. But that took time: time for him to work through his powerful negative feelings; time to learn new ways of coping with frustration; time to learn how to play with his peers; time to learn how to deal with his parent's self-destructive tendencies as they affected him; and, finally, time to achieve a sense of self-esteem and autonomy, rather than the self-deprecating attitude and bossy, controlling stance he had brought to the play therapy process.

Perry's reaction to a household devoid of structure was to compensate by trying to take charge of every facet of his life. Changes were painful and fraught with anxiety, threatening his stability. Many changes were in store for Perry as the months wore on.

Understanding Aggression and Its Impact on Perry's Life

Perry's family history of violence, lack of routine, drinking, and drug abuse set the scene for his aggressive outbursts, reinforced by the example of his parents' behavior. Research has demonstrated that children learn to imitate aggressive behavior. In one study, children who saw a film in which a large plastic toy (a Bobo doll) was hit and knocked down by a teacher imitated these aggressive responses. Before they had seen the film, they were mildly frustrated as part of the experiment. Later, they accepted the adult's behavior in the film as appropriate, as was evidenced by the way they pounded the doll in direct imitation of the teacher's methods, including using a toy hammer. Similarly, Perry had seen Bill strike Patty and Robert on numerous occasions and had himself been the victim of many of Bill's brutal attacks; as a result, Perry had tried to inflict the same pain on Robert and his school playmates. Perry's style was a carbon copy of Bill's: when angry and frustrated, he struck out, often using the same gestures and expletives.

When frustrated in attaining a goal, each of us reacts in a specific way, depending on our past experiences with obstacles, our own coping skills, our previous successes or failures in similar situations, and our knowledge of the particular obstacle and the reasons for it. If, for example, it involves an aggressive act or a threat of force (perhaps the threat of punishment by a parent, like Bill or Patty), we become more aggressive when frustrated than if the obstacle involves no threat and is merely difficult to overcome or ambiguous.

Frustration may also lead to regression. In a study done almost fifty years ago, young children were deprived of desirable toys, which they could see but could not reach because of a barrier. These children, being frustrated, became disorganized, banged objects, and moved aimlessly around the playroom; their play lacked organization and constructive goals. Often, Perry reacted as these children did. If he could not have his way, he would start to throw toys in the playroom, or his organized pretend story would deteriorate to talking gibberish, knocking down his block buildings, scattering his figures, and shouting at me. I needed to be alert and often found myself holding Perry's hands to prevent him from inflicting harm on me or damage on the toys.

It is important to differentiate between anger and aggression. Anger is a basic human emotion, and aggression is only one method of expressing our anger. Anger may also result in flight, anxiety, repression, depression, or even distraction by other activities (keeping our minds off the annoying stimulus). Aggression implies an intent to do harm to another person or to property. However, aggression may also occur in the absence of anger. There are two forms of aggression: angry aggression, which is intended to make the victim to suffer (the aggression Perry displayed), and instrumental aggression, which is the result of competition or of the desire for some reward, such as food, money, status, or military victory.

When does aggression begin in a child? We can't truly consider the behavior aggressive when an infant pushes its mother's arm out of the way while trying to feed itself or when, as a toddler, a child grabs another child's toy. An infant who bangs a toy against a table or tears a page in a magazine doesn't fully understand that he or she is causing minor harm to an object. It is only when a child grasps the notion of *intent*—that is, that one event can cause another, and that people are instrumental in causing events to happen—that we can label an act aggressive. Perry certainly acted with intent, wanting to destroy property or to harm his brother or other children.

When we hear two-year-old children yell, "Mine, mine, mine," in the playroom, we see the beginnings of involvement with possession, the beginning of children's sense of autonomy and clarification of their own identity, but we do not see these toddlers attacking or forcing each other to give up the desired toy. The struggle seems to focus on the toy itself, and there is no clear means of getting it except by grabbing. Only later, as children become three and four, do they try to attack the possessor of the toy and strike out at this obstacle to ownership, the other child.

As children become more mobile, they encounter restrictions imposed by their parents. "No" is frequently heard; certain areas are off-limits, and the rules that are imposed must be followed. The socialization of the child takes place with the parents' use of praise or punishment to reinforce desirable behavior. Unfortunately, Perry had received more punishment than praise during his young life.

In my many hours with Perry, I constantly tried to get him to use words, not his fists, and to restrain his desire to kick or throw things when he was angry or frustrated. Using words to express his feelings seemed alien to Perry at first, but gradually, as therapy progressed, he began to relinquish his physically aggressive means of self-assertion. He used arguments, bargaining, and even compromise or compliance to attain his goals. Usually, at the end of a session, the children I work with may pick out a charm or a sticker as a reward for cleaning up. Perry decided one day that he wanted two charms.

▸ How about I take two charms now so you won't give the ones I like away?
▸ Perry, you can have one now and tell me which one you like. I'll save it for next time.

Perry thought about this.

▸ I *really* want two now.
▸ I know you do, but we have a rule. I know it's hard to follow rules, but you're learning. Can you wait until our next playtime?

There was a long pause while he thought again.

► I guess so, but *don't you forget.*
► I won't.

Perry chose one charm.

Words were not the tools used to settle disputes in the Donne household. The parents' frustration was resolved by chemical abuse, which often resulted in violence directed at each other or at the children. This pattern of behavior was similar to Patty's and to Bill's own childhood experiences and hopefully would cease to be perpetuated by Perry.

Dan Olweus, a psychologist in Sweden, interviewed and observed hundreds of parents in order to ascertain the origins of aggressive behavior in their sons. He found that not only did these boys differ in temperament (their levels of activity and impulsivity from birth), but their mothers had been rejecting and negative toward them early in life. The mothers had also permitted these children to be aggressive. In addition, both the mothers and the fathers, like the Donnes, had used physical punishment and threats or violent outbursts as methods of control. Children reared in this kind of atmosphere were found to be bullies or consistent aggressors and to have few controls or inhibitions. Olweus followed these boys up to the ninth grade and found that they not only were aggressive but tended to initiate situations that would lead to fighting. For example, they would tease, poke, take another's possessions. Frequently, like the boys in this study, Perry provoked incidents that resulted in a physical fight.

There are incidents of violence within families that are acceptable to our society. If a child is doing wrong and won't listen to reason, hitting is thought to be justified. Until fairly recently, physical punishment was considered acceptable even in our schools. Many American families regard spankings as an obligation. The Donnes obviously accepted this premise.

The amount of violence considered excessive in a marriage or in the disciplining of children varies with the individual and with the subculture. Generally, Bill and Patty were drunk or under the influence of drugs when they fought with each other, or when they hit their children. But on many occasions when they were completely sober, they still physically abused the children. Bill's father had beaten Bill; both her father and her mother had beaten Patty. Much of the family violence in our society occurs because males are brought up to think that they have the right to the final say in family matters, and that the ultimate resource of physical force may be used to back up their authority. Certainly, physical violence had been an established pattern in both Bill's and Patty's families as they grew up. Unfortunately, they had learned that hitting solved problems. The Donnes' parents had suffered from chronic stress; similarly, Bill and Patty faced numerous crises in their marriage.

The notion of *family privacy* in our society, I am sure, had discouraged the Donnes' neighbors from complaining about them and perhaps about other families like them over the years. As media publicity has made us more aware of physical and sexual abuse in our society, there has been a greater willingness (in some states, it is a legal necessity) on the part of family members, teachers, neighbors, and physicians to report suspected child abuse. What was fascinating, although not unusual, was the Donnes' reluctance to recognize—and their need to deny—that they were indeed spouse batterers and child abusers. Raised in dysfunctional families themselves, they simply assumed that their methods of discipline were within normal limits. It was only through counseling that they began to accept their pathology and their need to change. When once they truly examined their style of interacting with each other and with their children, they were ready to begin the healing process. The turning point came when they recognized that Perry was disturbed, a victim of their disastrous relationship and in need of professional help.

The Therapy Process

Our second session began with Perry's desire to play "volcano" again. I asked him to draw some things: the simple House-Tree-Person Test. I felt that Perry would reveal feelings to me as I questioned him about his drawings. Perry drew a tall tree with one huge coconut: "Here's my tree. It's a coconut tree, and you know what? This coconut is going to fall and hit *you* on the head!"

He seemed delighted and tried to gauge my reaction to his aggressive remark.

> ▸ Well, you want to hurt me, I think.
> ▸ No, but I could.
> ▸ Why do you want that coconut to hit me?
> ▸ Because—oh, I'm only fooling. It would be an accident.

This term *accident* was one I would hear again and again over the year. Often, Perry's deliberate attempts to hit me or to drop something or throw an object or a toy were followed by "It's an accident. I'm sorry," as if that would excuse his behavior or make the act more acceptable to both the victim and himself. I speculated that Perry was often spanked for his outbursts and his destructive acts. His defense was the "accident" excuse. Was Perry afraid that I would hit him as Bill and Patty had? This second session came too early in our relationship for me to truly understand or to attempt an interpretation of his remark, and only later, as trust began to develop, was I able to explore the meaning of *accident* in Perry's mind.

Perry's "house" drawing was of a primitive, lopsided one with a huge door and one window. The door was almost as large as the whole house. Was he inviting me in to share his emotions? Or was he barring me out? The lack of any details on the house perhaps symbolized feelings of a lack of warmth or intimacy. Finally, Perry would not draw himself; the "person" he drew was me, a great big face with an open mouth: "This person is you, talking to me." Often, children draw a significant other. At this point, that was what I was: a person entering Perry's life, someone whom he needed to trust, but of whom he was still leery.

Next, Perry gravitated toward the cabinet where the Play-Doh was kept.

> ▸ Okay, now I'm going to make more volcanoes. They'll explode.
> ▸ You sure like making volcanoes.
> ▸ Yep, I like explosions specially.
> ▸ How come?

Silence. My question was too direct. Perry worked diligently, lips pressed together, a frown on his forehead, and made his volcano larger and larger, using four cans of clay. He finally broke the silence:

> ▸ Robert kicked me. I didn't do anything to him. He just kicked me.
> ▸ You felt bad, I guess, when he did that and maybe angry, too.
> ▸ Yep. I even kicked him back, and he cried.
> ▸ He's younger than you. Maybe you could tell your mom about it and try not to kick Robert.
> ▸ She won't believe me.
> ▸ How do you know?
> ▸ 'Cause. That's how!

Perry soon left the volcano and donned the space clothes. He took the miniature "space guys" from the box and, while dressed in his space outfit, constructed a "planet." Once all the "guys" were lined up, Perry knocked each one down with shouts of glee, until all the "good guys" were "dead."

> ▸ This bad guy, he's He-Man. He's going to knock down this girl—that's you, Dorothy. Then, Willy, that's the He-Man's name, is going to chop her up into pieces. That's 'cause she hit Willy.
> ▸ Well, Perry. Willy is sure mad at the lady. Why did she hit Willy?
> ▸ 'Cause she did. That's why. Into pieces she goes!

With that remark, Perry scattered the small spacepeople all over the floor. I reminded him that we had only a few minutes left so that he could finish his game and clean up. It was clear to me that Perry was ambivalent about his feelings toward women: his mother, his teacher, and now me. This "chopped-up" girl could be "Mommy" perhaps, the person who hit "Willy," the substitute for Perry. We would return to this theme again.

As Perry cleaned up, he said, "I want an hour with you. I want to come a whole year—two—three years." A surprise to me! But I welcomed his willingness to come.

Our sessions were to be a half hour, twice a week. Perry obviously enjoyed our time together. He needed to unleash his fury and eventually come to understand that he could do so through words, play, and art. But it was crucial for him to learn the difference between self-control, or autonomy, and controlling others. In the playroom, Perry tried at first to control me: he ordered me to do things and generally refused my help or suggestions. He tested the limits in many of our early meetings, but he slowly began to understand and comply with the rules, which I firmly delineated in the therapy sessions.

I also wanted Perry to know that I could accept his feelings and could help him develop a sense of independence, that he could ask for help and could rely on adults and trust them. We were making clay dinosaurs, for example, during one session, and Perry was having trouble with the shape of the *Tyrannosaurus rex*.

▸ May I help you with his face?
▸ No, don't touch it. You do yours.
▸ Well, Perry, I'm here if you need help.
▸ I don't need help. OK?
▸ OK.

Perry picked up his clay dinosaur and moved to the other end of the room with his back to me. My question "How are you doing?" was greeted with silence.

I tried to get his attention by saying, "I'm making a baby dinosaur. Do you want to see it?" He ignored me.

▸ I guess you like to do things yourself.
▸ Yes! (*He was still having trouble.*)
▸ That's good. But it's also OK to ask for help. Even grown-ups need help sometimes.

Perry glanced at me, too stubborn to accept my offer. We both worked quietly. He finished making his dinosaur, but the face was still a problem and he reluctantly came to my table. Perry didn't speak. He was too proud. I silently reached for his clay figure, and he gave it to me. I worked on it and, when I felt the face was fairly complete, returned it to Perry for the finishing touches. He accepted it back.

There would be other times when Perry again refused my help, but gradually he began to see that I posed no threat to him, and that seeking help was not a sign of weakness. I understood why Perry needed his facade of bravado: Too many times he had been made to feel small, weak, and powerless.

Perry eventually began to understand that adults are not all abusive and that they may control and still love and accept. Perry would learn how to cope with the turmoil that his parents had imposed on him, and he would learn that he did not need to avoid closeness and intimacy.

Perry's comfort in working with various art forms triggered my decision to offer him art materials as part of each session. This decision was fortuitous. Generally, Perry shared his deepest feelings while engaged in drawing, building with clay, or using materials in an arts-and-crafts kit, such as beads, feathers, pipe cleaners, construction paper, flannel patches, wool, and small sticks.

I have found that when a child is blocked verbally, art often serves as an outlet for expression. It has been a useful adjunct in my work and certainly was successful with Perry. Specialists in art therapy conceive of artwork as supporting a child's ego, fostering a sense of identity, and encouraging steps toward maturation in general. Perry not only expressed his deepest feelings through art but was also intensely gratified by making his numerous products, often hanging pictures on my walls or taking them home as gifts for his parents and even for Robert.

Pioneering research with children seen in the psychiatric outpatient department of a hospital found that children's use of imagery and then later drawing the objects or people they had imagined helped them express their feelings in discussions with their therapist. When once I had found that Perry enjoyed artwork and seemed less defensive when he drew or constructed objects, I continued this approach. Sometimes Perry "drew" his "problem" instead of talking about it.

Once, when angry, he drew a series of family pictures: Mother, Father, Robert, and Perry. All had large faces with big mouths and huge hands; they were monsterlike in appearance.

The theme of destruction continued to characterize our first six weeks of therapy. Perry like to play spaceman and frequently tested my response by deliberately turning the "space box" upside down and scattering the "guys" all over the room. He administered "poison" to his guys, built "forts" that were demolished in a frenzy, gave "powerful" shots of "medicine" to a teddy bear, and used the dollhouse as a place to "punish" the "children." Perry would put "all the kids in one room. They must go there. They are all bad; they kick and punch. They are so bad."

Often, Perry would vacillate between saying to the teddy bear, "I love you" and "I hate you." One time, he administered "sixteen thousand shots" to the bear and shouted loud "ouches" as the bear received them.

▶ I'm only *playing* mad. I'm really not mad.
▶ You like to play "mad." I see you're mad at Teddy, at the space guys—anyone else?
▶ Tell my mom I can have TV all day. She won't let me now.
▶ So you're mad because you can't watch TV all day.
▶ Yep. I need to watch "Ghostbusters," "Masters of the Universe," even "Mister Rogers' Neighborhood."
▶ Well, maybe we can let you watch some TV. I'm glad you like Mister Rogers.
▶ I watch him and "Mr. Wizard."
▶ You seem to watch a lot of stuff.
▶ Yep. I want TV all day.

One of the subjects I had discussed with the Donnes was the amount of TV watched by both Perry and Robert. The chief source of entertainment in the Donne household was television, including the rental of movies several times a week. Bill and Patty exercised poor judgment about television. The children had unlimited access to the medium when they were home, and their parents had very little awareness of the programs they watched. Research by others and by my colleagues at Yale carried out since the early 1970s indicates that watching excessive violence on television and in the movies increases the likelihood that at least some viewers will behave more violently.

Perry was especially vulnerable to the negative portrayals on television. He watched approximately five hours of television a day, slightly more than the average American five-year-old, and the programs he favored were cartoons and action-adventure programs that contained many acts of physical aggression. Perry often used TV scenes as scripts for his own behavior. Television stories seen the night before our sessions were acted out through his use of the miniature characters, or through his attempts to "shoot" me or hit me with any object he imaged as a weapon. However, Perry's aggressive outbursts no longer depended on a particular TV scene. Because of his repeated exposure to television violence, his memory store provided cues to specific acts as well as a more generalized aggressive behavior pattern. In addition, Perry's current family life, dominated by arguments, physical aggression, and an absence of warmth and nurturing, exacerbated Perry's predisposition to aggressive behavior. Thus, a number of factors, including television, had led to Perry's use of aggression as a response to frustration and stress.

When his parents complied with my suggestion to limit the number of hours Perry watched television and to select programs suitable for a five-year-old, Perry was angry at first, as his behavior in the playroom showed, but he gradually accepted the rules imposed by his parents. He continued to watch "Mister Rogers' Neighborhood" and "Mr. Wizard," but nighttime adult dramatic programs were off-limits.

After his access to violent programming was curtailed, a shift occurred in his play. The space theme faded and was replaced by a desire to play board games such as Candyland and Chutes and Ladders. This desire indicated that Perry was able to handle rules more easily and was more in control. His pretend play had unleashed strong emotions. Certainly the repitition of volcano and space play had afforded Perry ample opportunities to vent his anger and had evoked memories of unhappy experiences at home. Now I wondered if expressing this new preference was Perry's silent way of telling me he was ready for a more mature kind of play, or what Jean Piaget called the stage of "games with rules." Perry's attention span was also increasing, and he was able to concentrate more than in our early sessions. This shift in play was not so much a cognitive one (he was still quite young) as a recognition of his need for structure and organization.

The Game of Checkers

After two months in therapy, Perry was able to sustain a longer play theme. He had not completely relinquished his desire to knock down buildings, but the passion that had previously accompanied these displays was less intense. I met with the Donnes once a month and during one of these visits was updated on his progress.

Bill spoke first as usual: "Things are better at home. We're both still seeing our counselors. Perry still picks on Robert but not as often, and it's not as miserable as it used to be."

Patty nodded but didn't volunteer much during our sessions. She looked more vacant to me than usual, as if she were miles away. When I tried to get her to talk and describe a typical day with Perry and Robert, she was not particularly informative. She gave me the briefest of responses: "It's OK," "It's good," "We're doing OK." I suspected that all was not "OK," but neither parent offered any more elaboration on life at home.

In the playroom, Perry still called Robert "bad, bad," and when he played dollhouse, he "locked" Robert in his room. But a new element had entered into our sessions: Perry spotted the checkers set on a shelf and asked me to teach him the game. Checkers became an integral part of our time together. The need to focus on this activity enabled Perry to talk to me about his parents and himself. In addition, as we played this simple game, I was able to observe how Perry reacted to structure, rules, taking turns, and on occasion, his triumphal winning. I was able to talk with Perry about cheating when he did so; lying when he told me, "It's my turn, Dorothy— you moved"; and his capacity to delay his actions and use self-control. Richard Gardner, a psychiatrist who has successfully used checkers as a diagnostic and therapeutic tool, feels that checkers is particularly useful in helping a child gain a sense of mastery and competence.

Although checkers falls into the category of competitive games, I used it because the very nature of the game tapped into Perry's major behavior problems. In our early play, Perry did become anxious when he lost pieces to me, but we were able to confront this reaction immediately, within the framework of the game, without his previous use of dolls to enact a power struggle between him and his parents, or his use of "spacemen" to dole out punishment after he had lost a squabble with Robert, or his attacks on the teddy bear, a substitute for Robert. The game of checkers also provided a safe climate in which Perry could allow his need to win and to be in control to emerge. For example, he thought of his black checkers as "soldiers" advancing, or when he crowned his kings, they were the "conquerors." Thus, Perry enjoyed his use of fantasy and his playful attitude in a structured game with a clear beginning and ending.

For a short time in August, my vacation suspended our checkers games. In September, we resumed our sessions and Perry was eager to come back to the playroom and also to demonstrate his progress in checkers. Bill had played checkers with him while I'd been away, and Perry had improved enough so that I knew he now genuinely understood the game. I played it straight, with no deliberate errors. On occasion, Perry would "forget" the rules, especially if he thought he was losing, but he also recovered quickly, and less sulking or weeping followed the loss of a piece or even a game.

His choice of checkers as the favorite game in September proved to be a good one. Perry was anxious about his new school but had repressed many of these feelings. He was more quiet than he had been during our sessions in the spring, needing to reassess our relationship after the August break. A brief vignette from one of our checkers games later in September illustrates how the game helped Perry to make his adjustment to school and to reestablish his trust in me:

▶ Dorothy, you be red. I'm always black, remember?
▶ I remember.
▶ (While moving a piece): Carl is a boy in my class. He throws things at me.

▸ What does the teacher do?
▸ She sends him to the principal.

Perry seemed more distant now and stopped moving his pieces.

▸ Perry, your turn to move.
▸ I'm stuck—no more places to go.
▸ You can move your men from your last row.
▸ I won't. If I do that, you'll get kings.
▸ Well, you can get kings, too.
▸ I guess so, but it's hard.
▸ Not if you concentrate and if you're careful.
▸ I can't win.
▸ That's not so. Remember, you beat me way back in July.
▸ I remember. I'll move this.

Perry made a bad move, and I was able to jump twice, landing in a place that made a king. Perry reluctantly crowned me and seemed weepy. He made another bad move, and I jumped him again. He reacted by throwing all the checkers on the floor and ran under the small slide to hide, watching me.

▸ Perry, that was not the way to end the game. I know you feel bad because you thought you were losing. Please come back. Pick up the pieces and put them away.
▸ No.
▸ Perry, one of our rules is that we don't deliberately throw things if we're angry. Come and talk about it with me.

No response. Perry's head was down, and he was feeling contrite.

▸ Perry, let's pick these checkers up together. This is only a game. Sometimes I lose, sometimes you lose. Come, help me.

▶ Perry came out from his "safe place," a label he had given this little boxlike spot weeks before when he crawled in after hitting me with a block. He now came to the table, picked up all the checkers himself, and set up the board.

▶ I'll leave this for next time, OK?
▶ Fine, Perry. I'm sorry that you threw the checkers, and I wonder why you crawled into your "safe place."
▶ Everyone is mad at me today. Dorothy, I told a lie. Carl didn't throw the block, I did.
▶ When you threw the checkers, I guess you remembered that you threw that block at Carl. Did you think I would punish you?

No response. Perry still couldn't tell me in words that he had been physically abused when he was "bad" at home; it is difficult for children to "tell tales" on their parents. What happened to Perry had taken place a long time before, in the days of the trailer camp, but perhaps those psychological scars had not yet completely healed and remained to haunt him. When he was disobedient, Perry's instinctive reaction was still to run and hide. However, I was pleased when he set the game up again. He was able to recover and restore, and through these positive steps, he had signaled to me his willingness to cope.

I wondered, however, if physical punishment was still occurring at home. When asked, the Donnes denied it, but I still felt that something was amiss. Patty's demeanor and lack of emotion conveyed negative messages to me.

We were moving into a new phase of therapy by November, approximately six months from my first contact with the Donnes and with Perry. Perry was able to accept me as a "friend" and seemed a relatively happier child. Instead of the volcanoes that he had drawn or sculpted out of clay or papier-mâché, Perry began to use watercolors and drew rainbows, and he constructed various gifts for his parents, such as a small "feather duster," a colorful horn made of a cardboard paper insert, and an Indian headdress. As he fashioned these objects, he talked to me more freely. He no longer called himself "bad," and I was gratified when he finally agreed to draw himself. The picture was a brightly colored portrait of a "happy " boy with a big smile, yellow hair, and blue eyes.

There were also some setbacks during the fall months. When Perry's teacher, who was pregnant, left her job in November, Perry was forced to make another new adjustment. And when his Uncle Ed moved to California at the end of the month, Perry felt abandoned by him, the only relative besides his parents whom he truly loved. These disappointments were reflected in Perry's regression early in December. Checker games were approached with hostility. "I'm going to beat you," Perry stated with a vengeance, or he would give up in the middle of a game if he appeared to be losing and flip the board over, causing the checkers to fall to the floor.

Many such "accidents" were occuring in school, at home, and in the playroom. Perry purposely spilled water on the playroom floor, hit me with a spoon, and knocked over a chair. All were labeled "accidents" by him, and we were able to explore the meaning of "accidents" as intentional acts on Perry's part, a major step in his treatment. Perry gained some insight into why he struck out when angry instead of talking about his feelings. He confessed one day:

▸ I was bad in school, Dorothy.
▸ What happened?
▸ I punched a kid. He bothered me. I just wanted to be by myself.
▸ Why did you want to be alone?
▸ I don't know. I just did.
▸ What happened when you punched him?
▸ I went to the principal's office. The lunchroom lady sent me there. I had to stay all the time, the whole lunchtime.
▸ Did you try to tell that boy *before* you punched him that you wanted to be alone?
▸ No.
▸ You can do that, Perry. Use words to talk about your feelings. You don't have to punch him.
▸ He's a jerk!
▸ Well, maybe, but you can still use words.

Perry listened. He was still defensive, but the message "Use words" was penetrating, if slowly.

During this period, Perry began to draw numerous pictures of hurricanes, with such rage that the paper would tear. We talked about his missing his Uncle Ed and his disappointment concerning his teacher's leave of absence. Talking helped. Perry's outbursts were briefer than in his early days in therapy, but more important, he was struggling to find the words to tell me about his "hurt feelings."

The School Visit

Perry adjusted beautifully to his new teacher, Ms. Sheffield, and was proud of the stickers he was bringing home from school for good conduct and for good work. I thought it would be beneficial for Perry if I visited his school to seek his teacher's help in reinforcing the progress he had made in therapy.

Bill and Patty arranged for me to meet Ms. Sheffield and to obtain permission for a classroom and playground observation. Perry was delighted to have a "special" visitor and was on his best behavior during my stay. He volunteered for many activities; he asked the teacher if he could "read" out loud and if I could sit near him. On the playground, Perry was a natural leader; only once did he boss another boy. Most of the time, he played appropriately, unlike the child described to me so many months before.

At the end of my visit, Ms. Sheffield and I discussed Perry's academic and social development while an aide supervised her class. According to Ms. Sheffield, Perry had progressed "beautifully" but was still subject to "the whims of his parents' behavior." Although she seemed to have some knowledge of Perry's background, I felt that I could not breach the Donnes' confidence and refrained from the elaboration of details. Ms. Sheffield added that Perry responded well to praise, liked to have a "job" in the classroom, and "loves being the center of attention." His responsibility for the distribution of crayons, pencils, and papers made Perry feel "important." On days when he sulked or became obstreperous, these monitor privileges were withdrawn. The rewards for good behavior were stars, stickers, or "happy face" drawings, which Perry relished.

I supported Ms. Sheffield's approach and emphasized his continued craving for attention, praise, and warmth. I explained my handling of Perry's outbursts and my constant reminder to use words when he was angry, not his fists or the hurling of some accessible object. Ms. Sheffield was a sensitive, caring teacher, I felt, whose allegiance was imperative if Perry was to continue his strides in therapy.

Buddy Joins the Play

Perry often asked me if he would live in his house "forever" and if his parents would ever fight again. The future was a scary place for Perry, and as we moved into our last stage of therapy, he could share these concerns with me. I became Perry's friend, his support, his sounding board. Perry again took a giant step when he began to use a large doll named Buddy as his alter ego to role-play scenes of sharing and taking turns, as well as to express his negative feelings. Perry called these scenes the "Buddy plays" using different "acts" for each segment of the playlets. One session we played "book":

► Buddy tried to tear Robert's book today, Dorothy.
► I guess he was real mad about something.
► Let's let Buddy pretend he's doing it.
► OK, Perry, you be Buddy. I'll be Robert.
► Buddy is watching TV, and Robert changes the channel. Boy, is Buddy mad! He grabs Robert's book.
► Where's Mommy?
► She's in the kitchen.
► Well, think about what Buddy could do instead of tearing the book.
► He could say, "Please put the channel back."
► Yes, that's good. What else?

▸ Well, OK, he can walk away and ask Mommy if he can see TV later after dinner.
▸ Perry, I like that. Would you like to try this out with Buddy?

We enacted this simple scene, using variations, until Perry felt comfortable with each resolution and had had enough. Generally, Perry drew a picture of Buddy doing some activity after we role-played. As he drew, Perry liked to listen to a recording of "Little Brave Sambo." This song, in which a child is empowered and conquers a tiger, seemed to have a special significance for Perry—perhaps the symbolism of the wilder side of one's nature, tamed and controlled at last.

Relapse

All that I had accomplished in therapy was about to come apart through Patty Donne's self-destructiveness. Perry obviously sensed the strained relationship between his parents. One day, as he was drawing, Perry remarked:

▸ I don't like it when Mommy and Daddy fight.
▸ Are they fighting?
▸ Sometimes Mommy is sad. She promised me she wouldn't fight. She doesn't go to her meetings. I don't know what they are. She doesn't go.
▸ You sound worried about Mommy.
▸ I got stuff on my mind.
▸ What stuff?
▸ Just stuff.
▸ Can you tell me about the stuff?
▸ Don't ask questions, OK?
▸ OK.

Perry was angry, and I could see that he needed to talk but couldn't find the words to tell me what was bothering him. He continued to draw: "This is Mommy. Mommy's mouth is big, bigger—bigger. She's yelling at Daddy."

Perry then scribbled over the face. He crumpled the paper and began to cry.

   ▸ Perry, you're so upset, and you're angry, too. Can you talk to me? Tell me what you feel?
   ▸ I can do it!
   ▸ Do what?
   ▸ I can hold Mommy and Daddy. Mommy can't go away. I can hold them!
   ▸ No one is going away, Perry. What do you mean?

Perry was now sobbing and put his head down on the crumpled drawing. He was unable to talk to me.

   ▸ It's OK, Perry, you can cry. I know you're upset about Mommy and Daddy. I'll talk to Daddy and try to find out what's happening. OK?

Perry continued to cry for a while and then wiped his tears and sat quietly. He looked small and lost. He wanted so much to be powerful, to keep his family intact, to hold his parents together, but he couldn't—and I couldn't. At that moment, I felt as frustrated and helpless as Perry. I suspected that the Donnes had been arguing about their relationship and wondered if Perry had overheard a conversation about divorce. I wanted to cry, too, but all I could do now was try to comfort this heartbroken little boy. When Perry seemed calmer, we went to the waiting room, and I asked Bill to phone me that evening. It was important that we talk.

I discovered later that Patty had not been honest in her monthly contacts with me. She had stopped attending NA in October and, unbeknownst to both Bill and me, had begun using drugs again. By the end of December, the drug abuse had become more frequent, and Bill suspected it when Patty lost her job and slept most of the day. When Bill confronted Patty, she used foul language, threatened to leave him, and told him to "butt out." Bill was frantic, short-tempered, and out of control with the children, and although I tried to convince Bill to be open with me when I told him that the dips in Perry's behavior might be related to something going on at home, Bill refused to confide in me.

When I saw Patty at one of our last sessions in December, she had gained a good deal of weight in six weeks; her face was puffy, her clothes unkempt, and she seemed sullen and withdrawn. Patty was abusing not only drugs, as I found out later, but alcohol as well.

By the middle of February, Perry was regressing further, becoming more anxious, less in control, and my attempts to get Patty back into her NA counseling (Bill finally told me she had stopped going) were unsuccessful. Patty now refused to come to our sessions, and Perry's behavior was a reaction to the turmoil at home.

Once again, Perry made his volcanoes and often hid under the slide in his "safe place." He appeared depressed and withdrawn and was reluctant to share his feelings. He announced, "I can get my own way at home. I can be boss and tell Mommy and Dad what to do."

Bill was now cooking, shopping, and struggling to maintain a sense of family, while Patty become more slovenly, more irritable, and less involved with the children. Finally, one night in late spring, Patty "short-circuited," as Bill put it. She left the house, managed to find drugs on the street, came home late in the evening, and "tried to tear the house apart." Bill called Patty's NA support person, who took her to the local hospital.

I saw Perry the next day. A neighbor was helping out at home while Bill tried to get some more permanent arrangement for the children's care. Perry came into the playroom like a cyclone. He would not talk but roamed around the room. He grabbed some crayons and drew himself with a large, open mouth and great big teeth. It was like the picture he had first made of Patty. He ignored my attempts to comfort him and hid behind a couch. I waited. He finally came out and sat near me. He then ran out into the waiting room and threw himself on the floor, sobbing. Bill and I tried to comfort him. Finally, he sat on my lap, asking if he could "play," and we went back to the playroom.

We tried to play checkers, but Perry dumped them on the floor, although he picked them up without my asking him to. He then built a "house." He put all the plastic dinosaurs inside and then attacked them all, knocking everything over. In response to my reflections about his anger, Perry simply ignored me and hid his face under a cushion. He then came out, found Buddy, and hid Buddy under the cushions, saying, "I want to lock up everybody. I don't like this family." He hit Buddy with a tambourine.

▶ Buddy is crying. (Pointing to the doll's freckles.) See his tears?

▶ Buddy is crying because you hit him, and maybe because the family is locked up.

▶ (Through a torrent of tears): The family is gone, gone, gone. Mommy is gone, gone in the hospital—forever. I want my Mommy. She won't be home for my birthday party.

▶ Perry, you can have two parties: one on your real birthday and one when Mommy comes home. If you like, I'll ask your dad about that.

Perry seemed to accept this suggestion, calmed down, and sat near me. I didn't want our session to end with such despair, and I offered to help Perry make a get-well card for Patty. Cheering up, he took the construction paper and crayons and accepted my help (a big concession for him) in spelling some of the words. He then decorated the card and made an "envelope" for it. By the end of our time, Perry's mood was lighter, but I knew that the next six weeks (the length of Patty's hospitalization) would be especially painful for Perry.

Indeed, they were. Our next two sessions were pivotal in Perry's therapy. Through words and actions, he unleashed all the mental and physical suffering that he had endured in his five and a half years. When he came into the playroom, I asked him how he was feeling.

▸ Two hundred!
▸ What does that mean?
▸ Two hundred means good, better than one hundred.
Daddy says that when Mommy comes home we can have
a party—one big one for me and Mommy.

My relief in hearing this was quickly dispelled by what happened
next. Announcing that he was "baking pies," Perry took the Play-
Doh out of the can. Then he aimed one pie at me, threatening to
"throw it in your face," and I knew that Perry thought I must have
failed him in some way: How could I, his friend, the one he had
come to trust, let bad things happen to him? Perry felt betrayed by
adults yet again.

After the pie threat, Perry was upset and withdrew, sniveling,
to his "safe place" under the slide. Eventually, he came out and
yelled at the top of his lungs, "It's my fault that Mommy went away.
I was bad."

I tried to reassure Perry, but he put his head on the table.

▸ Perry, you weren't responsible. You didn't do anything
that put Mommy in the hospital.
▸ Dad says I didn't do it, but I know I did. I was bad.

Perry crawled into a large cardboard box and repeated, "It's my
fault." Finally, he came out, and we were able to talk about being
"bad." Perry confided that once Patty had told him he caused all her
problems and "drives" her nuts." Perry rejected all my attempts to
ease his guilt and pain, and our session ended with discomfort on
both our parts. When Perry and I entered the waiting room, Bill
sensed that something was amiss. I phoned him that evening, and
he told me that Perry was withdrawn and weepy, and that he, too,
was having difficulty reassuring Perry about his role in Patty's illness.

Our next session took place two days later, and I knew it would
again be a difficult one. Perry ran into the room and hid behind a
chair: silence. I waited and waited. He finally emerged with a shout.

▶ Did I scare you?
▶ Were you trying to?
▶ Yes.
▶ Why?
▶ For fun.

Perry was restless, and I knew that he could relate his deepest troubles when he was using his hands. He spotted a large cardboard box and asked if he could make a "caterpillar house" out of it. When I assented, he took the scissors, started to cut out a window, and, as he did so, said in a flat voice, "Mommy is dead!"

▶ Perry, Mommy's not dead, she's just ill. Why do you say she's dead?
▶ I know. You go to a hospital only when you're dead.
▶ No, Perry, you go there to get well.
▶ No, she's dead. I made her go!

Perry got angry at me. Why didn't I understand? he seemed to be saying. He tried to throw the box at me, yelling again at the top of his lungs, "I want my mommy." Perry ran out of the room to his dad, and I followed as he hollered, "Tell Dorothy there was a fight at school. Tell her how I scratched a kid. Tell her, tell her!"

Perry was now out of control and ran back into the room. Bill asked if he could come, too. We followed Perry, who now tried to throw a large plastic toy at me. Bill tried to hold Perry. I put my hands on Perry's shoulders and asked him to look at me. I told him that I knew he was unhappy and angry, but that he could not hit me; he could use the box to let the anger out. Perry struggled out of Bill's arms, and we both watched as he ripped, pounded, stepped on the box and tore it. Like this cardboard box, Perry's world was falling apart.

We watched until Perry had had enough. Crawling like a baby, he went to the slide and sat under it. I waited a few minutes and then went to his "safe place" and reached out to him. Perry came out, put his head on my lap, and let out a sob like a wounded animal. Bill was crying softly, telling Perry how much he loved him, and that he, too, was sad about Mommy, but that no one was to blame for Mommy's illness—not Perry, not Robert, not Daddy. Perry hugged his father and seemed more composed. I spoke to Perry: "It's OK, Perry. We know you're angry and you miss Mommy, but Mommy will come home when she's feeling better. None of this is your fault."

I felt we needed to repair the box. Our session could not end with the "caterpillar house" in a shambles. Bill watched as Perry and I mended the box with tape. Perry agreed that we could leave it for our next session, when we would paint it.

▶ It will be for Mommy. A surprise for her when she gets home.
▶ Yes, I like that idea.

That evening, I called Bill, urging him to get the hospital staff's permission for Patty to talk to Perry; he needed to hear her voice to confirm that she was truly alive. Perry felt reassured after Patty spoke to him, and in his next session with me, the healing process began again.

Termination

During Patty's hospitalization, my work with Perry focused on helping him relieve his guilt, and on building up his self-esteem. Perry was able to talk about his mother and to recognize that what she did was not his fault. At first, Perry labeled his mother "bad"; then, gradually, he understood that she was unhappy and sick. He knew that drugs were involved but could not, of course, fully comprehend the implications of drug abuse.

Just before Patty was to return home, Perry announced once again, "I put Mommy in the hospital, Robert did, and Daddy did." Once again, he needed reaffirmation and tried to throw a toy steth-

oscope at me. I warned him that he would have to leave if he did
so, and he settled down.

> ► Remember, I threw a pie at you.
> ► I remember. You were angry and sad, angry at Mommy
> because she had to go away, and angry at me because you
> thought I could help her stay home.
> ► Yes, and when she comes home, I'll put her in the time-
> out chair.
> ► Why?
> ► 'Cause she went away.
> ► I guess you want to punish her.
> ► Maybe. Will she go away again?
> ► No. I don't think so. I hope not.
> ► Will she be the same when she comes back?
> ► Yes, Perry, she will be the same mommy, only she will
> be well again, like before, when she went to her meetings.
> ► Will she fight with Daddy?
> ► Perry, Daddy and Mommy will try to get along. I'm
> sure they will try hard.
> ► Dorothy, when do I stop coming here?
> ► Are you worried about that?
> ► A little.
> ► Well, you can still come for a while, until you feel really
> ready to stop.
> ► OK.

Perry needed reassurance that our relationship would continue after
Patty returned; he needed to know that there would be a safe place
for him. He still required support, and it was important to maintain
therapy after Patty's return until the family readjusted. Yet, I felt it
was time to begin thinking of reducing our sessions to test whether
Perry could begin to handle difficulties on his own. Bill and I agreed
that the twice-weekly sessions should continue for another month
or two, and then, gradually, we would reduce our visits, depending
on Patty's progress and Perry's reactions.

   After six weeks, Patty came home. She joined her support group
again and was on a strict regimen of diet, exercise, and therapy. The

roller-coaster ride of Perry's family situation was on an uphill turn. Bill evidenced great strength throughout the ordeal, faithfully bringing Perry to play therapy, and continuing in AA. He offered Patty his own strength now, and he no longer behaved toward her in a brutal, macho way. A sweetness emerged that I would not have predicted from my early encounters with him, nor from the history of physical abuse in the family. I can only surmise that Bill had profited from his counseling, gaining insight concerning his role as father.

Perry had learned alternatives to aggressive responses and, if he lapsed, recovered quickly. I began to phase out the therapy in late spring, almost one year after we had begun. Perry announced, half-joking and half-earnest, that he would "be bad so that I can come forever." Although Perry was making preparations to end our sessions as well, his reluctance was evidenced in his alternating between minor regressive behavior and a bravado stance: "I don't need to come. I have no troubles."

One day, Perry announced he had a secret that he could now share with me. He told me that he had been sucking his thumb at night and rubbing his blanket: "Now, Dorothy, I stopped—just like that!" He was very proud, and I realized that he was also telling me that he was better, more grown-up. Shortly after, Perry asked if he could take some of his drawings down from the bulletin board and walls. Again, he was letting me know that he was ready to leave me and this room, where so many outbursts of anger, tears of sadness, and also funny things had taken place. Perry left me one picture, a drawing of himself with a big smile, two missing teeth, and his arm raised in the air.

▶ Perry, what are you doing in the picture?
▶ I'm saying, "good-bye."

And we did say good-bye soon after that. I met with the Donnes several times as I ended the therapy with Perry. Patty was also conscientious about attending her own therapy sessions. She was on a strict diet, had begun to dress more neatly, had a new hairdo, and seemed more comfortable with me than she had been over the past year. At this point, I was seeing Perry only once a month. He would still announce that he had "talked out in school," hit Robert, or messed up his room—all said in a teasing way, and always followed by "I'm kidding. I just miss this room."

By summer, Perry and I had said our final good-byes. He brought me a photo of himself: a big grin, missing upper front teeth, and holding a small plant I had given him. I thought all was well: his report card was excellent. Patty and Bill were both keeping away from alcohol and drugs, and discipline was no longer a beating, but a time-out or the denial of TV or a treat. I told the Donnes that if ever Perry needed me, I would be here for them.

Unfortunately, in October, the phone rang. It was Bill: "Patty left me. The marriage is over. Can Perry come to see you?"

Perry came. He said, "I miss you." He had the beginnings of one new front tooth, but the smile was gone. He looked like a bent old man, his spirit and vitality diminished. We talked about Patty and Perry's sadness. He told me that he "never wants to see Mommy again." Perry was building up his defenses. He wanted to come back to see me, but that never happened: Perry did not come for his next appointment. When I phoned, Bill told me they were moving to California to join his brother Ed, and that eventually he would divorce Patty and start a new life again. Perry was lost. I fretted about his vulnerability. My reaction to Perry and Robert's loss was one of frustration. I felt once again as helpless as Perry did, but I hoped that whatever strength Perry had found through play therapy would enable him to deal with his new life without his mother.

CHAPTER THREE

TOM'S SCARY WORLD

A Case of Sexual Abuse

Introduction

There are times when it is difficult for me to separate my role as therapist from that of a parent. Working with Tom, a five-year-old boy, created that conflict in me. I can describe my immediate reaction only as outrage when I heard about what had happened to him. Hearing his mother, Ellen Kaye, tell me over the telephone that Tom had been sexually molested by her cousin Eddie made my stomach knot in pain. Outwardly, I remained as calm as I could and tried to reassure her that I would work with Tom in play therapy.

Here, once again in my practice, an innocent child had been the victim of an adult's perversion. And once again, I needed to control my anger and disgust, that someone had continued to violate a youngster over a year's time and no one had suspected it. And yet, once again, I also tried to understand, as a psychologist, the aberration of a person like Eddie. What had driven him to invade the lives of Tom and his parents with such a foul act?

I remember, too, feeling the urge to say to Ellen Kaye, "Where were you? Didn't you know? Didn't you even suspect? How could you let this happen?" And then, the more rational, controlled me, the therapist, responded appropriately, as I had on many similar occasions over the years, and as I undoubtedly will again when the next sexual abuse case is referred to me.

The parents were Eddie's victims, too. I listened to Ellen with sympathy and concern, and with the knowledge that often, the parents are trusting, especially when a family member is the abuser, and that, as a result, the abuse continues. Tom may have believed that what was happening to him was normal, perhaps even a sign of Eddie's love. After all, no one was concerned about it or stopped it. In Tom's mind, his parents' silence must have meant that they condoned Eddie's actions. But after a year, as Tom grew older, and as the incidents became more frequent and were accompanied by pain and threats, Tom had broken the silence himself and told his parents about his disturbing experiences with his cousin.

Tom's Story

It was evening bathtime in the Kaye houshold. Tom's two-year-old sister, Maureen, had just come out of the tub. She was dressed in her pajamas, and Ellen was reading her a story. Jim, the children's father, was washing Tom's hair while Tom squirmed, wiggled, and protested about the soap getting into his eyes. Then Tom said, "Soap comes out of pee-pees." At first, Jim thought that Tom meant the shampoo that now made bubbles and floated in the tub. Tom persisted. "Eddie pee-pees in my face, and my eyes get stuck together." Jim quickly pulled Tom out of the tub, dried him, and carried him into his room. He shouted for Ellen to join him. Together, they tried to remain calm questioning Tom further.

> ► Tell me, just tell me what you mean about "pee-pee" in your face.
> ► After you and Mommy go out, Eddie comes into my room and lays down on my bed, right next to me. He

jumps up and down on my heinie. He pulls my pants
down. Eddie's pee-pee is hard. He puts soap on my eyes
with his pee-pee.

Jim and Ellen listened to this, tried not to panic, and continued to
probe. Tom told his parents that this happened whenever Eddie came
to baby-sit. Eddie, Ellen's cousin, had been looking after the children
for about a year and a half, since he had turned sixteen and was able
to drive to the Kayes'. He had lived with Ellen's parents from the
time he was an eleven-year-old, when his own parents were killed
in an automobile accident. Ellen's mother and father had legally
adopted him about a year after the tragedy. The Kayes described
Eddie as a loner and a poor student, but a "good kid" who seemed
to love their children. He was saving up for his own car and needed
the baby-sitting money. Jim had felt that Eddie was somewhat
"strange," but Ellen felt comfortable with him as a sitter and trusted
him completely.

As the Kayes questioned Tom further, he described in greater
detail what Eddie had done, including rubbing Tom's penis, "smell-
ing" his "heinie," and "biting" his penis. Evidently, when Tom
resisted, Eddie pulled Tom's hair, "squeezed" his face, and
"punched" him. Once, he had "kicked" Tom when Tom resisted
him and had also threatened to hurt him. These threats had become
more frequent, and so Tom had decided to tell his parents. Just the
weekend before, Eddie had "twisted my nose and twisted my pee-
pee. He held his hand over my mouth so that I wouldn't holler, and
he squished my face."

Ellen and Jim put Tom to bed, reassuring him that he was a
good boy, and that Eddie was "bad" and would be "punished."
They promised not to hit Eddie or Tom. Both parents left the room
and collapsed into each other's arms, crying, heartbroken, and bewildered. Ellen then remembered that six months before, Tom had
kept talking about a "hard pee-pee" and she had assumed that he
was referring to his awareness of his own erections. She also recalled
that just three weeks before, he had mentioned a "soapy pee-pee."
Again, she thought, as Jim had, that Tom was referring to the soapy
bath bubbles and made no connection between his two attempts to
reveal what had been happening to him. As Ellen put it, "Such things
as Eddie did to Tom never occurred to me."

The Kayes were in a state of shock. Their world seemed to be crumbling around them. Jim's next reaction was fury, and Ellen had to restrain him from going out to find Eddie. "I'll kill the bastard," he shouted over and over. When he finally calmed down, they called their pediatrician, who advised them about the procedure to follow.

The following morning, the Kayes reported the incident to the Connecticut Department of Children and Youth Services, as their pediatrician had advised. A social worker visited the Kayes and questioned Tom, who repeated the story just as he had told it his parents. The Kayes did not want to involve the police until they had spoken to Eddie and to Ellen's parents, the Kellers, but they took Tom to the pediatrician for an examination. The social worker had given them a referral to the child abuse unit at the local hospital for an evaluation, but the Kayes preferred that Tom go to a private therapist. Their pediatrician referred them to me.

The Kayes also took Maureen to the pediatrican for an examination. They had asked Tom if Eddie had ever "touched " Maureen, but Tom hadn't seemed to know. Doubt was raised, however, and now Ellen and Jim were afraid that their daughter might also have been victimized by Eddie and was too young to tell them.

The pediatrician's examination of both children showed no evidence of abrasions or infection, and he was able to ascertain that there had been no penetration of Maureen's vagina or of Tom's anus, ruling out coitus and sodomy. Eddie's acts seemed to have involved mostly touching or stroking Tom's body, and perhaps masturbating by rubbing against Tom. Fellatio may also have been part of the abuse.

Eddie agreed to begin therapy with a psychiatrist ("only because I'm unhappy") but kept denying the Kayes' accusation. In a dramatic scene, Ellen's mother implored the Kayes not to press criminal charges, saying that the "whole family would be disgraced." She promised that Eddie would continue in treatment, and she hoped that he would eventually be able to confess what he had done and confront his illness. The Kellers were as shocked as the Kayes and also expressed considerable guilt to Ellen, blaming themselves for "not bringing Eddie up right." They all agreed that there would be no further contact betwen Eddie and the children.

Jim was more inclined than Ellen to press charges. He was unhappy with the family's decision to keep the incident quiet, but for Ellen's sake he went along with it. As required by law, the social worker did report the incident to the police, but as the family did not press charges, no arrest was made.

It was agreed that Tom would begin play therapy immediately.

The Kayes

"Find out, please find out," Ellen begged me at our first parents' session. "Please find out. Maybe it's not true. Maybe this is all a dream and Tom was never touched."

During this first session, I took down all the facts as the Kayes presented them to me, but I made it clear that my role was trying to help Tom overcome his present emotional state and that I would not pry; I would not play detective. Tom had been questioned by his parents, his grandparents, the social worker, and the pediatrician. Enough! Now it was time to begin the healing process. If the Kayes wanted an evaluation to determine whether or not the abuse had taken place, I suggested that they get one at the hospital's child abuse unit. I wanted to concentrate on working with Tom to help him deal with the trauma—or, if it was not real, on discovering the reasons for his allegations and his current distress. If Tom revealed his "secret" to me through play, he would do so on his own terms. He needed a respite from the constant probing, and he needed someone he could trust and a place where he could just be Tom. He was a little boy who needed to regain a sense of himself, and who needed, as we shall see, to "wash away" the "bad things."

Once the Kayes had agree to accept my terms and were willing to regard me as Tom's therapist, not their "detective," I continued to inquire about Tom and his family.

Ellen and Jim were very young, both only twenty-three. They had been in high school together, "not real lovers," but "good friends." They had had occasional sex and had married a few months after Ellen discovered that she was pregnant with Tom, about five and a half years before. Ellen had dropped out of school, but Jim had continued and learned a trade. He was now a draftsman. Ellen had learned word processing and had a thriving free-lance business typing reports and manuscripts.

Tom had started nursery school; he was enrolled when he was four and a half because "he needed friends, and he fought too much with Maureen."

As the Kayes talked about Tom, Ellen cried continuously. Jim was more in control, stony-faced and less overtly distressed. At one point, when Ellen and Jim described the bath scene and Tom's "confession," Ellen broke down and became hysterical. She shook, screamed, and then sobbed with deep sounds like rattles as she gasped for air. Jim sat there, watching and weeping inside.

"Why don't you hold her?" I wanted to shout. "Don't just sit there. Hold her. Comfort her. Cry yourself. It's all right. Hold her—hold each other."

But I didn't. I offered the tissue box to Ellen and tried to soothe them both.

"It's all right," I said. "I know how much pain you must be feeling. It's all right, cry."

I, too, felt pain. How could I not feel compassionate? I wanted to cry as Ellen did, but my crying would hardly have been useful. What I was there to do was offer strength, some suggestions that would help, and an opportunity to talk, to let the Kayes' feelings come out: anger at Eddie; guilt because this had happened and they, as parents, had not stopped it; helplessness because they couldn't go back in time and have their child the way he had been, unsullied and "innocent."

And now hints of Tom's distress over the past year began to form a clearer pattern for his parents. Ellen recalled the incidents when Tom had tried to tell her about Eddie: the "hard pee-pee" and the "soap in the pee-pee." Why hadn't she listened? she asked. His behavior too had changed. He had nightmares more frequently, and there had been occasional bed-wetting. Ellen: "I thought it was because he was jealous of Maureen. She gets a lot of attention. Were these signs of the abuse?"

> ▸ Bed-wetting and nightmares can indicate many things:
> the new school and, yes, even some regression because of
> the rivalry with Maureen. You're too hard on yourself,
> Ellen. You had no real reason to suspect sexual abuse.

▸ But I'm his mother. I should *know* these things. I should sense them, feel them. Where was I?

▸ Ellen, you were there, doing your best for your children.

Over the months to follow, Ellen continued to wallow in her guilt despite all my efforts to reassure her. Jim remained stoical, seething with anger toward Eddie and, as I later found out, toward Ellen. He seemed to blame her for using Eddie as the sitter, and for not, as he put it, "being tuned in to the kids." I witnessed their disputes in my office: the recriminations, the making up and forgiveness, and then the arguments all over again. It was a growing disease they could not cure, a disease inflicted on the Kayes by Eddie's emotional disturbance, acted out on Tom.

"Why," Jim asked, "why in God's name would someone do this to a child?"

I gave the Kayes the reasons that research offers. There are men who, for one reason or another, feel inadequate in relationships with females. They have a poor self-concept, have poor relationships with others, or may even feel threatened by women.

Contrary to popular belief, most sex offenders are not "dirty old men"; they are young and respectable. Most child molesters are also well know to their victims, just as Eddie was well known to Tom: three quarters or more of the offenders are friends, neighbors, or relatives. The research tells us, too, that most abusers were abused themselves as children.

Ellen reassured me that Eddie had never been abused. His parents had been "wonderful people," and her parents were religious, law-abiding, simple, decent folk.

Jim continued, "But Eddie is scared of girls. He talks a good game and even has pin-ups in his room, but he has never once had a girlfriend or even a really close friendship with a guy. All he does is fiddle with motors. He asks me about cars all the time. He never goes out on weekends. He rents porno videotapes from stores. I know, but so do a lot of guys. He always has his head under the hood of Gramp's car, and when we're over visiting, he pokes under the hood of my pickup truck."

"He's a good kid," Ellen said. "I still can't believe this, but in my heart, somehow, I know it's true. It's killing my folks, and it's killing us. Can Eddie be cured? Can Tom be cured?"

In our society, despite the openness about sex in the popular media and in conversation, it is difficult for many children to understand what is "appropriate touching." The numerous books, videos, and classroom discussions about self-protective skills that reduce children's vulnerability to assault are certainly good preventive measures for the school-aged child, but the preschooler also needs help in recognizing and resisting sexual exploitation. Unfortunately, Tom was a child who received such information too late.

Over the months, I offered the Kayes more information about sex offenders, but during our early sessions, I felt that it was important to focus on Tom and to get a sense of how deeply he had been wounded.

Tom was one of the estimated 500,000 children who are sexually abused each year. For sexually abused children, the abuse continues over a long time, and many remain scarred in some way, by loss of self-esteem, anger, guilt, and depression. Older children who have been sexually abused over long periods of time not only harbor these feelings but may also have problems later in life in forming appropriate sexual relationships. In many cases, they become involved in drug and alcohol abuse and even in prostitution.

The Kayes told me more about Tom. He had always been an active child. Once, Ellen said, when he was two and ran into the street, she had "whipped" him because she was afraid he would do it again and she needed to "teach him a lesson." For most of his five years, Tom had been "wild," and "aggressive when kids came over."

As Jim put it, "He does have behavior problems. That's why we thought nursery school would be good for him. You know, teach him how to get along with other kids. We do yell at him a lot—he's always teasing Maureen. I sometimes hit him, send him to his room, or make him stand in a corner. He's been really awful these past six months. Like I said, I thought it was because Maureen gets into his things, and she tries now to fight back. I never, ever thought it could be anything else than just normal kid fighting.

"Tom is an awkward kid, he can't throw a ball; he can barely skip or jump. His speech is not clear. We can understand him, but sometimes the words are hard to figure out. It's getting a little better since nursery school, and since he has more kids to play with. Tom liked to play with me at night, but lately he wants to watch TV when I offer him a game. TV seems to be the only thing he concentrates on. He can be mean and ornery or as sweet as sugar—his moods change so darn fast—but mostly he's 'hyper.' The nightmares have been more frequent, but like Ellen said, we had no reason to suspect anything unusual."

Ellen and Jim both had praise for the Kellers. Tom adored his grandparents and always wanted to visit.

"Lately, we've noticed that Eddie hasn't been around when we came over," said Jim. "We thought it was a good sign—maybe he'd found a friend at last. We had no idea that he was avoiding us. God, if only I'd know earlier what that bastard was doing to my kid!"

"Do you think this will stay with Tom all his life?" Ellen asked. "Do you ever get over something like this? Is Tom's life ruined?"

These were questions I had heard from many distraught parents in cases of sexual abuse, but just as I had told other parents, I told the Kayes that each child is different, and that with good parenting and professional help, a child as young as Tom had a fairly good chance of regaining a positive self-image and feelings of self-worth.

Tom's Scary World

Tom came to see me a couple of days after my first session with the Kayes. He looked like a miniature professor. He wore glasses with thick lenses that hid his dark brown eyes; he sported a bow tie, a crisp white shirt, and long gray flannel pants; and his expression was serious, almost doleful. But when he spoke, the image of the scholar was immediately shattered. He was difficult to understand because of a lisp, misprounciations of words, a singsong quality, and a tendency to swallow the last words in a sentence.

Tom was of average height for his age, but very thin. His brown hair was neatly combed, but he had a cowlick that added to his comical appearance. To top it all off, Tom's nose was runny and well acquainted with his sleeve. I realized that Ellen had groomed Tom for his visit with me, and I let her know that day that it would be perfectly all right if Tom wore jeans or play clothes in the future. He did so after that and appeared more relaxed.

When Tom entered the playroom, he asked me if it were Pee-Wee Herman's house.

> ▸ Mom said I was going to a place like on TV.
> ▸ No, Tom, it's not Pee-Wee Herman's house, but a place where we can play and talk together. You can tell me how you feel about things, what makes you feel good, and what makes you feel not so good. OK?
> ▸ OK. Can Mom come in here, too?
> ▸ If you want her to, she can.
> ▸ Well, can I go and show her this?

Tom had found a small box of miniature figures. I went with him to the waiting room, where he quickly showed Ellen the toys and then, reassured that she was there, ran ahead of me to the playroom to explore its contents. I had planned to use our first day just to get acquainted and explain the rules, so that I could observe Tom. He was curious about the toys that I had set out for him, opening some drawers and cabinets to look for others, glancing at me each time to be sure I approved. Settling down with one toy seemed to mean to Tom that he would have to forgo the possibility of playing with the others. I explained that he would have time to use all the toys in the future, but he didn't seem to grasp this idea. He was like a child in a candy store, finding it difficult to make a choice, wanting to sample each item, and attracted to the next before he had even finished savoring the previous one.

Tom rarely smiled, and he maintained his serious expression throughout our first session. He listend as I explained who I was but asked no questions; and he seemed guarded and standoffish with me. When our session was drawing to a close, I told him it was time to clean up. He ignored me and grabbd the doctor's kit and a small bear, jabbing the bear with the plastic hypodermic needle. This was a favorite activity of many of the children; I made a mental note to begin our next session with these particular toys. Perhaps Tom was trying to tell me something. If indeed he was, we didn't have time that day to explore this play more fully. I also felt that I didn't want to create any further anxiety at our first meeting. Tom jabbed the bear once more.

▶ The doctor does this to me.
▶ Are you playing doctor?
▶ Yep, and here goes a shot!
▶ Tom, you can play doctor next time. Now it's time to clean up.

Tom threw the bear and the kit, scattering its contents all over the floor. He just stared at me.

▶ Tom, I know you feel angry because you have to stop playing, but time is up. Remember, we clean up before we go. That's a rule here. Please put the toys on the shelf.
▶ I don't want to.
▶ I know you want to play, and we will again next time. We can start our time together playing with the doctor's kit and the bear. But now it's cleanup time.

Tom ran out of the room, hid behind the door, and waited.

▶ Tom, please come back. I'm waiting for you. We can clean up together. But you must pick up the toys.

Tom peeked around the door at me.

"Tom," I repeated in a firm but nonthreatening voice, "please pick up the toys. Remember, I explained that we do this so that we can easily find the toys we like again, and so that other children can find them."

Tom came out of his hiding place and looked at me sheepishly. "He's through testing me," I thought as he picked up the toys and glanced at me for approval.

"Good job, Tom," I said. "Now let's go to Mommy. She's waiting for you."

I thought about this incident long after Tom left and made notes about my conjectures. Was he angry because I had missed a message he was trying to convey to me about the "shots" and the bear? Or was he angry because he couldn't have his own way? Was he trying to find out what my role was, how strict I would be about imposing the playroom rules, and how far I would go if he didn't comply? After all, someone else in his life had made him comply. Would I twist his nose?

These thoughts worried me, and it occurred to me that, in Tom's eyes, because adults had power, he needed to learn what difference there was in the kinds of requests and demands that adults made. Tom needed to know when he should say "no" to ensure his physical and mental safety. Right now, it seemed that his aggressiveness at home and his defiant stance with me were his way of asserting himself, as well as his way of expressing the guilt and anger he must feel about what Eddie had done to him. And of course, Tom may have felt that he had been "bad" because he had participated in the dreadful secret. Sometimes, children who have been abused feel that they are to blame, that they are "dirty" or "bad," and that's why they continue to be victimized.

I would wait and watch as Tom, in his own way, directly with words or mutely with toys revealed his story to me. Perhaps this first day with him was the beginning of the unraveling of his scary experience. Tom's parents believed him completely; rarely can a child of Tom's age make up the details he described to his parents. My job was now to help him recognize that he was not at fault and that he could learn which adults he could trust.

The next time he came, Tom eagerly ran into the playroom. He was wearing a baseball cap, jeans, and an "Alf" T-shirt, looking more like a boy of five than he had on the previous visit. Before I could stop him, however, he had dumped all the plastic cups and saucers out of their small bin, spotted some cans of Play-Doh, and announced that he wanted to "bake cookies." This was fine. I watched as he rolled the clay.

▸ This feels good.
▸ You like to make things with Play-Doh?
▸ Yep, I have some at home, but Mommy got mad.
▸ Why?
▸ I throwed it at Maureen.
▸ Well, you must have been pretty angry to do that.

Silence.

- ▶ Do you fight with Maureen a lot?
- ▶ She starts.
- ▶ Does she? How?
- ▶ She's a ninny.
- ▶ How does she start?
- ▶ She takes everything.

Tom stopped "baking." As he was putting the clay away, he saw the doctor kit that I had placed on the couch near the bear. Very carefully, he examined the bear, took a spoon from the tea set, and fed the bear. I watched as he played and talked out loud: "Now Teddy, eat your beans. If you don't you get a shot."

Tom handled Teddy brusquely, turning him upside down and giving him a "shot" in his back. Tom did this several times, wearing an angry expression.

- ▶ Well, you're really giving Teddy a lot of shots.
- ▶ Yep, he's so bad, so bad. He won't do anything I say.
- ▶ What do you want him to do?
- ▶ Listen, listen, listen!
- ▶ Listen to what?
- ▶ Nothing!

Tom finished the doctor game and, without my reminding him, picked up all the contents of the kit as well as the plastic dishes and put them away. Tom was again telling me something about the bear, and I needed to be patient. I sensed that his emotions were rather close to the surface, and that he was now just trying to figure out whether or not he could let these feelings emerge in my presence.

Noticing that he was now fingering the crayon box, I asked Tom if he would like to draw. He nodded yes, and I gave him a large pad. This was the beginning of what I called the "missing body series." Tom drew a large round face with the usual features and lots of brown hair.

▶ Who is this?
▶ Me, of course.
▶ Well, it's a good face. Can you draw the rest of you?
▶ Don't want to.
▶ Well, I like this face. Do you want to write your name
on the top?
▶ I can do my name. I can print *Tom*.

He laboriously printed his name in large letters, slanting upward,
typical of a five-year-old. He then gave me the picture.

▶ Here, put it up on the wall.
▶ We can do that together. Just show me where you want
it.

Tom found a place he liked on the wall and taped his drawing to it.
He stood back, admiring.

▶ Now I'm here.
▶ Yes, you are here.

Tom and I played his two favorite games for the next few sessions:
baking cookies and playing doctor. He made more elaborate cookies
and alternated between feeding the bear and giving it "shots." His
nose was never dry. I showed him how to use tissues and how to
blow, but he still preferred his sleeve. If I reminded him about the
tissues, he would use them, but the sleeve was more convenient.

At the end of each of these sessions, Tom would draw a "face"
for me. They were always the same: big brown eyes, a little round
nose, and a mouth that was a straight slit across the bottom of the
face. He did not draw a body. We put these faces in a folder. Tom
wrote his name on the front of it and told me to keep him "safe"
inside. He then took his first picture off the wall and added it to the
folder so it, too, would be "safe."

Would Tom ever draw the rest of him? I wondered when that would be. He evidently felt some trust in me, giving me his pictures to keep in the "safe" place, but he was obviously having difficulty dealing with his body image. The lower part of his body was perhaps a part he wanted to deny, and until he could trust me and begin to feel more positive about himself, Tom would remain "bodyless."

I had no idea whether or not Eddie had used Tom passively, to masturbate with, or had tried to arouse Tom and evoke some sexual response. If so, the sexual abuse had been all the more traumatic. Research indicates that children who have been traumaticaly sexualized, a process in which, according to Finkelhor and Browne, "a child's sexuality (including both sexual feelings and sexual attitudes) is shaped in a developmentally inappropriate and interpersonally dysfunctional fashion as a result of sexual abuse," may later develop confusion and misconceptions about themselves, inappropriate repertoires of sexual behavior, and sometimes unusual emotional associations with sexual activities.

Eddie had used affection, attention, and later, it appears, threats to maintain his relationship with Tom over the year. Certainly, Tom must have been confused by what was happening, especially after he began to attend nursery school: Later, I found out, that the school did have a simple "sex education" program consisting of stories about "good touching" and "bad touching," and I believe this program was what finally motivated Tom to tell his parents about Eddie.

Tom felt betrayed by Eddie. Eddie had been someone he loved, someone to whom his parents had entrusted him, someone who had given him gifts and had often taken him for a ride in the car to "buy ice cream or hamburgers." Eddie had been like a big brother to Tom, and now he couldn't see him anymore. This young man, whom he had adored, had treated Tom with a complete disregard of the effects his behavior would have on Tom and the family.

As the therapy continued, Tom's attacks on the bear became more violent. I interpreted his behavior as meaning that Tom had been made powerless by Eddie. His territory and body space had been attacked against his will, and now Tom was venting his anger on the toy bear. Perhaps, early in the year, Tom had been passive and more agreeable, but later, as Eddie's abuse continued and as Tom felt more guilty and, perhaps, resisted, these attacks became more frightening and more ugly. Tom had tried to stop Eddie but must have been frustrated in his attempts to do so. He had been trapped by fear and even, to some degree, by a strange kind of loyalty to Eddie. Tom had kept his secret for a long time.

Now, Tom felt "badness," shame, and guilt. We also didn't know whether Eddie had conveyed these feelings to Tom in words. Tom must surely have been sensitive to his parents' reactions when he told them about the abuse. As calm as the Kayes tried to be, shock, disgust, fear, anger, and a desire for revenge—all powerful emotions—had come pouring out. And then there was the visit from the social worker, discussions about police, and finally Tom's visits to me. Tom had seen his grandparents cry; he had been denied further contact with Eddie. Surely, he knew that something of great proportions had occurred and that he was at the center of a family tragedy. He must have felt stigmatized in some way. Fortunately, no one "blamed" Tom, despite the general hysteria. He was not treated as "bad" but given support and love, unlike some sexually abused children who are viewed as "spoiled goods" and even assigned such negative characteristics as being "oversexed." They may be treated as being as blameworthy as their abusers and may be made to feel ashamed. If there are strong religious and cultural taboos in addition to the usual stigma, a child may feel even more different, more estranged, and more morally corrupt than a child who is clearly told that what happened was not his or her fault. Fortunately, Tom was young enough not to comprehend many of the ramifications of his victimization. But it was clear to me that he needed help in regaining his sense of himself and in shedding his anger and guilt.

After a month of building up trust and allowing Tom to take the lead, I introduced into our play a small bathtub and "anatomically neutral" rubber dolls. I wanted to see what he would do with these before I introduced an "anatomically detailed" boy doll.

Originally, these more realistic dolls were designed to prepare children for the anxieties aroused by surgery. Now they are used by mental health professionals, physicians, and law enforcement personnel with children who they suspect may have been victims of sexual abuse. Unfortunately, many people using these dolls have little training in their correct use. Research suggests that there is too little agreement about exactly which interactions between a child and a doll indicates that sexual abuse has very likely taken place. When, for example, a child uses a doll to reenact digital penetration of the vagina or the anus, surveys show that most police view this action as an indication that actual penetration has taken place. A mental health professional may interpret it only as exploratory play or curiosity where, indeed, no actual abuse may have occurred. Unfortunately, there are no standardized protocols similar to those in other tests, such as those of intelligence, achievement, aptitude, vocational preference, or even creativity. However, dolls, along with other play materials, such as drawings, and in the context of therapy, appear to be useful in detecting whether a child has been abused.

It is important that any evaluation of the sexual abuse of a child be done over time. As I had told the Kayes, I would use dolls and other materials to offer Tom relief, not to investigate the details of his experience with Eddie. I explained that dolls could be used to help Tom learn about good or bad touching, a continuation or reinforcement of what the nursery school teacher had tried to convey. I believe, too, that dolls should not be used in therapy if a court case is pending. Such use may interfere with the admissibility of evidence based on the child's interaction with the doll during the initial investigation or even when the child testifies during the trial, because the continued play may alter the child's memory of the actual experience. It is appropriate to use dolls in therapy as part of the healing process only after the investigative phase of the case has ended. Tom's parents definitely were not pursuing legal action. Therefore, my decision to introduce the dolls seemed to be justified.

After six visits, Tom was eager to come into the playroom. He usually ran ahead of me and then would wait, owl-like, peering through his thick lenses. Just before his seventh visit, I had placed the small rubber tub, with water in it, on the table and had put a small rubber doll next to it. The doll was naked. Tom enjoyed putting the doll into the water, washing it, and then drying it. He put it "to sleep" on a cushion. I didn't expect any reaction to this doll; after all, it was sexually neutral. Immediately after this rather benign doll play, Tom gravitated toward the doctor's kit and the bear. He jabbed the bear with the "needle" repeatedly.

▸ Hope you feel this and this and this!
▸ Tom, you sure like to hurt that bear. Poor bear.
▸ Well, give it some pills.

Tom took the "pillbox" out of the kit. It was empty. He made believe there were pills in it and gave them to the bear.

"I'm glad you're making the bear feel better," I said. "You really gave him a lot of shots."

Tom threw the bear down and, grabbing the rubber doll, threw it across the room.

▸ Tom, remember, you can't throw the toys. Please go and get it. You seem angry at Teddy and angry at the doll.
▸ Yep. I hate them, hate them.
▸ That's a strong feeling, Tom. Can you tell me why you hate the bear and the doll.
▸ They're "bad," "bad," "bad."

Tom grew silent and sat on the floor with his head down. I waited. Finally, he looked up at me and told me to pick up the toys.

"No," I said. "Please pick them up, Tom. You threw them, not I."

Tom waited, looked at me again, and reluctantly got up and gathered the toys from the floor. He put the doll back on the cushion and put the bear on the shelf. He then asked if he could take a toy home.

▸ Well, you know you can have a charm or a sticker, Tom, but that's all. The toys stay here so that other children can share them.
▸ OK, OK. Are you mad at me?
▸ No, Tom, I'm not mad at you. I like to play with you, but you must follow the rules.

Tom's time was up for the day. He chose a dinosaur sticker, put it on his shirt, and said good-bye.

Jim was in the waiting room. He told me that Eddie had been skipping his therapy sessions and that Ellen and he had been fighting a lot lately about it. I set up an appointment to see the Kayes. It was important that we review Tom's progress.

Tom came to see me one more time before my scheduled appointment with Ellen and Jim. I decided to offer Tom the anatomically detailed doll to play with (but not as an investigative technique). I was curious to see his reaction after his experience with the neutral rubber doll. I felt that he trusted me now, and I was concerned about his many "bodyless" self-portraits and his rage against the bear and the doll.

I placed the boy doll, fully clothed, near the tub. I left the neutral doll there as well.

▸ Tom, would you like to give this doll a bath?
▸ What's his name?
▸ Whatever name you want to give him.
▸ I'll call him Stevie.
▸ OK.
▸ Can I take his clothes off?

Tom proceeded to undress the doll. When he removed the overalls, he shouted, "He's got a pee-pee!"

He jumped back quickly, put his hands over his own genital area, and said, "I don't have a pee-pee. My daddy took it."

Tom was clearly upset and looked very pale, but he put the doll in the small tub. He then put the neutral dolls in the tub as well. Tom bathed the neutral doll, assiduously avoiding "Stevie."

▸ Why does Daddy have your pee-pee?
▸ He has it forever and ever and ever.
▸ Will he give it back to you?
▸ Never! Can I play doctor?

Tom clearly did not want to talk about his "pee-pee," and I felt that it would not be helpful to continue questioning him now. It seemed wiser to let Tom just play, work out his feelings about his "missing" penis, and also deal with "Stevie," the doll.

Tom left the dolls in the tub and played "cook," using Play-Doh to make "hot dogs" and "hamburgers." He then fed the neutral doll, ignoring Stevie.

> ▸ Isn't Stevie hungry?
> ▸ No, he never eats. He's sick. I'll take him to the doctor.

Tom took Stevie out of the tub, dried him, and took him to the table. He then gave Stevie all kinds of "medicines" and "shots."

> ▸ I guess Stevie is really sick.
> ▸ Yes, sick in the pee-pee.

Tom now put the medicine on the doll's penis and then jabbed the "hypodermic needle" into the penis. After each shot into the penis, Tom asked the doll, "Is your pee-pee OK? Does it hurt?"

Tom then pretended he was going back to his "office." He took the doctor's kit and rode around the playroom on a Big Bird "car," shouting.

> ▹ Pee-pee is gone. Pee-pee is sick. Pee-pee is gone. Pee-pee
> is sick.
> ▸ You're making it better, Tom. You're a good doctor.
> I'm glad you're making it better.

Tom came back to the dolls, and I told him it was time to start cleaning up. Tom took Stevie to the couch and carefully dressed him. Then he put the other toys away.

> ▸ Will you come home with me and play at my house?
> ▸ No, Tom, I can visit with you here. I'm pleased that you
> would like me to come home.

▸ Yes, I have no friends. Not even one. Not even two!
▸ I'm your friend, Tom. Maureen and Mommy and Daddy
are your friends.
▸ Eddie is gone!

This was the first time that Tom had mentioned Eddie to me.

▸ Eddie is still at Grandma's house, but you know that he
needs help so he won't do "bad" things to anyone.
▸ Eddie is bad. Mommy says so.
▸ Eddie did some things that were bad, I guess. Now he is
getting some help.

Tom headed for the waiting room, a clear signal to me that he did
not want to talk about Eddie any more that day.

I felt this session had been a breakthrough for Tom. It was the
first time he had displayed verbal concern about his body. In their
omission of his body, his drawings were significant, but now he had
revealed his rejection of his penis—the part of him that reminded
him of Eddie and the molestation and the anxiety of the family,
which had focused so much attention on the genitals.

Tom's response to the anatomically detailed doll had been one
of surprise, shock, and overt anxiety. Generally, when chidren do
find the doll in my room and play with it, they giggle and become
somewhat self-conscious, but they do not react as Tom did. The
sight of the penis had been unexpected, true, but Tom's reaction
suggested to me that he harbored many negative feelings about his
own penis. He no longer had a "pee-pee"; his father had it. Did that
mean that, in Tom's mind, Jim was protecting Tom and "guarding"
Tom's penis? Did it mean that his memories of Eddie's sexual acts
were so horrible that Tom needed to deny the part of him that had
been contaminated by Eddie? Tom's avoidance of the Stevie doll and
then, later, his need to see Stevie as sick suggested that Tom felt
"sick," too, and in need of "shots," "medicine," and some help to
restore his feeling of well-being. All the anger Tom had previously
expressed at the bear was now directed at Stevie. Because Stevie had
a penis and was a "little boy," the memories of Tom's experience

over the past year came to life and resulted first in Tom's avoidance of the doll, and then in his furious attack on the doll. He desperately wanted both to attack and to cure Stevie—to punish himself and to cure himself. Tom's reaction did not "prove" the truth of his story or Eddie's guilt, but it was suggestive. It may also have reflected Tom's reaction to his parents' concern about his story.

It was interesting, too, that Tom had wanted me to come home with him after the session. He had revealed much about himself more directly than during our previous visits. In a way, because of his disclosure, I believe that some signficant bonding had taken place. Perhaps Tom felt closer to me, more trusting, and viewed me as his protector and friend. He was able now to invite me home: I was an adult whom he could trust.

I saw the Kayes soon after this session. They were upset because Eddie was skipping his therapy appointments. He had confessed to his parents that he had touched Tom but had refused to go into details. The Kayes had sworn to him that they would never involve the police and had urged him to resume his therapy. Jim was less sympathetic toward Eddie, and during their session with me, the tension between Jim and Ellen was palpable.

"How long will Eddie be in treatment?" Ellen asked.

"That's hard for me to answer," I responded. "We don't know much about Eddie's sexual orientation, nor do we know if there have been other such incidents. I'm inclined to doubt it, however, from what you've told me about Eddie."

I did briefly describe the various approaches that have been used with persistent male sex offenders. Jim asked me about Depo-Provera, the controversial synthetic hormone that reduces sexual desire. He had read about it in *Newsweek* and was curious. I told him that it is used in some prisons, but that it has risky side effects. Conventional therapy is the approach more generally used with child molesters, but research tells us that there is really no cure for the perpetual molester, only varying degrees of self-control. Jim felt that the Kellers did not believe Eddie was capable of such "wickedness," as they called it, and that they were not "firm enough" in demanding that Eddie keep his appointments with his therapist.

Ellen was weeping now for her son and for Eddie: "All I want to do is hold Eddie, comfort him. No one is comforting him. I feel so rotten. I wish I had been there for him, really there, as a sister or even a mother. He's been through a lot. Tom's been through a lot, too. Did he tell you everything? Is there more stuff we need to know? How I wish I had listened when he said Eddie's pee-pee was hard!''

Ellen was suffering with mixed emotions: pain for Tom, pity for Eddie, and guilt that she had not heeded Tom's signals. But I repeated my position: I would try to help Tom feel better about himself, but I would not question him directly about details. I shared the main elements that had emerged in my last session with Tom, and I asked Ellen if she and Jim were giving Tom some information about "good and bad touching." I gave them a book to read geared to Tom's age level and an accompanying pamphlet that offered suggestions to parents concerning how to tell children about touching, and how to get children to talk if they are worried.

> ▸ It's important that you continue to support Tom if he talks about Eddie and his feelings to you. Research tells us that the one factor that helps children recover from sexual abuse—regardless of the kind, regardless of the duration, and regardless of who abused them—is their being able to talk about it to someone they trust, and that person's being supportive and caring.
> ▸ He told us, didn't he?
> ▸ Yes, that was good. He trusts you.
> ▸ But he's clammed up now. Why?
> ▸ Sometimes, after children do tell, they draw back. Putting the incident into words may be overwhelming. It makes the incident more real and stirs up anxiety. Tom also responds to your reactions. He knows what happened was serious. Now he needs to learn that he was not to blame. In his play, he's acting it out, trying to get rid of all the bad feelings. I suspect he'll do this for a while and will also try to accomplish self-healing through play.
> ▸ How long will this take?
> ▸ You both want "time" answers from me: How long will Eddie's "cure" take? How long will Tom's cure take? To be honest, I don't know. When we see Tom accepting his body, playing less aggressively, balancing his mood swings, sleeping better, and smiling more—we'll know.

Jim responded with an outburst: "That dirty homo—that's what he is. Why didn't he find another seventeen-year-old homo!"

Ellen was extremely upset by Jim's remarks; she got up and ran out of the room to the car. Jim and I followed. Ellen was now in tears: "Don't touch me. How could you? How could you?"

Jim and I both tried to lure Ellen back into the office, but she refused to go.

"Please, please, Ellen. I'm sorry. I'm sorry," Jim begged.

Ellen refused to speak. I told them to call me and to come back again because we needed to talk further. Jim shook my hand and got into the car, and they rode off.

I was distressed by Jim's accusations and also by the visible strain between the Kayes—over Tom, over Eddie, and over the Kellers' lack of support for Tom and their belief in and sympathy for Eddie. I was worried about the Kayes' relationship and would need to refer them for counseling. Like the child, the parents often need help when sexual abuse occurs. The Kayes had been devastated by this upheaval in their lives, and Ellen was especially distraught by the rift that the incident had caused between her parents and Jim.

Ellen called me the next morning and confessed a few things over the telephone: Eddie had been in therapy two years before and had actually been hospitalized for depression and an attempted suicide. Ellen believed he had been suffering a delayed reaction to his parents' deaths. That was why her folks were so protective of Eddie. She assured me that even though she and Jim had notified the police of the sexual abuse, all charges had been dropped, one contingency being Eddie's continuation in therapy. Ellen also said that the possibility of Eddie's being homosexual had occurred to her, too, and that when Jim had said it out loud, her own fears had simply erupted. She apologized for her emotional outburst.

This seemed like a good opportunity to recommend some counseling for the Kayes, and Ellen willingly took down the names of some therapists whom I suggested. We agreed to meet again in a few weeks to discuss Tom's progress.

As we ended the conversation, Ellen said, "Everyone is being punished: Tom, Jim, my folks, me, Eddie. It makes me want to scream!"

"Ellen, please try to see a counselor. It will help," I urged.

We said good-bye, and I felt uneasy about the Kayes. Would they be able to weather this storm?

Tom's Anger, Despair, and Repair

At our next session, shortly after the Kayes' visit, Tom came in with a new haircut—a crewcut—and looked less bookish. He ran to the shelf, grabbed a bin of plastic spacepeople and some blocks, built a wall, and put the spacepeople behind his wall.

- Everyone will be safe.
- Safe from what?
- Safe from bad people.
- Who's bad?
- Bad people are bad. Stevie's bad. Don't take his clothes off.
- I won't if you don't want me to.
- I don't want that doll to be naked.
- You were the doctor last time and tried to help him, didn't you?
- I helped him. He can stay on that chair. No more baths for you, Stevie.
- No more baths.
- We're not supposed to see his pee-pee, and (shouting) no one touches it! I love Stevie. Stevie is my baby-sitter.
- You have a new baby-sitter named Stevie?
- Well, not for real, but this Stevie can be my baby-sitter.
- This Stevie with his clothes on?
- Yes, this Stevie with his clothes on.

This was a remarkable session. I remember feeling elated and yet a bit anxious. It was all happening so quickly, even though I knew that Ellen was reading about sexual abuse and talking to Tom about it.

Tom was earnestly working through his feelings about Eddie. The Stevie doll, fully clothed, was acceptable and now was a mixture of both Tom and Eddie. Tom had indeed confused his and Eddie's penises and also felt confused about his feelings toward Eddie and himself. Now he was trying to sort them out. He played with the plastic spacepeople for the remainder of the session but maintained the wall between them and Stevie, who was now perched on a small chair behind the wall, separated from Tom and the miniature figures.

- ► Stevie is watching you play.
- ► Yes, he can watch.
- ► He's a good watcher.
- ► He can take care of us, but he can't come over here.

No, Tom was still not sure he wanted "Stevie," or any "sitter," to come very close despite his protestations of loving the Stevie doll. Progress was being made, however. Tom was beginning to acknowledge that he could begin to trust another sitter, or another grown-up male.

Our next session came after a two-week break during which Ellen, Jim, and the children went off on a short vacation. Unfortunately, at the end of their trip, without alerting the Kellers, the Kayes stopped off to see them. Eddie was home and in the living room. This was the first time Tom had seen him since revealing the molestation to his parents.

Tom was visibly shaken, and Jim asked Eddie to go up to his room. Eddie refused, and the Kayes left after a horrible scene with the Kellers. Jim swore he never wanted to see "the whole damn lot of them again."

Needless to say, Tom's next session demonstrated a setback. He ran around the playroom as if he had gone berserk. He threw "Stevie" on the floor and refused to comply with my attempts to stop him or control him. He ran into the waiting room and just cried. We sat there for a while, and then, nose running, shirt out, shoe laces undone, and face streaked with tears, he asked if he could come back and play. When we did go back, he stood in the middle of the playroom and announced with tremendous assertion, "I have a pee-pee."

I was startled, delighted, flabbergasted. I must admit that I had not anticipated this announcement after the previous scene.

Tom stood there and said it again.

- ▸ I have a pee-pee. No one can touch it but me or Mommy and Daddy.
- ▸ Well, that's the way it should be.
- ▸ Yes, that's the way.
- ▸ Would you like to tell Stevie that?
- ▸ Yes.

Tom went to the doll, held it, and made his announcement again. He then told me he would like to draw. He drew himself with a whole body! He asked if he could show the drawing to Ellen.

I was pleased, but apprehensive. What would happen next? Just as Tom was beginning to heal, the Kayes' marriage was floundering.

Unfortunately, my apprehension was accurate. Ellen and Jim had begun counseling, but Jim had refused to continue after a few sessions. He kept telling Ellen that he was OK: "It's your rotten cousin who's to blame." Ellen tried to continue alone, but she, too, stopped after only six sessions.

Tom's behavior in the playroom now began to reflect his anxieties about his parents. He played numerous "monster" games in which the "family" in the dollhouse was attacked by the monster, a plastic spaceman. The Stevie doll was also labeled a "monster" now and was "scary." Tom would knock the family figures down and throw Stevie on the floor. His play seemed to reflect the disruption he was experiencing at home.

Ellen told me each time she brought Tom to therapy that she "was a wreck" and "had to get away." I tried to persuade her to resume the counseling sessions so that she, at least, would get some relief.

Her response was, "What's the use? Jim won't cooperate. He hates my family now and I think he hates me and, I'm ashamed to say this, I think he can't stand to be around Tom. Tom reminds him of what Eddie did. Jim needs help more than I do, I guess. Now he's really reacting to the whole event, when at first, I thought he was in control."

Ellen phoned me often just to talk, and I did try to be her sounding board, but I knew she needed more consistent and sustained help. Meanwhile, Tom began to regress. During the next month, he became preoccupied again with the doctor kit and liked to inflict pain on the Stevie doll. It was as if he needed to exorcise the entire year's experience. He would jab the syringe into Stevie's belly button, penis, and "heinie" repeatedly. He used a lot of scatological language, for example:

- ▶ [Tom shouted]Stevie is pooh-pooh, pee-pee.
- ▶ You sure are mad at Stevie lately.
- ▶ He's pooh-pooh, caa-caa.
- ▶ Why is Stevie pooh-pooh, caa-caa?
- ▶ Because he is!

At this point, Tom turned to the bear and gleefully called the bear names. He began to lose control, screaming at the bear, then giggling, then screaming, and giggling again. I felt it was time to stop him, and I held him by the shoulders until he calmed down, saying, "Tom, you're really upset today. Can you tell me why?"

Tom was sobbing, the first time in a while that I had seen him cry. He sat on the floor, and I took two puppets out of the puppet box. Tom liked the rabbit and the cat best.

"Tom, would you like to play with your puppet friends?" I asked. "Here, put these on and talk to me if you can."

On occasion, Tom had put these puppets on his hands, changed voices, and carried on silly conversations in baby talk. Most of the time, his words were made up and completely unintelligible to me, but he always seemed quiet and peaceful when he played this way. I wanted him to calm down so that perhaps he would reveal what was upsetting him that day. Gradually, Tom stopped weeping and told me that he had seen Eddie on Sunday. Evidently there had been another visit to the Kellers that I didn't know about. I found out from Ellen that evening when I phoned her that she had taken the children to her parents for the weekend to "get away" from Jim—and, of course, Eddie had been home. I told Ellen about Tom's reaction to the visit and begged her not to repeat it until I felt that Tom had gained more strength.

When Tom came for his next session, I asked him to tell me more about the visit if he wanted to, and he was eager to talk about it:

▶ Daddy didn't come with us. Grandpa bought me a new baseball glove and played with me.
▶ That's good. You do love your Grandpa.
▶ Yes, and Grandma, too.

A long silence.

▶ What is it, Tom?
▶ I don't love Eddie. No more. He's so bad.
▶ I know you are angry at him. Did you talk to him on Saturday or Sunday.
▶ Once. He said, "Hi," to me and went out.
▶ Did you see him again?
▶ No. Mommy cried a lot and Grandma cried a lot. Can we play?
▶ Yes, Tom, we can play.

Tom chose to play with water. He filled the tub but didn't want to use the dolls. He took the plastic pitcher and cups and simply poured water back and forth. He seemed perfectly content to feel the water and did not want dolls intruding on his pure water play. However, after a while, Tom took the girl doll (also anatomically detailed), undressed her, and asked if he could wash her hair. He then took Stevie, undressed him, and washed his eyes—only his eyes. He poured the water over the girl doll and then dried her and put her on the table.

▶ This boy (*meaning Stevie*) needs water on his pee-pee—on his heinie. A pee-pee goes in his heinie.
▶ Tom, who says a pee-pee goes in Stevie's heinie?

▸ God says so! *This* doll (*pointing to the girl doll*) has no pee-
pee.
▸ No, she doesn't. She's a girl.
▸ No pee-pee. She's a girl. I have a pee-pee.
▸ Yes, you do, Tom.
▸ I can wash her heinie. I can wash Stevie, too, and clean
him all up.
▸ Yes, you can.

I said to myself, "Tom wants to 'wash' away all the bad memories."
    Tom searched in the toy box for something, found a red belt on
the dress-up rack, and spanked the girl doll on her "heinie."

▸ She doesn't listen. I'll make her cry.
▸ Why doesn't she listen?
▸ I'll hit her again—not too hard!
▸ Does someone hit you on the heinie?

Tom did not respond but picked up Stevie and brought him to the
girl doll: "Watch this, Dorothy. Stevie is peeing on the table."
    Tom dipped Stevie in the tub, turned the doll over, and shouted,
"Look, pee-pee comes out. Oh, is he bad. Don't pee-pee on the
table."
    Tom was attempting to re-create through his play some of the
unpleasant experiences he had had with Eddie. This play, however,
was more calm, more deliberate, than before, when Tom had been
more upset, angry, and frightened. As I watched him, I saw that he
was the one in control now. He needed to repeat his game until he
could master his fears and anxieties, and the more he played, the less
worried and anxious he became. What had happened to him could
now be talked about with less guilt, less self-blame. Even "God"
was the authority who made decisions. Where Tom had got this idea
of "God" making the rules about sexual acts, I didn't know. Perhaps,
Eddie had told him this, or perhaps, as many children believe when
they need explanations for events that are too confusing or are beyond
their ken, "God" had become the source of knowledge.
    We were to have many more "doctor" games over the next few

weeks. Tom fluctuated between adoring the bear and the Stevie doll and inflicting numerous shots on the "heinie," on the "pee-pee," and on the belly button. At one point, Tom decided to "repair" the doll's penis.

▸ Is it sick?
▸ Yep, we need to fix it. There's a splinter in his pee-pee.

Taking the tweezers out of the kit, Tom pulled the imaginery splinter out of the doll's penis.

▸ There, he's better. All better. No more boo-boo.
▸ Good, Tom. Stevie's pee-pee is all better.
▸ Yes, no one touches it. Only the doctor and his mommy and daddy.
▸ Yes, you told me that no one touches your pee-pee either, right?
▸ Right (*shouting*) *no one!*

I felt that we had come a long way in the few months of therapy—at least in terms of Tom's acceptance of his body. His drawings were now of a "whole" boy: face, body, arms, and legs. But I was still concerned about his aggressive behavior. He was disobedient in school, fought with Maureen, and, as Ellen said, "still can't obey the rules in the house."

It was time to meet with the Kayes again. I felt that I would like to work more on modifying Tom's aggressiveness. I would still help him deal with his body image and his identity, but I believed that Tom was self-healing as far as the sexual abuse was concerned. I set a time for our session, wondering if both parents would come. According to Ellen, she and Jim were barely speaking to each other. Surely, the tension in the household must be affecting Tom. It was unfair. Just as he was making some progress, was it possible that he would have to deal with another trauma?

Surprise

Ellen and Jim both came for their session with me.

Despite my warnings, Ellen had taken the children to her parents' home again: "Tom spoke to Eddie. It was like normal. Look it's my family. Eddie's my cousin. He's getting help."

Jim interrupted her: "That's bullshit! He's drinking, and he's driving while he's drinking. I know from the group in town. He's a mess, and I don't want my kids near him."

"*Your* kids," Ellen said. "You don't ever talk to them or play with them. We might as well be on another planet."

I tried to tell them about Tom's progress and my concern about his reactions to their family squabbles.

Jim interrupted me: "Don't you know? I've moved out!"

"No, I don't know," I answered. "That's important information. I need to know these things, so that I can understand what Tom is experiencing at home, what he has to contend with. How can I help him if I don't have all the pieces in place?"

Ellen said she was "sorry," that she "just forgot" to tell me. Clearly, she hadn't had the courage to tell me when she brought Tom to therapy twice a week. She hadn't really forgotten but was ashamed and embarrassed or may not have fully understood the impact that this separation would have on Tom. Tom already blamed himself for the part he had played in Eddie's drama, and now I was very much afraid that he would blame himself for his parents' breakup. Being at the center of so much distress, he was fully aware of the disruptions in his parents' and grandparents' lives.

I felt numb and helpless. Unfortunately, the many facets of the lives of clients are beyond the control of the therapist. I asked the Kayes if they would consider marriage couseling. Both shook their heads.

"No," Ellen said. "This goes way back. Jim knows I never loved him. We married because I was pregnant." Here again, Tom had been the innocent "cause" of unhappiness.

"I just want to be totally free of Jim," Ellen went on. "He can visit the kids if he wants to, but I'm filing for a divorce."

Jim sat there stony-faced, as he had on other occasions, and finally agreed that divorce "was for the best," saying that he "could never feel right about Ellen's family again."

Years of resentment toward Ellen, toward Tom, and toward the Kellers had now come to a head: "I just want out. I'll do what's right for them all financially, but I need space."

"Will you please let Tom continue with his therapy?" I asked.

They both agreed. But they were adamant in their refusal to try any form of counseling for themselves.

The Kayes left. With a sinking feeling inside, I sat there long after they had driven away. This is the unpredictable nature of psychotherapy with children. Just as I was making progress with Tom, his parents had shattered his world. There was not much that I could do except hope and pray that Tom would continue to see me. I was annoyed and resentful, and I felt betrayed. Why wouldn't Tom's parents try to continue in marriage counseling? Why weren't they concerned about how their divorce would affect Tom? Why hadn't Ellen been more open with me? Did she think of herself as a failure? First, she'd been unable to prevent the sexual abuse of her child, and now her marriage was falling apart. Perhaps she felt inadequate as a parent and as a wife. These were painful issues for Ellen herself to confront. But what would be their impact on Tom?

Ellen brought Tom to see me one more time and then decided to terminate his therapy. If her reasons were financial, I told her, I would continue to see him at a much reduced fee, or she could bring him to a clinic.

Her answer: "No, it's not money. I just can't deal with all this now. Please try to understand. I just don't want to think about any of this until I know where I'm going."

In his last session, Tom was unusually quiet. I explained that we would say good-bye now, and he asked me if I would keep his pictures in my playroom: "Keep them here where I play. Keep them safe, Dorothy. Keep my pictures where no one can touch them. Keep them in the folder."

I promised that I would.

Tom wanted to play a special game this last time. It was a game called "fishing." He sat the Stevie doll on the couch near him and spread out the seashells from a bucket all over the rug. He pretended he had a "fishing pole" and gave a "pole" to Stevie.

> ► We're fishing for big fish and for gold and silver treasure.
> ► Great. You have a friend, I see, fishing with you.
> ► Yep, we're friends.

And so they sat there, quietly "fishing," sharing a little make-believe game—the kind of wholesome play that I hoped would continue for Tom. We said good-bye and Tom gave me a big hug. As he and Ellen drove away, he waved from the car window and threw me a kiss.

One Year Later

Approximately a year later, I had a phone call from Ellen. She was divorced and had moved to another state. She was now visiting her parents and wondered if I could see Tom: "He isn't sleeping well. He has scary dreams and wakes up in a cold sweat. I don't know if he's thinking about Eddie again, but I need help. Can we come? I need you to give me the name of someone where I live now. Please, can we come?"

Of course I would see Tom. I was curious about him. I had not heard from the Kayes since our last visit.

Tom remembered the way to the playroom and ran right in. He had grown taller and heavier, but he still had his cowlick. He was missing a tooth, his glasses were as thick-lensed as I had remembered, and he was still awkward in his movements, but his speech had improved significantly. I had been so used to deciphering his difficult speech pattern that it was pure pleasure to be able to understand him so easily.

Tom told me that he saw Jim "a lot": "Dad lets me come every two weeks, and all Christmas and Easter. I can stay with him this summer for one month." He also told me that he liked his new school, missed his grandparents, and had a cat named Tweezer. Tom was in first grade and reading now.

Gradually, Tom told me that he "can't sleep" and had "scary dreams of monsters and mean people who come to hurt me."

▸ Is there something bothering you, Tom?
▸ No. I can't remember anything that bothers me.

Tom was certainly bothered by something but, whatever it was, was denying and repessing it. I asked him if he would like to draw another picture for our folder.

▸ Do you still have it?
▸ Of course, I do.
▸ OK, I'll draw two pictures: one of me and one of anything.
▸ Good.

Tom drew himself: a face with two dots for eyes, a dot for a nose, and a slit for a mouth, very much like his first face drawing for me of so long ago. He added a square torso—no legs, just a square under the face. Protruding from the square about midway, he drew what looked like a stump for an arm. When I asked Tom if it was his arm, he wouldn't answer and instead asked to draw another picture: dozens of circles, one with features added that made it into a face.

▸ What is this, Tom?
▸ It's me all over.

Yes, it was Tom—all over the page, as if he were coming apart. Tom then read a story to me, choosing a book about a space adventure and reading very well. Finally, when our time was up, I told him to write to me if he wanted to. I also said that I would help Mommy find another "play" person for him nearer to home so that he could talk about what was bothering him. Reaching into his pocket, Tom brought out an apple: "This is for you. When I knew I would see you, I saved it from lunch for you."

I accepted this apple with as much love as if Tom had given me a great treasure. It was, I believe, a sign of the trust he had in me.

How I wished we could continue to work together toward a more permanent healing.

I gave Ellen the names of people in her area whom I respected, but I haven't heard from her since.

I put Tom's drawing in his folder among the many drawings of bodyless faces and the few of a whole person. Would Tom ever become that "whole person"?

I often think about Tom and his struggle to restore himself and to find his own identity. I wonder how he is doing now, and I ask myself repeatedly if I could have done anything more for his family, but I realize that a psychotherapist who chooses to work with children is subject to the whims and vagaries of their parents. Like Tom, I was powerless over the events in his life and had to accept my limitations. It is a help to believe that, wherever he is, Tom still preserves both in his memory and in his fantasies, some of the mutual trust and sharing that characterized our relationship. Perhaps it sustains him as he faces new challenges.

~~~~~~~~~~~~~~~~

CHAPTER FOUR

MARTY, THE LITTLE CYCLONE

Attention Deficit and Hyperactivity

Marty's Background

"He tried to choke me—can you believe it? My own child tried to choke me. Marty climbed up on a chair to get at the cookie jar, and when I reached up to get him down, his hands went around my neck with a hold so tight I couldn't breathe. He's as strong as an ox and as destructive as a cyclone." These words, spoken by his mother, were my introduction to Marty, three and a half years old.

Helen and Craig Newman had been referred to me by a pediatrician who had just treated Marty for a severe laceration on his leg that required ten stitches. Marty had jumped off a high rock behind the Newmans' house and had landed on a sharp stone jutting below.

Helen said that she had just turned her back "for a minute" when the accident occurred: "We can never, never leave him alone. I'm worn out physically and mentally."

The pediatrician characterized Marty as a "whirling dervish," a child with a limited vocabulary and a short attention span, impulsive and "hell on wheels." Helen Newman was at her wit's end, exhausted, frustrated, and concerned that Marty was "defective." The Newmans described Marty as "difficult from birth" in contrast to Louisa, their six-year-old daughter, who was the "perfect" child: "smart, sweet, kind, and quiet—a joy to live with." Marty had "always" been "active, walking early, but still not speaking clearly. He has no friends and can't sit still a minute."

According to the Newmans, Helen had been in good physical condition during her pregnancy with Marty and had not smoked, drunk alcohol, or used any drugs. Her diet had been proper, and there had been no undue stress in the household. The delivery had been normal, without the use of drugs or forceps.

Helen admitted, however, that as Marty grew older, she had "nagged" him continuosly, demanding from him "proper" behavior like Louisa's. Louisa had been an easy, good baby, nondemanding and compliant, according to Helen. Marty's behavior was a complete contrast. Helen lost patience with him, and his lack of language skills exacerbated their difficulty in communicating with each other. Helen was ever-vigilant with Marty, never able to relax. This necessity had to have built up some resentment in her. Indeed, she knew, "in my heart of hearts," that she was being "unreasonable" and contributing to Marty's emotional problems.

The Newmans went on to add to my picture of Marty, each parent contributing details.

"We have tried to enroll Marty in the local nursery school," Helen said, "but that didn't work out. On visiting day, I sat with the other mothers while all the children were being observed. Most of them played with the toys, but Marty ran around the room, touching toys, dropping them, banging on the piano, trying to turn the lights on and off—he even tried to grab the fire extinguisher, tugging at it. A teacher trailed after him, picking up the toys, trying to hold onto him. He was like a cyclone, leaving disaster in his path all around the room. Finally, the director, as politely as she could, told me that Marty wasn't ready for her school, and perhaps we should leave. Well, we left, with me dragging—and I mean dragging—Marty across the parking lot, and struggling with him to get him into his car seat. I was a wreck, crying, embarrassed, feeling terrible.

That wasn't the only place that wouldn't take him. I tried the library story hour, and the librarian asked us to leave after about ten minutes. She tried hard to keep Marty interested but it didn't work. I tried a local exercise group for preschoolers. I thought Marty would do well where he could just use his body, but that didn't work either, because he wouldn't listen to the instructor. He just wanted to tumble on a mat, hit the other children, or run around the room upsetting the routine."

By now, Helen was in tears: "He's a failure. I'm a failure. I can't seem to do anything right. Is Marty retarded? Is he crazy?"

Craig looked beaten and forlorn: "This is my only son. He's big and, as Helen said, strong as an ox. He weighs over fifty pounds, and he's tall for his age; we just had him measured, and he's forty-three inches tall! So everyone thinks he's five or six and expects him to behave. Isn't it OK for a kid three and a half years old to have a lot of energy?" Craig wanted reassurance that Marty was not abnormal, just overly "rambunctious."

I told the Newmans that I would see Marty, assess his needs, and help them make some plans for the coming year. It was late in the spring, and nursery schools were setting up their fall schedules of classes. From both the Newmans' and the pediatrician's assessment of Marty, expecting him to fit into a typical nursery school didn't seem realistic.

I gathered more information from the Newmans. Marty was a good eater, was toilet-trained, and slept through the night. In general, aside from the frequent cuts and bruises sustained in his many wild adventures, he was in excellent health. The Newmans seemed to be a devoted couple who were at a loss over Marty. They obviously needed help—especially Helen—with his daily management. Their concern about his mental ability was a realistic one, given his inability to "relate" to people, to adhere to rules, to control his temper, or to sustain any prolonged play. Television was the thing that could keep Marty "under control," and as a result, he watched television nearly all day so that Helen could "get relief and get chores done." His behavior in church had been a "disaster," so now he didn't accompany his parents, who attended services separately. He couldn't go to birthday parties or to visit relatives because a "scene takes place," in which Marty "grabs his cousin's toys, hits them, or shouts gibberish at everyone."

Helen had become a recluse, remaining at home all day, standing guard over Marty like a "jailer," and feeling totally incompetent and depressed: "I can't handle his temper tantrums. There seems to be a couple each day—even more if I cross him. He rules us completely."

Three nights a week and on Saturday, she worked as a waitress, "just to get out" while Craig took over. Craig insisted that Marty was much better when he was around and even "showed affection." Much of Marty's wild behavior was apparently more subdued when Craig was in charge: "There are times when Marty can be on the swing or kick a ball, and even smile, and seems like every other kid—just normal. There are also times when he's able to sit and concentrate for a long time and seems busy and intense, like when he moves his cars along or uses clay. What does all this mean?"

"It sounds as if Marty can concentrate when he's motivated to do so. That's not unusual," I said. "When children find that a task is difficult or boring or that it offers no satisfaction, they often tune out. Even children who have attention deficits or who are described as overactive sometimes become engrossed in a game if they can understand it or if it offers them pleasure."

Helen appeared to accept my explanation and listened quietly as Craig continued: "I have my own roofing business and enjoy making things with my hands. I tried once to interest Marty in making a bird house, but after exploring the toolbox, he tried to run off with a hammer. I chased after him, afraid that he would throw the hammer at me. I really want my son to be able to do things with me when he grows older, but it looks as if that's just a pipe dream. Is there a test to find out what's wrong? Maybe he'll just outgrow this. Or maybe I'm kidding myself. I've been saying he'll outgrow this for a long time now, and you know what? It's just getting worse, especially since he's been getting so big."

Indeed, Marty probably would grow to be a tall boy. His father was over six feet and huge of build. Helen was also tall, about five feet ten. It seemed that Craig's prediction about Marty's size, at least, would be fulfilled. I was less comfortable with the notion that Marty would "outgrow" his behavior pattern.

We agreed that I would see Marty to determine whether I would work with him, and that I would give them some ideas for Marty's management. The Newmans left. During this interview, I had felt their frustration and their sense of defeat and worry. From their description, Marty sounded like a hyperactive child with an attention deficit. A child diagnosed as having this disorder often fidgets with his or her hands and feet, has difficulty remaining seated when required to do so, and is easily distracted by any stimulus in the environment. According to the Newmans, Marty often had difficulty sustaining his attention in play or in completing the tasks his parents demanded of him, such as putting away his toys or helping with simple chores. In addition, he did not seem to listen to what was said to him, appearing to be in his own world. He shifted from activity to activity before he had completed one of them. Finally, he engaged in physically dangerous activities. The incident with the hammer, his jumping off high places, and his riding his tricycle into the road were further indications of his lack of awareness of limits and boundaries.

The only thing that kept Marty quiet was television; its short scenes, loud music, changes in voices, funny characters, action, and movement seemed to keep him focused on the screen. These are just the elements, research tells us, that lead to hyperactivity in children. According to Helen, Marty "loved cartoons" but could not sit still during a program like "Mister Rogers' Neighborhood," which has a slower pace. The Newmans owned a videotape collection of animated stories and simply used the VCR to fill those hours when TV cartoon programs weren't scheduled. Without television, Marty ran around the house, used the couch as a "trampoline," or threw a temper tantrum if he was crossed in any way. Marty was the "ruler" of the Newman household, and clearly, the family needed help in handling his behavior, as well as some guidance concerning his future.

A verse from an old German children's book translated into English as *Slovenly Peter* came to mind as I listened to the Newmans:

Phil stop acting like a worm
the table is no place to squirm
Thus speaks the father to his son
severly say it, not in fun.
Mother frowns and looks around
although she doesn't make a sound.
But Philip will not take advice
he'll have his way at any price.
He turns and churns
he wriggles and jiggles

here and there on the chair,
Phil these twists I cannot bear.

Would Marty, unlike Phil, ever take advice?

Marty, the Cyclone

When Helen brought Marty to me for his first visit, she announced at the door, "Here comes Marty, batten down the hatches."

She was right. He was on a rampage as he tore into the waiting room, tried to knock over the lamp, grabbed the magazines, pushed over the wastebasket, and ignored me completely.

Setting things to rights, I asked, "Marty, why don't you come with me to see the toys?"

Helen urged him to go with me. He refused. I then asked if he would like his mother to come, too. Marty nodded yes, and all three of us went into the playroom.

Marty was indeed huge for three and a half years old, exactly as Craig had described him: physically, more like a five- or six-year-old. He had a mop of curly brown hair, hazel eyes, and a short nose covered with freckles.

Helen sat to the side of the room and watched as Marty began his "investigation," her expression a mixture of resignation, embarrassment, and "I told you so." Marty touched everything. I decided just to observe him and to interfere only when I thought he might get hurt or do damage to some object. I told Marty that he could look at the toys and choose something to play with. He glanced sideways at me as he explored the room, seeming to be fully aware of me and wondering how far he could go. He finally picked up a doll and threw it.

Jumping up, Helen yelled, "No, no. Stop that, Marty. It's Dr. Singer's toy."

I motioned to her to be quiet and observed Marty's reaction to her and to me. I also kept quiet. Marty looked puzzled and leaving the doll on the floor, went over to Big Bird, a plastic scooterlike toy. He sat on it and rode around the room.

I commented, "That's a good ride, Marty. I like the way you ride."

Marty rode awhile and then rode the toy into the door. He did this several times, aware that he was bumping into the door and creating a loud bang. Helen looked quite anxious. I just watched.

"Well, getting no rise out of these grown-ups" Marty's expression seemed to say. "This is boring. I'll stop." We were ignoring Marty's negative behavior, and he stopped his "bumping."

During that first hour, each time he acted negatively, I ignored him. After repeated attempts to elicit a response from me for behavior that was not constructive, he appeared more subdued and stopped. (However, his therapy was not to be as easy as I had thought after our first visit. The worst was yet to come.)

Marty seemed willful, out of control, and angry, but responsive to praise. I wondered what he was all about. What was causing his recalcitrant behavior? Why wouldn't he sustain attention? Could he play imaginatively instead of stereotypically, as in that first hour? What was his speech like? He had barely spoken, and I needed to know. Could I try a behavioral therapy approach with Marty? So far, so good: When I had ignored his negative behavior, he had stopped it. When I had praised (reinforced) his positive behavior, he had repeated it. I knew that Marty was interested in the playroom but needed help in learning how to play.

First Steps

My plan for Marty's psychotherapy involved four steps. First, I wanted Marty gradually to become able to separate from Helen, and come into the playroom by himself and remain there for the entire session. Second, I planned to try behavioral therapy to get him to eliminate his destructive behavior and play more appropriately. Third, I wanted to reinforce any play that involved sustained attention. If I could keep Marty on-task, perhaps I could evaluate his intellectual functioning. Fourth, I felt that Marty needed to learn "how to play." His parents told me that he often seemed to be talking to himself, and I wondered if he had an imaginary playmate.

My goals involved plans for Marty's parents as well. Helen needed support and guidance in her handling of Marty. In addition, she needed some daytime relief from him, and I planned to suggest that she use a sitter for some hours each week. As nursery school had been ruled out, Helen had the responsibility for Marty's care all day, every day, except when she went to work in the evenings and on Saturday.

Helen did not socialize with her friends during the week: "When I take Marty over to play with my friends' children, it's always a disaster. He can't share or play in a nice way. It ends up with me screaming at him. Or if he doesn't fight with a child, he just runs around my friend's house. That makes her mad. No one calls me to come for coffee, and I can't blame them. Marty's hard to take.

"I try to read to Marty, but he won't sit still long enough to listen to a story. Maybe that's why his speech is so backward; he doesn't learn any new words. When I point to something in a picture book, he just wriggles out of my arms and pushes the book away. It gets me so upset, I just give up." Helen reported this to me at our second parents' visit.

How, then, to begin? Marty and Helen came two days later for his second session. He again refused to remain in the playroom alone with me. Helen had walked him in, said she would be in the waiting room and tried to leave. He screamed at her, "Me go. Me go!" My telling Helen to stay quieted him. He needed her presence for a sense of security. He found the Buddy doll, then gave it to his mother, going from toy to toy and handing each to Helen. I took Buddy and put him on the slide. At first, Marty ignored me, but gradually he came over to watch my "game." I made Buddy climb up the stairs and let him slide down, talking about this activity all the while. Marty then tried to help Buddy climb the stairs but threw him down the slide and then ran around the room.

Well, he was not about to play *that* game with me. He was curious but clearly wanted me to know that he was not going to join in *my* game. He now tugged at the curtains, tried to turn the lights on and off, and touched everything he could, always darting a glance my way. "What is she going to do about this?" he seemed to be asking himself. Helen watched, clearly upset, but controlled and quiet.

Marty then needed to go to the toilet to "pee-pee." Helen got up and led him across the hall to the bathroom. I waited and listened.

Marty asked, "Where she is?"

Helen said, "Dorothy is in the playroom. Finish, wash up, and we'll go back."

Marty wanted to know where I was? Good. He was aware of me and interested. Was he making a connection with me?

Marty came into the playroom again, picked up Buddy, went to the slide, and let Buddy slide down.

"Do," he commanded.

"Yes, thank you," I said. "I'll play too. Good boy. I like this game."

We "played" this primitive game repeatedly. Up and down the slide. No variation. No further conversation on Marty's part. A more typical three-and-a-half-year old would have used more words than Marty and would have elaborated on the game. There would have been "tricks" on the slide that Buddy could do, conversation with Buddy or about Buddy, and more involvement with me. This game lasted about three minutes. Marty ended the game by tossing Buddy across the room.

"Marty, it's OK if you want to stop this game. Just tell me, but don't throw Buddy."

Marty picked up Buddy and threw him again. I remained silent. He threw him again. No response from me. Marty took Buddy to Helen. We both praised him, and he smiled.

I suggested to Helen that we would begin a simple behavior modification program at home and in the playroom: she would try to ignore the negative aspects of Marty's behavior except when it involved potential danger and would be effusive with praise whenever he complied with her requests, or whenever he did something positive on his own. I was in no hurry to wean Marty away from his mother because I could serve as a model for Helen in my handling of the child. She would have an opportunity to watch me as I taught Marty how to play; as I encouraged his use of vocabulary; and as I shaped his behavior through reinforcing acts that were more social and ignoring those that were destructive or offensive.

At our next parents' visit, I explained to Helen and Craig what I meant by a behavior modification program.

Parents have been successful "change agents," people who can carry out a behavior modification program with their children. They can easily learn to use behavioral techniques to improve or change a child's specific (targeted) behavior. Parents have access to numerous books that will acquaint them with the general theory of behavioral therapy, including exercises that will help them develop skills in analyzing their reactions to their child's behavior and that offer concrete information on how to achieve a particular goal. I gave the names of several of these books to the Newmans. Videotapes are also available that demonstrate behavior modification techniques for nonprofessionals.

While I was working with Marty and trying to get a clearer picture of his problem, it seemed appropriate to begin a program aimed first at getting his trust and then at bringing some of his hyperactive, negative behavior under control.

I suggested to the Newmans that the first step in working with Marty would be to keep a log to determine both what were his quiet times and what led to an outburst of screaming, when it occurred, how long it occurred, what Helen or Craig did about it, and how it stopped. I also told the Newmans to be aware of any purposeful, postive activity of Marty's and, when they "caught" him at it, to reward him immediately with verbal praise. I also suggested "modeling," like mine with the Buddy doll on the slide, so that Marty would begin to imitate the play behavior they wanted. Speech is important, and wherever possible, Helen and Craig needed to urge Marty to ask for something rather than grab it and to tell them how he felt rather than to react with anger and demands. Again, I suggested that Helen and Craig use the very words that they wanted Marty to use, so that he could learn how to interact socially.

Most of all, I asked them to be patient and consistent, to ignore the tantrums, and to reward correct responses immediately. I knew they would need much encouragement and support from me, as it was very difficult to ignore one of Marty's full-blown tantrums which consisted of throwing himself on the floor, kicking everything near him, and trying to bite; it generally took two people to move him or lift him.

I began to think about a diagnosis for Marty. His physical examination had ruled out any gross organic deficits, including hearing impairment, but there still might be some subtle brain dysfunction that caused his excessive, purposeless movement. This type of dys-function is difficult to detect even with sophisticated brain-scan tech-niques. Some allergists even claim that specific foods contribute to hyperactive behavior, but there has been no scientific evidence to support this theory.

I did not completely rule out autism. However, whereas autistic children generally seem to lack awareness of the existence of others, Marty seemed to be aware of me and of Helen. His awareness of me was obvious from his question concerning my whereabouts when he went to the bathroom, his constant glances, and his willingness to play at the slide with me. On the other hand, he found it difficult to play with another child, preferring solitary games. Socially, he was grossly impaired. For example, he did not comply with social conventions, could not make appropriate contact with his peers, and displayed no understanding of how to behave in a structured situa-tion, such as the library story hour or the exercise class. Marty tended to perseverate; that is, he would repeat an action endlessly, another characteristic of autism. Also, he would tolerate few deviations in the format of our games of hide-and-seek, his favorite activity early in therapy. And like many autistic children, Marty could sit for "what seemed like hours," according to Helen, moving the same car or ball back and forth.

Marty had speech, although it was somewhat babyish for his age. Autistic children have marked abnormalities in their speech— in its volume, pitch, stress, rate, and rhythm. Marty's intonation was not completely normal, and at times, I detected a monotone or a questionlike pattern. Despite his capacity to communicate verbally in one- or two-word phrases, he seemed unable to sustain a conversation.

According to Helen, Marty sometimes played by himself and seemed to be talking to a "friend." Later, I discovered that Marty's "friend" was "Petey," an imaginary playmate, atypical of autistic children, but not an impossibility. Marty did not present any evi-dence of the stereotypical autistic body movements, such as hand twisting, spinning, or head banging. He was, however, interested in mechanical objects and was upset by changes made in his own room or even in the rest of the house. Later, I found that to be true in the playroom as well. He insisted that I keep a storybook on a certain shelf. If another child had removed it or misplaced it, Marty became frantic, and we could not continue our session until the book was returned to its original spot. Only as therapy progressed, and as Marty became more flexible, was I able to move objects around the room without his reacting with distress.

Marty also could not tolerate transitions from one activity to another for example, from undressing to bathtime or to bedtime, and he was upset if times were changed in his daily routine. If meals were not on time, or if Helen shopped at a different hour or took him to see her parents in the evening rather than on a Sunday, he was distraught. Shopping with Marty in tow had become increasingly difficult over the six months before his therapy began. He constantly tried to run down the aisles or fingered groceries on the shelves and dropped them into the cart. Finally, the Newmans decided that Helen would shop in the evening, while Craig baby-sat with the children.

So, Marty showed a mixture of autistic symptoms (solitary play, perseveration, poor speech, an interest in mechanical objects, rigidity, difficulty in relating to others, and no sense of danger) and a pervasive developmental impairment (behaving like a much younger child).

Marty's hyperactivity was also a serious problem. He found it impossible to sit still, and he was easily distracted by the objects in the playroom. If he picked up one toy and began to play with it and another toy caught his eye, down would go the first as he examined the second. I found it extremely wearing to keep Marty involved in any structured task, such as drawing, molding clay, or even playing at the dollhouse. His drawings immediately became scribbles, the clay was rolled into a ball and hurled onto the floor, and the dolls set up to play a game were thrown out of the dollhouse.

Marty didn't seem to listen to me. I often had to repeat what I said or gently hold his shoulders to get him to look at me and to pay attention.

Often, Marty tried to do something dangerous in the playroom. For example, he would stand on the slide platform and, instead of sitting down to slide, would try to jump off backward or to run down the slide. I needed to be constantly alert to keep him from jabbing himself with a pencil or sticking it in his ear. Helen reported that he had no sense of danger at home either. He was not allowed to ride his tricycle even on their dead-end street because he was unaware of cars. He was allowed to ride it only in the yard and only when she or Craig was present. He tried to leap off anything high, as he had on the day he needed stitches.

Thus, at the beginning of therapy, I had a rather confused picture of Marty's condition, but it also seemed to me that a label was not crucial that early. My objectives were helping Marty to become more socialized, to control his temper tantrums, and to use speech to make his needs known, rather than action, such as kicking, hurling objects, or running away. I hoped that I could engage him in make-believe play for longer periods each session, and that I could keep him focused on one game for a sustained amount of time. But first, as I mentioned, he had to trust me enough to separate from Helen and play alone with me.

I was seeing Marty three times a week, and when he came for his sixth session—surprise!—he wore a big smile. His smile told me that he liked to come and that, despite my rules, he was finding some pleasure in our encounters. I think too, that he felt some relief in being with a person who didn't say "no" all the time. However, he still wanted Helen to come into the playroom with him. In advance, I had set up some miniature people on the table, and I asked Marty to come and play. He did come to the table, knocked the figures down with one sweep of his hand, and stood there staring straight at me, waiting for my reaction.

"Well, I guess you didn't want to play with these people," I said.

No response.

"You can *tell* me that you don't want to play with them, Marty. Can you tell me that? Can you use words?"

No response.

"Shall we pick these up, put them away, and play something else?"

Marty reluctantly came over, picked up a few of the figures, and dropped them into their basket.

I praised him profusely. Progress. At least he had picked the toys up; Marty had understood my request and followed it through. But then, in his typical manner, he moved around the room sampling the toys, unable to stay with any activity for more than a minute or two. He tried testing me again by playing with the light switch, banging Big Bird into the door, spilling the plastic spoons out of their holder, and touching everything without purpose or plan. He was more fully aware of my presence, however, and I noticed that his exploration of the room and his tossing of materials had less of the frenetic quality than he had displayed on previous visits. But he still moved like a whirling dervish.

As the days went by, I began more and more to think I was dealing with a child who, although he had some of the autistic symptoms I have described, was more like a child with a severe attention deficit and hyperactivity, which led to emotional problems. His restless behavior, limited speech, and inability to sustain a game suggested that there were some learning deficits that might have a neurological cause. Marty seemed to have trouble processing information. His receptive language (his ability to understand or interpret what others said to him) was faulty. When he was told to do something or even when he was asked a question, he seemed unable to comprehend the request or to make sense of it unless the words were repeated, slowly and simply. I decided that the language of adults and of his peers must often seem blurred and even foreign to him. Hence the confusion, the untamed behavior, the seeming ignoring of others. No wonder Helen and he were at swords' points: much of what Helen demanded was a mystery to Marty.

Marty's large motor ability, however, was excellent. He could jump, hop, and do a sort of a half skip. He threw and caught a ball extremely well, and he could balance himself on one foot. He rode a tricycle with ease. His fine-motor movements were a complete contrast: he could not properly grasp a crayon or a pencil, and it was hard for him to do puzzles, stack blocks, or put pegs into a board geared to his age level.

At the end of each of Marty's sessions, I was physically exhausted and confused. There were moments when he seemed to be listening to me and would maintain eye contact—and then he would drift away, not heeding my words or my presence. I began to empathize with Helen's frustration and confusion, her feelings of impotence, and even her anger. She wanted to help Marty and didn't know how. I hoped that some of my skills and tehniques would begin to make a difference in both their lives.

At this sixth session, Marty found the Play-Doh again, and we actually made a "cookie." I showed Marty how to feed Buddy, placing the "cookie" close to Buddy's mouth, and I "talked" for Buddy: "Mm, this is good. Marty, please give me more!"

As Marty watched, I repeated the game and urged him to feed the doll, too. Finally, he joined in the game.

► Cookie, here, cookie, good cookie.
► Yes, Marty, you're a good boy to feed Buddy.

Marty gave the cookie to Buddy once more and then threw it on the floor. Helen jumped up to retrieve it, and I motioned to her to stay seated. I ignored Marty as he watched me out of the corner of his eye. Making another cookie, I continued the game with Buddy. Marty slowly advanced toward me. I kept feeding Buddy but acknowledged Marty's presence now: "Good boy, Marty. You want to play, too!"

Marty came closer, took the cookie from me, and fed Buddy. I gave him effusive praise, and we repeat the game. It was soon time to clean up. I waited to see if Marty would pick up the cookie. He did! Helen clapped her hands, and we both praised him. He grinned from ear to ear.

These small moments of success served to reinforce *me* in the therapy and helped to soften my feelings of defeat each time Marty left.

And Marty—what must the world seem like to him? It must be confusing, overwhelming, full of sights and sounds that he could not always decipher. As a result, he responded in a way that appeared to others to be willful and inappropriate. Certainly, he was different from Louisa, Helen's "sunshine child." His tantrums were responses to his frustration—shrieks, I believed, for understanding: "Why isn't anyone listening to me? Why isn't anyone helping me sort out this confusion?" But he hadn't the words to ask these questions.

His play excluded me for the most part, as if he had his own script, his own dialogue, his own direction. I would be the observer, and hopefully the facilitator. If Marty began to understand that the playroom was nonthreatening, that I was willing to listen, and that I would not punish him but would be consistent and firm, perhaps he would eventually respond. Meanwhile, he didn't ask who I was. He was wary of me, but not fearful. What was his inner experience? How could I reach him to find out? Could I become an echo of his language and his play? Would I ever be able to interpret Marty's true meaning, the content of his mind?

Marty Comes into the Room Alone

Feeding the Buddy doll must have been a critical experience for
Marty. The next session, two days later, was a triumph of sorts.
Marty took off his jacket in the waiting room and ran on ahead of
me into the playroom without his usual refusal to be separated from
Helen. I signaled her to stay in the waiting room. Marty immediately
found the Play-Doh, made a crude "cookie," and fed Buddy. I was
delighted. I praised him, but he was more absorbed in his game than
in responding to any reaction from me.

Marty "fed" the doll for a few minutes, then suddenly looked
around and realized that his mother wasn't there. He scooted out of
the room, yelling "Help, help," and ran to Helen in panic. She kissed
him and soothed him. Then, looking at me, he reached for my hand
and returned with me to the playroom. He stood there, arms akimbo,
as if to say, "Well, here I am. What next?"

He was funny in a way, signaling to me that he was ready to
enter into a relationship with me—alone, in this room. But would
I be able to keep him there? It was Marty's silent challenge. He came
to the table and rolled out more cookies. I commented on what a
good job he was doing but got no response. Soon, bored with the
clay, Marty went to the slide and hid his face against the side.

> ► You count.
> ► Count what, Marty?
> ► You count.

I didn't understand this game, but I counted, "One, two, three,
four."

> ► You hide.
> ► You mean hide-and-seek?

Marty nodded his head vigorously. I had made a good guess. He
wanted to play hide-and-seek! Later, I found out from Helen

that this was the only game he played with Louisa or Craig. He could play it "forever," Helen said. "He can't count, but yells out numbers at random. He likes to hide best of all while someone else counts."

Helen was right. Marty loved this game, and this first day that I was alone with Marty, we played it over and over. At least, he was able to separate from Helen and remained in the room for the rest of the session.

The next visit was a carbon copy of this one. Marty wanted to play hide-and-seek again, and I complied. Soon I introduced some variations. I hid Buddy, and Marty had to find the doll. When he did so, he shouted with joy.

Marty "hid," too, but not very successfully. He would leave his feet exposed as he crawled under a chair, or behind the couch, or behind the drape, unaware that he was only partially concealed. I counted to ten and made a pretense of not knowing where he was. When I found him, Marty insisted that I shout too: "Here you are! I found you!" He preferred hiding himself to my hiding or hiding Buddy. This game made me think of the more primitive peekaboo games of infancy and toddlerhood, which babies adore as they discover that we go away and come back. It's the beginning of what Jean Piaget, the psychologist, called "object permanency," the notion that objects maintain their existence even when they are out of sight. Marty, perhaps, wanted confirmation that he existed and that I existed. He could appear and disappear in this game, playing out his need to verify his own existence, to find "himself," the child who was now so diffuse and without substance or inner core.

From this point on, from Marty's willingness to remain alone with me and trust me a little, our sessions began to change. His parents were learning how to reinforce any positive act on his part. The tantrums were subsiding, and when he did have one, it was shorter than previously. Our play now consisted of my attempts to engage him in games of role playing, such as doctor, firefighter, and mailman. These games gave me the opportunity to use language with Marty and to help him carry out simple scripts that were related to everyday events. I wanted him to begin to develop his imaginative capacity. Through play, he could increase his vocabulary and learn a sense of order and sequence; he could learn how to delay gratification, take turns, cooperate, and share; and he could learn how to empathize. If we played doctor, he could see how we would take care of the hurt doll, bandage it, give it "medicine," and put it to bed. If he could begin to take another's point of view, communicate with me, vary his behavior, and relinquish some of his perseveration, I could begin to rule out the autism diagnosis.

With the use of simple props, I would enact short scenes with Marty. For example, I gave him a cap, some old envelopes, and a small bag, and we "delivered" mail to all the dolls in the playroom. I constantly used simple phrases, urging Marty to repeat them: "Here's a letter for Buddy, here's one for Peggy doll, here's a letter for teddy bear," and so on. Marty's speech was actually improving and becoming less singsong and monotonous. He could sustain our vignettes for only a brief time—no more than four or five minutes—but this was a vast improvement. When he threw a toy, I ignored him. When he picked up the toy or cleaned up, I praised him. As he began to play more, his interest in random touching and turning the lights on and off gradually subsided.

Over the next two months, I saw Marty's parents every three weeks to get an update on his progress, and to reinforce their behavior modification program. Of course, I also saw Helen three times a week when she brought Marty to therapy, and I would spend a few minutes with her then, encouraging her to continue her work with Marty.

For two afternoons a week, Helen had a sitter, a college student whom I had recommended because of her ability to deal with a child like Marty. As a result, Helen began to visit her friends, shop, and have an afternoon coffee break. She began to "feel like a human being again."

As Helen relaxed, Marty seemed to respond to her more calmly. Because of the changes in Marty's behavior, Helen asked if she could take him to her nephew's fourth birthday party. I suggested that she prepare Marty by telling him what would take place. I also advised her that, if he started to get excited, they should leave immediately, while things were still upbeat, rather than wait until Marty got out of hand. I wasn't sure it would work, but Helen was eager to try it.

Unfortunately, Helen did not follow my suggestions, and Marty was unable to handle the confusion at the party—too many children, too much stimulation. When his cousin opened his presents, Marty started to scream and tried to grab all the gifts. He threw himself on the floor in a typical tantrum, kicking in all directions while Helen tried to pick him up. Finally, she managed to get him to the car and into his car seat. She was "mortified" and "so angry that I slapped Marty across the face."

Helen called me that evening, crying and ashamed. She had felt humiliated in front of her family and asked me repeatedly, "Why is he like that? All the other kids sang and played nicely, and all Marty did was run around touching the balloons, poking at the other kids, and ruining the party."

I tried to explain to Helen that Marty wasn't ready for such a prolonged event, and that the stimulation in the room was more than he could handle.

Helen said, "You told me he was better."

"Yes," I answered, "Marty is better, but he's not ready yet to play the way other children his age do. It takes time. Remember, Marty is alone with me, and I'm prepared to handle his outbursts. Even though you're doing a good job, there will be setbacks. Don't get discouraged. Marty will gradually be able to spend longer periods with other people."

Helen listened, but I knew she felt as if she had failed. In her eagerness to have a normal child, and to do what other mothers did—attend birthday parties, take their children shopping, go to restaurants, and go visiting or to the library—she had moved too quickly and had suffered a defeat.

In the meantime, I decided that I would test Marty and, perhaps in the near future, set up a new plan for him. If he was of normal intelligence—and I suspected that he was, (he was moving along satisfactorily, and he was more responsive than during his early days with me)—I would try to enroll him in a nursery school that I knew accepted children of normal intelligence who had emotional problems. If we started him with a five-minute period at the school each day and built up his time as he progressed, I hoped he would eventually be able to stay for the whole morning. An aide would be assigned to Marty to help him adjust to a structured classroom with other children.

I decided to test Marty before I described my plan to the Newmans because I didn't want to disappoint them. Marty and I had been together now for almost five months, and he was more compliant with me, played for longer periods of time, and only rarely refused to clean up or to pick up a toy he had thrown down. He was able to relinquish his fixation on the book that had formerly been his symbol of safety in my room, which had at first been a strange and unfamiliar place to him. We rarely played hide-and-seek now; Marty enjoyed our role-playing games, especially "postman."

I decided to give him a test that required no expressive language of him. On a day when Marty was relaxed, I gave him the Peabody Picture Vocabulary Test, a crude measure of intelligence but one that has proved to be nearly as accurate as more refined measures. All he had to do was point to the correct picture on a page as I asked him the stimulus word. Marty seemed pleased with this "game," pointing proudly as he responded, and wearing a big smile of satisfaction with his accomplishments: he was aware that he was doing well. In this way, he conveyed to me that he had a sense of himself and pride in his successes. This was not the same little boy who had originally not seemed to care about himself or about how others reacted to him. It was important now to Marty that I valued him—and perhaps he was beginning to value himself. I was delighted to find that Marty was of average intelligence and that I could now proceed with the arrangements for this next phase in Marty's therapy.

I spoke to the Newmans about my proposal. Marty was now doing much better in a one-to-one situation with me. It was important, too, as he was approaching age four, that he learn how to play with a peer and conform to a group. I could not provide this experience for him, and I felt that preschool would be a beneficial adjunct to his play therapy.

The Newmans were apprehensive at first, especially because of the birthday party incident and because of Helen's prior visit to the other nursery school, where she had had such a bad experience. I explained that it would take time to make all the arrangements: I wanted the Newmans to meet Mrs. Langdon, the director; visit the school; and then have Marty meet the teachers and the aide. It as important, too, that Marty have time alone with the aide, Karen, before he began attending the school. Karen would play alone with Marty each day before he entered the classroom, so that she could calm him down and prepare him for the classroom activities and the presence of other children.

Preparing Marty for "School"

Marty came into the playroom alone, as he had for the past few months. He approached the teddy bear and took the doctor's kit form the table, motioning me to join him.

"Do you want to play doctor?" I asked.

Marty nodded yes.

> ► Say "yes," Marty. You can ask me to play doctor. Can you do that?
> ► Play doctor.
> ► Good, Marty, that's very good. We can play. Can you say "yes"?
> ► Yes.
> ► Good. We're talking to each other now!

Marty smiled, placed the bear on the couch, and pretended to examine it.

> ► Petey sick, too.
> ► Petey? Where's Petey?
> ► Here Petey is.

And Marty pretended he was examining Petey, his imaginery friend.

This was the first time that Marty had introduced Petey into our play; he was feeling enough trust in me to share his friend. I watched as Marty "talked" to Petey and to the bear. His speech, racing along, wa unintelligible to me, filled with nonsense words, his own private vocabulary, but obviously affording him pleasure. He was peaceful as he played—for the longest time he had remained with one game. I watched. Fifteen minutes went by. I was pleased by Marty's progress, but cautious; we'd had our setbacks before.

Petey was Marty's "friend." Petey made no demands on Marty.

It didn't matter if Marty used gibberish to communicate with him. Marty was in control and enjoyed his game. And I was delighted that Marty had an imaginary friend because it demonstrated that he had imagination and the ability to respond to another person, even if that person was not real. Marty was using Petey to compensate for the real friends he didn't have.

I capitalized on this "friendship" to help Marty continue to interact with the dolls in the playroom, hoping that eventually he would be able to transfer his skills to interactions with other children. When next we played doctor or postman, I urged Marty to take Petey along. Sometimes Marty tried to bathe a doll and pretended that Petey was in the tub as well. Gradually, he began to feed the dolls, put them on the slide, and put them in the wagon with Petey, interacting more with the dolls and with me. I knew that I had to prepare Marty for preschool and that our doll play would make a good transition to playing with other preschoolers.

Marty finished playing a game with Petey one day, and I asked him to come and sit near me.

"Marty, would you like to go to playschool and play with other children?" I asked.

Marty didn't seem to understand. I described the playschool, mentioning the toys, the sandbox, and the big sink where he could play with toy boats. He liked the idea of boats, so we took two plastic boats and filled my small rubber tub with water, and I urged him to "sail" the boats. As we played, I told him about the school, and about how he could sail his boat in the big tub there. I asked if he would like to visit the school with Mommy and me. We would meet Karen, I told him and the teacher, Mrs. Langdon. I was not sure that Marty comprehended the idea of playschool and decided to keep on talking about it during our next few sessions.

In the meantime, Helen had arranged for a visit to the school, and I agreed to join her and Marty. Helen had phoned me every day since I had presented my plan to her, her apprehension about Marty's reaction palpable as we talked.

Mrs. Langdon, Karen, and I had spent much time discussing Marty and how they would proceed. They were just as nervous as Helen, even though Mrs. Langdon had taught other children with emotional problems over the years, and despite Karen's obvious skill in working with similar children at this school and at others. Mrs.

Langdon told me that she had seen Marty in church about a year before and remembered a "scene." In a small town, word travels fast, and nursery school directors do know each other. Nevertheless, she was looking forward to the challenge. Mrs. Langdon was a woman of tremendous vitality, astute, sensitive, and patient. I felt that Marty would be in competent hands.

Our visit was scheduled for ten in the morning. As Marty and Helen came up the walk together, I was waiting with Mrs. Langdon and Karen, and we could see them from the office window. Marty bounced along, face shining, curls framing his round, snub-nosed face. Helen followed right behind, wearing a look of dread. She had had so many failures with Marty, each one causing her to doubt her competency as a mother. As they came to the door, she looked as if she was uttering a silent prayer. Mrs. Langdon guided Marty with her usual warmth and charm, and Helen smiled and began to unwind. Karen showed Marty his cubby and took his hand to lead him into a small room where she had a few toys. They would play with these toys first and then take them into the larger room where the other children were. We waited in Mrs. Langdon's office, out of sight, but nearby in case Marty wanted Helen. I was delighted that Marty had been able to separate from Helen so easily and accept Karen. After about ten minutes, Karen and Marty came back, and Marty ran into Helen's arms, clinging to her. I felt that this was enough for one day and suggested that we wait until tomorrow, the day of our next scheduled session, for Marty's introduction into the larger room with the other children. We all praised Marty, and he obviously basked in the praise. He sat on his mother's lap, beaming with joy over his success: he had been able to stay with a new person alone—and he had survived!

Nursery School

Karen kept a daily record of Marty's progress that was helpful in my work with him. I was able to identify trouble spots before they grew. The teachers and I had numerous contacts about Marty by phone or note, and I continued to work with him, emphasizing speech more and more so that he could communicate with the other children.

In the beginning, Marty's time in the large room was short. He could tolerate only five minutes among the children before he began his "touching" of objects and running around the room. Karen was his shadow. She stayed closeby, ready to intervene if Marty tried to hit a child or destroy property. She offered praise when he sat quietly, or when he found a toy that engrossed him. Gradually, his time in the class was extended to ten minutes. If there were any wild moments, Marty was removed from the group to a "time-out" chair. At first, he would get up from the chair, but Karen put him back each time, explaining calmly why he had to be separated from the other children.

After Marty had been in the school for three weeks, I decided to observe him there. He had been able to remain in the class without incident for ten to fifteen minutes on average but, on some mornings, for as long as twenty or thirty minutes. I was curious about his behavior in the classroom, as he was now talking more to me, playing with more toys in the playroom, and generally appearing to be more composed. I arranged to observe Marty on a day between his visits to me, so that I could let him know I was coming to see him, and so that we could talk about the visit afterward.

I arrived at the school at 9:30. Marty was due at 10:00, to have time alone with Karen, and then time in the large room. Our plan was to see if Marty could stay for snack time that day, an extra fifteen minutes that, it seemed to me, would be a good time for socializing. The chidlren were all seated at tables, about eight at each, for a distribution of juice and crackers; there was relative quiet—no one squabbling over toys, and no one in an active game. Marty could even help clean up. He was getting quite good at this in my playroom, and I hoped he could transfer this "skill" to the school.

I observed Marty from behind a one-way mirror. He entered the room with Karen. They had just had their usual quiet time together. Marty was holding a puzzle, and he sat at a table near some children who were playing with some pegboards. He did not talk to the other children, but as he put his puzzle together, he watched the children, and if they giggled, he did, too. His attempts to become part of the group were usually imitations of what the other children did. He didn't ask any questions, initiate any conversation with the children, or respond if one asked him a question. He seemed content to sit near them, engaged in what is called *parallel play*, that is, play near another child, but without social interaction. This reminded me of his crude version of hide-and-seek, which was also characteristic of a younger child. Karen sat nearby, smiling with approval or praising Marty for his appropriate behavior.

Marty soon left his puzzle and began to roam around the room, always on the periphery of other children's small play groupings. I felt this tremendous urge to change my form and become a dybbuk, a spirit that could enter Marty's body and use the words that would give him access to the world of the other children. I watched and felt a mixture of pride because Marty had come so far and sadness because he didn't yet have the tools to become like the other four-year-olds.

Marty came back to his puzzle, put it together again, and gave it to Karen. She took his hand and led him to the sandbox, where three other little boys were involved in an elaborate game of "construction." They wore yellow plastic hard hats and moved their small trucks and cars around with much noise and shouting. As Marty sat on the wooden rim of the box, Karen offered him a car. He moved it in a desultory fashion, eyeing the other boys, and then throwing the car at one of the small trucks, upsetting the pile of sand. The boys all yelled at him, and Karen, speaking to him gently, took him to his "time-out" chair. I couldn't hear her, but she told me later that she had told him he must not throw cars. Marty, I believe, wanted to play with the boys but didn't know how to make the proper overtures. Throwing the car was his method of making contact. I decided that we must practice role-playing "how to join a game." Marty needed both the language and an awareness of the other person's reaction to a request.

Soon, Karen gave Marty permission to leave his chair. He went to the block corner, and while he started to build a tall tower, Karen sat on the floor and watched. A little girl, Lisa, came along and sat next to Marty. He seemed oblivious of her. Again, I felt myself aching inside.

"Marty, please," I murmured to myself. "Say, 'Hi,' say anything! Don't just ignore her. Here's a chance to respond."

Silence.

I was keenly aware at that moment how crucial language was for Marty. Without the easy flow of words typical of four-year-olds, he would remain isolated from his peers. He didn't talk to the child; he continued his block building, content to be alone, but at least he didn't run around aimlessly, as he had during his first weeks in the large room.

It was time to put away the toys and come to the table for snacks and juice. Well, this was a success. Marty lived to eat, and he was on his best behavior for this little feast. He sat betweeen Karen and Lisa, drank his juice, ate his graham crackers, and looked like a contented pussycat. He helped clean the table, scrubbing with vigor. His time was up now, and he willingly left on a positive note.

I left, too, suddenly realizing that I had been tense and in a cold sweat for the entire forty-five minutes of my observation. My identification with Marty was more powerful than I had realized. So much of me was invested in his success. He had come so far, and yet he still needed so much help. It's true, his attention span was now lengthened, and the hyperactivity was less in evidence, but he was in a structured situation at the school, with one-on-one attention. What was happening at home? I looked forward to finding out in the Newmans' next session.

Marty came for his session the day after my school visit, and he wouldn't get out of the car. Helen urged him, begged him, and finally, dragged him to the door. When I opened it, Marty lay down on the waiting-room floor, stiff as a board, and refused to move. He then began to cry and throw a tantrum. He shouted, "No go in, no go in."

I asked Helen what had happened. She told me that she and Craig had gone to a movie the night before and had used a new sitter. Marty had been asleep and usually did sleep through the night. He awoke, however, at 10:30, and his parents were not yet back. He was terrified of the sitter, a "perfectly fine young woman," according to Helen, and had cried until the Newmans returned. He hadn't gone to school that morning.

"This has been the worst day," said Helen. "He's been driving me crazy all day. I couldn't wait until we got here."

Marty remained on the floor. We ignored him and just sat until he calmed down.

I spoke to Marty. "I think you were upset when you woke up last night, Marty. You had a new sitter. Laurie couldn't come last night. It's all right now. Everyone is here who loves you. Will you come and play?"

Marty sniffled and wouldn't budge from his prone position. I told him that it was all right; we could skip our time together, and he could come back next time to play. Marty got up, hit his mother hard in the face, and tried to run out to the car. Helen looked stunned.

I ran after Marty, who now sat down in the driveway and cried: "Sorry, sorry, sorry."

Helen came out and picked up Marty, and we all came back in. I gave them each some water. Helen dried Marty's face, but her cheek began to swell. When I offered her some ice, she refused, and just sat there, looking small, despite her size, and helpless.

I talked to Marty about the episode, explaining again that when he was upset, he must use words, not his fists. I told him that I understood how upset he felt. Marty looked contrite but refused to speak to me. We canceled the session, and I asked Helen if she and Craig could come to talk to me that evening. She was eager to come. We said good-bye, and Marty waved to me as they drove away.

I especially regretted that Marty had missed school this day because his time the day before had been extended to include "snack," his most successful event in the school's schedule.

The Newmans' Visit

Helen and Craig came in the evening. Helen's mother was sitting: the Newmans weren't taking any chances! I told them about Marty's progress in school and what I had observed. I urged them to use language continuously, and not to respond to Marty's pointing or gesturing, but to make him ask for what he wanted. I offered them support and commended them on their continued efforts to reinforce his appropriate behavior and ignore his negative acts. The Newmans were using the time-out technique at home rather than sending Marty to his room.

"This works out much better," said Craig. "He never thought his room was punishment because he has so much stuff in there to keep him busy. And I think he really didn't mind being alone, away from us. He always had 'Petey.' "

I agreed that the time-out form of discipline worked well for Marty.

We talked about Marty's behavior in the waiting room. I tried to explain that Marty did his best when he had structure, when there were no surprises, when he had a steady routine, and when he was with people he knew.

"It was pure chance that he awoke the one night when you used a new sitter, but this was scary for Marty," I said. It was almost as if a sixth sense had alerted Marty to some change in the household.

"It would be best if you make sure that Marty knows your sitters beforehand," I continued. "He tried to retaliate and punish you, Helen, for leaving him with a stranger. That's why he hit you, and that's why he wouldn't go to school or leave you to play with me today. He needs to know that you're there for him. It's too soon for Marty to adjust to new situations. He's doing well in school, but he's not ready for situations that involve any new changes or unfamiliar faces."

The Newmans understood this and agreed that they would be more vigilant in the future. Helen told me that she had actually been feeling better since Marty started school; it gave her a short respite in the morning. She stayed at the school but had a cup of coffee and relaxed. And she "loved" her afternoons when Laurie came. She could go the hairdresser, or shop, or visit a friend.

I suggested that she try again to take Marty to the library. I explained that she should prepare him first by setting the ground rules, telling him what to expect and what they would do there, and leaving immediately if he was not "good." I explained that this preparation would be similar to the way we had approached his going to the playschool.

It was simply a question of time before Marty could extend his time at the school and transfer his appropriate behavior to a new setting. We were "shaping" his behavior, just as trainers shape the behavior of animals so that they perform certain feats. The Newmans had been reading enough to understand what I meant and did not take offense. They understood that the behavior modification program had its roots in experiments in animal laboratories, and they were cooperative parents who obviously cared deeply for each other and for Marty. Just as we were shaping Marty's behavior, the Newmans were learning new approaches and techniques to use in coping with him. In effect, they were breaking their old cycle of responding to Marty's negative acts and were reinforcing his behavior that was socially desirable. We parted with the library "assignment" for Helen.

Helen was able to separate from Marty at school the next day, phoning me from the school office to report. Marty also came that day for his next session, racing into the playroom just as he had been doing. For several sessions, we played "library," and soon after, Helen felt ready to try the library visit.

She prepared Marty for their outing, describing exactly what they would do: look at books, borrow some at the desk, always talk in whispers, and stay close to each other. It worked. Helen kept the visit short, and Marty had a good experience. He brought one of the books, *Mr. Tall and Mr. Small*, to our session and curled up next to me while I read the story, urging him to point at each object or character described. He also took the book to playschool to show to Karen, and Mrs. Langdon permitted him to sit through storytime while she read it to the class. She explained that this was Marty's library book and that he had gone to the library and had chosen it himself. Marty was the center of attention, "loving every minute of it," according to Karen. As Mrs. Langdon read to the children, he sat close to her. When she finished, the children commented on the story, and Mrs. Langdon talked about libraries as special, friendly places. It was a good morning for Marty and the beginning of his being able to stay a longer time at school.

Marty was still shy about talking to the other children, and they were still a bit wary of him, never quite knowing what to expect. His unpredictability put them off. Although Marty could talk to me more in the playroom and could role-play with the Buddy doll, he was still unable to ask another child to play. Helen had tried inviting a neighbor's child over, and Marty had ignored him completely. I explained to Helen that Marty felt less comfortable playing with another child than with Karen or me. His isolation from other children because of his hyperactivity and aggressiveness, coupled with his language deficit, caused him to be socially inept. He didn't know what to expect from other children, and their demands would be difficult for him to understand and to meet. He feared rejection and would not chance it. I assured Helen that gradually, as Marty got more used to the school and was more accepted, he would venture to play with another child. On the playground, he had let a child push him on the swing, and he had also taken turns riding in a wagon with another child. These were major accomplishments for Marty, compared to where he had been eight months before.

The question ever-present in the Newmans' mind was whether Marty would be ready to enroll in the local kindergarten. He was now four years and two months old, and we had a long time to work with him before he would be of kindergarten age. I felt that it was important to go slowly, and if need be, he could remain with Mrs. Langdon until he was ready for kindergarten—even if it meant starting when he was older than the other children. In connection with this possible delay, the Newmans were concerned about Marty's huge size—he was, indeed, the tallest child in playschool. His size created many problems because people expected him to behave more maturely. In a strange way, this child was hindered by his height: his speech and manner were incongruous with his body build.

Saying Good-bye

Over the next months, my work consisted of further role playing, continuous behavior modification, and targeting different kinds of behavior trying to extinguish negative ones such as hitting, biting, and tantrums. Marty's speech became clearer, less singsong, and less jumbled. He could speak in full sentences when he took his time, and he no longer made errors in his subjects and verbs. His relationship with Louisa had also improved. She was willing to play with him and even to read stories to him.

Helen and Marty made a weekly visit to the library and attempted to stay for story hour. It worked. Marty sat quietly while the librarian read a story, but he did not join in the singing afterward. Helen knew she had a long road ahead, but her spirits were better, and she was more optimistic each time she came with Marty.

It was time to begin decreasing the frequency of our sessions. The Newmans and I met to discuss this process. Over the months since Marty had enrolled in playschool, his behavior had become increasingly stabilized. My notes on our earlier sessions when I had pondered over Marty's diagnosis, now seemed to describe another boy. They demonstrated to me how difficult it is to draw conclusions about a young child's intellectual or emotional behavior. Yes, Marty was still unable to remain in his classroom every day for an entire three-hour morning session, but he had made enormous progress: his attention span was longer; the hyperactivity had been substantially reduced; the autism-like symptoms were no longer in evidence; and he spoke in sentences to let us know his needs. He was still fragile, however, and could benefit further from professional help that would consolidate his gains and help him compensate for his developmental impairments.

Fortunately, the essential ingredients had been present to enable Marty to make such strides: His parents were intelligent and concerned and had changed their approach to him so that his deeply entrenched negative behavior patterns had gradually subsided. And Marty's pediatrician had wisely refrained from using the medication that is so often prescribed for hyperactive children even before an accurate diagnosis has been reached and before therapy had been attempted.

So many children are overmedicated, so that the symptoms diminish, but not the underlying causes. Some physicians suggest that medication be used as the sole treatment for hyperactive children with attention deficits. Others suggest a combination of medication and psychotherapy. Although medication may be effective in diminishing the hyperactivity or distractibility of some children, their learning disabilities and social behaviors still need to be addressed.

My emphasis in play therapy was on helping Marty to develop language and social skills. Mrs. Langdon would continue to reinforce Marty's cognitive development, and of course, there would be ample opportunities at the school for Marty to engage in social interactions. Mrs. Langdon and Karen were essential partners in contributing to Marty's improved behavior. He had responded well to therapy; it was time to see if he could sustain his gains without my frequent intervention.

We agreed that Marty would now come twice a week instead of three times. Gradually, we would reduce these visits to once a week. I would continue to monitor his progress in playschool through observations and telephone talks with Mrs. Langdon. Helen and Craig were pleased with this arrangement. If Marty regressed, I would increase the session frequency. It was important to be flexible because Marty was still testing the water. I felt that one more year in playschool, combined with a weekly play therapy session, should be enough to maintain Marty's gains.

Now it was time to let Marty know that we would be together less often. I told him that he would still come to play with me, but not on Wednesdays anymore. At first, he seemed confused. We marked off the days on the calendar, and Marty, with my assistance, drew a circle around Wednesday. Wednesday would be "library day" for Marty. Helen and I thought the library visits would make a pleasant substitute for his therapy session and would still afford him structure and regularity.

The twice-weekly sessions went along smoothly. Marty would turn five in January and would remain with Mrs. Langdon until fall, when, if he had adjusted to the full morning schedule with only minor mishaps, our plan was to enroll him in kindergarten. He would be slightly older than some of the children, but socially and emotionally he would probably be more like the younger five-year-olds in the class.

Marty had made progress, but I knew that there would be setbacks for him. He was a calmer child and more tractable, but he was obviously more immature than his peers. There were still developmental lags in his speech and in his social behavior, but compared to where he was when I first met him, his gains had been remarkable. His growth in language and his willingness to communicate by words rather than by negative acts had made a substantial difference in the way others responded to him. In this regard, the school environment had been an essential part of his therapy program, along with the change in the Newmans' behavior toward him. The Newmans had learned how to handle him, relying in part on behavior modification techniques and using charts to document his progress in specific areas, and in part on their own willingness to accept my suggestions about relief for Helen (the use of sitters), more consistent handling of Marty in terms of preparing him for changes in his schedule, generally slowing the pace of his routine, and of course, constantly using language, in songs, reading, storytelling, and explanations of the events in Marty's life.

As the months passed, Marty's sessions were reduced to once a week. He was now spending a full morning at school and only occasionally had a tantrum. Usually, these took place when there was a change in routine, such as a visitor, a field trip to the park, or a classmate's birthday party. Slowly, Marty learned that sometimes a day can be different. With preparation beforehand and Karen's support, he was soon able to respond appropriately when a child celebrated a birthday at school.

In our sessions, Marty and I read books about birthdays, drew cakes and candles, sang "Happy Birthday" to the Buddy doll, and made a Play-Doh cake for him. Marty drew a picture for Buddy— primitive, but his first picture. It was a "ball" for Buddy, simply a round circle that Marty colored red. We hung it up in the playroom. Marty's pride in this picture led to other attempts to draw, both with me and at school.

The birthday preparations in the playroom had facilitated Marty's adjustment to parties at school, and I knew that Helen was eager to take him to the birthday parties of his numerous cousins. She also wanted him to have his own birthday party in January, even though she remembered with trepidation how embarrassed she had been by his behavior at her nephew's party when he was a "holy terror." I reassured her that Marty had improved, and that taking him to a party would be worth a try. It was crucial, I told her, to remove him immediately from the party if necessary, even if it was before the cake and the present-giving "ceremonies." I suspected that having to leave the party would be a sign of defeat for Helen because she had been telling her family how well Marty had been doing. I reminded her that it was essential to keep up the behavior modification program since it had been so successful with Marty. I also suggested that she forwarn her relatives of her intentions.

Marty's cousin's birthday came. Helen phoned that evening. I could tell by the lilt in her voice that Marty had done well.

"Do you think I can invite a few children from school and give Marty his own party" she asked.

"Yes, try it," I responded. "Keep the party short and simple. If things get out of hand, just ask the mothers to leave. Again, explain to them what you plan to do, so that everyone will cooperate. Helen, they're parents and they know Marty; they'll understand."

Marty's birthday party was a huge success. Helen kept it short— about an hour and a half, just enough time for a couple of games, songs, cake, ice cream, and the opening of presents. Marty proudly gave each child a small gift to take home.

At our next session, he brought along one of his presents, a plastic tape recorder. He put the tape into the proper slot, pushed the "play" button, and smiled when the song "On Top of Old Smokey" began. He insisted that I listen to it twice, and he sang along, trying to learn the words. He was able to tell me in his own way about his party, his other presents, and his cake with five candles. We then relived his experience by making a Play-Doh cake for him with five "candles." Marty "blew" out the candles, and we both sang "Happy Birthday." It was a happy time for Marty. He sat there grinning at me with his goofy smile. I felt like grinning, too. This had been a long, hard eighteen months for both of us. We would still see each other regularly until the August break. Then I planned to see him once a week to help him make his adjustment to kindergarten, and after a couple of months, just once a month.

When August came, we said good-bye.

"Next time I see you," I said, "you'll be a big, big boy. You'll be in kindergarten."

Marty was ready. He had passed the kindergarten screening test in the spring, and we had spent May, June, and July talking about what to expect. I had tried to make the connection for him between Mrs. Langdon's school and kindergarten. Marty, Helen, and I had visited his new school and had toured the building, the playground, and the classroom, Marty had met his new teacher, and I could see that it was love at first sight. Helen and I were concerned about the bus and agreed that Helen would drive Marty to school until we felt that he was ready to go on the school bus.

Six months after Marty started kindergarten, where he was fitting in well, he and I said our final good-byes. He hugged me for the first time and gave me a picture: it was a stick figure of me—a gift from his heart.

CHAPTER FIVE

BARBARA, WEDNESDAY'S CHILD

Divorce and Its Effects

Monday's Child is fair of face
Tuesday's child is full of grace
Wednesday's child is full of woe
Thursday's child has far to go
Friday's child is loving and giving
Saturday's child works hard for a living
But the child who is born on the Sabbath day
Is blythe and bonny and good and gay.

First Meeting

The saddest little face peered at me through the car window. Lillian Crawford urged her daughter, Barbara, to open the door and come into the waiting room, and reluctantly, Barbara complied. She kept her head down, but when I reached for her hand, she took it and slowly walked with me into the playroom. Barbara looked quite thin—undernourished—and had a sallow complexion and long dark hair badly in need of a washing, and yet, she was dressed in expensive clothes. The incongruity between her clothes and her physical appearance was striking, but as I learned more about Lillian Crawford and Barbara, I was less surprised.

Barbara was five years old when she started therapy. A colleague of mine was treating Lillian Crawford, Barbara's mother, for a long-term depression and was concerned about Barbara's depression as well, manifested by threats to Lillian that she would "kill" herself, by her constant weeping, and by her feelings of being "unloved" and "unwanted."

When Lillian first came to see me, she had been separated for two months from her husband, Arthur, Barbara's step-father. An impending divorce and arguments about Barbara's custody had exacerbated Lillian's own depression and suicidal threats, as well as her neglect of Barbara and a younger brother, Raymond. Therapy had been suggested for Barbara four months before my first contact with the family, but Lillian had resisted, believing that Barbara was only echoing her own complaints and was actually a "healthy child." Money for treatment was not an issue; Arthur Crawford was a wealthy stockbroker who was providing for the family's financial needs during the separation. Barbara and Raymond were visiting Arthur on weekends and, according to Lillian, were "confused" about what was happening. To further complicate matters, Arthur had a seventeen-year-old daughter from his first marriage. She also visited him and, Lillian said, "detested" Barbara, whom she had labeled the "snot."

The Family Background

Before my first contact with Barbara, Lillian Crawford came to see me. Her husband had refused, stating that "therapy is for the birds." An attractive woman in her late twenties, Lillian was meticulously dressed in expensive clothes, and her bleached hair was cut short and carefully coiffed. Although she looked as if she had stepped off a page in *Vogue* magazine, her voice, diction, and mannerisms (like popping chewing gum) were characteristic of someone from a less affluent class.

Lillian's face was devoid of expression during our session. She told me facts in a monotone, as if she were talking about another person: "All my life, I've had tough breaks. My life is like a soap opera but even worse. As a kid, I watched my folks fight. My mother drank every day. My father took care of us kids—four of us, all losers. When I was fourteen, my mom died and my three brothers and I were raised by an aunt and uncle because my father just up and left us. I dropped out of school at sixteen and began working as a typist in this brokerage firm. I was good at that. Arthur worked there, too. I've know him since I was nineteen, and I think he always loved me. He's older, by twenty years, and had just been divorced when we met. He wanted to marry me when I was twenty, but I didn't really love him. Because he urged me to find my own apartment, eventually I moved out of my aunt and uncle's house. Arthur helped with my rent, and sure, we did become lovers.

"I began to dress better and look better. By watching the girls in the office, I learned a lot. Arthur gave me presents and took me out, but I wanted more—more adventure in my life before I married. So, I saved my money.

"My dad came back when I was twenty-two. Imagine. He just walks in one day as if he never left—the bastard—and wants his family together. Well, my brothers wouldn't give him the time of day. I was the youngest and a softie, so I let him come live in my apartment. He was OK. As a matter of fact, he was a good cook, and that helped me. He cleaned, cooked, like he was trying to make up for all those years that he was gone. We had some fights—about my dating Arthur, my choice of men (he felt they were too old for me), clothes, you name it! He didn't want me to be like my mother, he said. It was OK though, I guess. I was lonely, and by this time, my aunt and uncle had given up on me. I think they thought I was too reckless, and maybe they worried that I would get too involved with the wrong kind of man. I had Arthur now, and my dad. But things were still going to happen. My dad gave me a present on my twenty-third birthday: a week's vacation in Florida at a fancy hotel. I was so excited. I had never been out of Connecticut before, not even to New York!

"Arthur wanted to go with me, but I said no. This was *my* big adventure. Dad now calls this present the 'Devil's doing.' Well, I guess in a way, Dad's right. I went to Florida with new clothes, a new hairdo—I looked like a million. That's where I met Barbara's father.

"It was love at first sight—for me, anyway. Anthony was in the army, stationed in Florida. One night, he and a buddy were at the bar of the hotel restaurant. We were together all weekend, and I was mad for him. I was also stupid; we didn't use contraceptives. When he left, he took my address and said he would write to me. We did write to each other, even after I let him know that I was pregnant. In my eighth month, he stopped writing. My letters were returned unopened. Later, I found out that he'd been transferred to Germany, and his buddy wrote to me that Anthony had deserted after two months there. I also found out that he had a wife and two kids.

"So, back home, Arthur steps in and asks me to marry him. I did, and he adopted Barbara legally. Barbara thinks he's her real father. We then had a child together: Raymond, who is three now. After Arthur and I married, my dad moved out. They just couldn't stand each other. Arthur and I bought this humongous old house, and I live there now with the kids. Arthur has his own place at the beach.

"His first wife lives in New York, and they have this daughter, Jackie, who used to come to stay with us on weekends. She's something else. I can't stand her. She's spoiled rotten and is mean to Barbara, but good with Raymond. She was always climbing out the window at night after we went to bed and meeting different guys and coming home early in the morning, mostly stewed, but Arthur shut his eyes to all this. Jackie and I fought like cats and dogs. She's jealous of me and Barbara and even hates her own mother. What a mess!

"Arthur and I fought a lot about Jackie, about my housekeeping, about the way I raise the kids. I think, too, he really favors Raymond and hates Barbara. He won't admit this, but I know he resents her. Even though he adopted her, she's really not his kid. Now he's giving me grief. He wants physical custody of my kids, just for spite, I think, but he says I'm an unfit mother. This is what's driving me nuts. I sometimes think if I died, everyone would be better off. Now my shrink says that Barbara is messed up. Can you help her?"

I listened to Lillian's story and wondered how she could tell me all this without shedding a tear. Either she had told this story so many times—to her therapist, her lawyer, her aunt and uncle—that by now the tears were gone, or she was using distance and insulation from these painful events as a way of defending herself from further anxiety and depression. I knew that Lillian was in good hands with my colleague, and that she had some psychological support from her father, her brothers, and her aunt and uncle. My own concern was Barbara. I asked Lillian to describe Barbara for me.

Lillian told me that Barbara really didn't like Arthur anymore: "She's so anxious that she grinds her teeth at night. She also cries when she has to visit Arthur on weekends. When I drop her off, she won't get out of the car, and if Arthur comes to my house to get the kids, he has to drag Barbara down the walk. She punched me the last time I tried to drop her off.

"She has a terrible temper. I told her to count to ten before she yells. I told her to put her anger in a basket and give it to Jesus; He'll know what to do. But she doesn't listen to me. She told me she'll kill herself if she has to go to Arthur's house, and she told me she really means it: 'I'll kill myself. I'm not joking.' That's just how she said it. Why should she have to go to his house? Arthur's lawyer told my lawyer that Arthur has legal rights. Well, he's not Barbara's natural father. I don't care if he did adopt her. He shouldn't see her at all."

This was the only time during my first encounter with Lillian that I saw her lose control and show emotion. Clearly, Lillian was angry at Arthur and resented his right to see the children. She continued to describe Barbara, emphasizing Barbara's "hate" and dread of Arthur; her difficulties with Jackie, whom Lillian saw as a "terrible role model"; and Barbara's refusal to "wash, eat, play, and be normal like other kids." Although Arthur gave Lillian money for the children and paid the bills for the house, her therapy, and her car, he was always "late" in his payments. Lillian was "sick and tired" of Arthur and his need to correct her constantly, his criticism of her mothering, and his loathing of her friends.

Lillian ended our session stating that she thought a detective was following her to try to prove that she "had other men" and was neglecting the children. She felt that Barbara was not really "disturbed," that Arthur was the real problem.

Barbara's Visit

When Barbara entered the playroom for our first session, she was quiet, shy, and listless. Rather than explore the room, she sat still on the couch, hands folded, eyes downcast, shoulders drooping. She had just started kindergarten, she told me, but "I don't know my teacher's name." When I asked Barbara if she would like to draw, she nodded and came to the table. She drew circles and squares and colored them in. She then asked if she could play with the dolls. She chose the Hart Family dolls, a mother, a father, and a baby. She played with them using different voices:

"Now I'm going shopping. You watch the baby," she said to the father doll.

"Come back soon for dinner."

"OK. Good-bye."

She played this scene several times: each time, the mother kissed the father good-bye, kissed the baby good-bye, and then went off. She brought the mother back in time for "dinner." As she played, she seemed to relax, became more animated, and enjoyed her little story. I watched with no comments. I just wanted her to feel comfortable before I intruded or made interpretations. As I watched Barbara, I was aware of her sallow appearance, her oily hair, and a slight stench as if her underwear were dirty. Her nails were jagged and dirty as well. Yet this child was wearing expensive sneakers, designer jeans, and a gold bracelet. I noticed, too, that Barbara had dark shadows under her eyes and seemed tired and lethargic by the end of the session. Once this brief, spirited play was over, she seemed spent. I led her back to the waiting room and told Lillian I would phone her that evening. As they drove off, Barbara waved good-bye from the car window.

I wondered what her home situation was truly like. Lillian struck me as so absorbed in her own psychological and physical needs that she was unable to expend much energy in caring for Barbara, who semed to be a victim of benign neglect.

That evening, I phoned Lillian and expressed my concern about Barbara's appearance, being careful not to sound accusatory; I didn't want to put Lillian on the defensive. To my surprise, Lillian listened, seemed grateful for my suggestions, and implied that she had just forgotten to wash Barbara that day, "because I was so worried and preoccupied with my divorce." Lillian said that she would take care of Barbara in the future, and that "it was really unintentional" on her part. She wanted to know if I thought Barbara would really "kill herself." I told Lillian it was too soon for me to have a good sense of Barbara, but that I would stay in close touch with her. Accepting this, Lillian said they would be back in two days for our next session.

Barbara's Drawings

I tried to make sense of Barbara's suicidal threats to her mother. It was possible that she had overheard Lillian talk about suicide to Arthur or to her father or friends. Children are perceptive, and Barbara may have realized that such a dramatic statement as "I'll kill myself" would attract adult attention and concern. I learned later from Lillian that Jackie often made suicidal threats to Arthur in order to "manipulate him" and had actually cut her wrists three years after her parents had divorced. According to Lillian, Jackie had told Barbara about this incident in order to "scare her."

When Barbara came for our second session, she was cleaner. Her hair was washed, her nails were evenly cut, and there was no odor, but she still looked tired and listless; her eyes still seemed sunken in the same dark shadows as before. Barbara went right over to the Hart Family dolls and began her little playlet. This time "Daddy" went to work, but he didn't "come home."

- ► Where did "Daddy" go? [I asked]
- ► I don't know. Far away.
- ► Won't he come back?
- ► When the baby is all grown up, she'll find him.

I thought Barbara was referring to Arthur and the impending divorce, and I continued to observe her as she played.

▸ This mother is crying now, big, big tears. Baby is
sleeping.
▸ The mother feels sad.
▸ Yes, everyone is sad. They never see Daddy, but they
have his picture and his name.
▸ What's his name?
▸ I can't remember.

Something didn't feel right, but I didn't know what was both-
ering me. Barbara knew Arthur's name. Why wouldn't she use it?
Meanwhile, Barbara put the dolls away and found the Play-Doh.
She rolled it out, made little balls, and seemed to like the texture of
the clay. I was still puzzled about her doll play and asked if she would
like to draw. She agreed, put the clay away, and drew "my family."
She asked for two pieces of paper. On one sheet, she drew
"Mommy," "myself," and "Raymond." On the other sheet she drew
"Daddy and Jackie. Dad has a beard, and a fat tummy. He lives in the
beach house. Mommy and Daddy are getting a divorce, and I'm sad."
Although Barbara had given me an accurate story of her family
situation in her drawings, it didn't match the doll play. I asked her
if that was Arthur who left the mother and baby dolls and went
away. She became silent, put her head down, and would not talk
about the dolls anymore.
I was confused. She seemed so open in her drawings of the family
with a clear separation of Arthur and Jackie from Lillian, herself, and
Raymond, but why wouldn't she say the "daddy's" name in the doll
play. In her own way, she had given me two stories. It was up to
me to figure it out, she seemed to say. She had communicated
enough. Now, no more today.
As our sessions moved along, Barbara continued to play the same
game: "Daddy goes away, and baby finds him." She was reluctant
to talk about where the father was and yet was open with me about
her feelings toward Jackie, Raymond, and Lillian. Barbara told me
that she was bothered by Raymond, who "takes her toys," "hits
her," and "is a crybaby and spoiled." She often went to the dollhouse
and put the boy doll to bed "with no supper" while "big sister
watches TV all night and eats lots of candy."
As the weeks went by, and as Barbara began to feel more
comfortable with me, she was able to tell me about her dreams. She

had a dream that was repeated several times a week. In this dream, "a scary gorilla comes to my bed. Then the banister falls down the stairs. Then the house shakes and falls down."

We talked about the dream, and through puppet play, Barbara was able to make one connection with her present situation. She pretended one puppet was the "gorilla," who chased Barbara, the girl puppet. She played this game with much excitement and intensity until she was able to laugh about it.

- ▸ Scary gorilla, go away.
- ▸ Who is the gorilla?
- ▸ Arthur is the gorilla!
- ▸ Why is Arthur the gorilla?
- ▸ He has a big beard.
- ▸ Is that why he's so scary?
- ▸ Yes. He came to our house with a bat and clippers.

In this session, our eighth one together, Barbara sketchily described an incident in which Arthur had come for the children but Lillian wouldn't let him in. Lillian later corroborated this story, at our second monthly meeting. Arthur had gone back to the car and taken out a bat, threatening to break the door in. When Lillian yelled that she'd call the police, Arthur went to the garage, got the hedge clippers, and said he would cut the telephone wires. Both children were now screaming. Lillian yelled at Arthur to go away, and he did leave. All of this was reported to the police and to Lillian's lawyer.

At our second meeting, Lillian also gave me some information that helped to explain Barbara's doll play. Because of Arthur's behavior with the bat, Lillian had been able to get a temporary restraining order that prevented Arthur from coming to the house. Further, she had been able to prevent the children's visits at Arthur's house until a court hearing decided on custody rights. The divorce papers had come through, and a date was to be set for the judge's decision concerning physical custody of the children. Lillian confessed that she was afraid that Arthur, out of vindictiveness, would tell Barbara that she was not his natural child. For this reason, she herself had told Barbara that her real father "had gone far away and one day would come back." Lillian had also given Barbara a photo of Anthony, which

"Barbara put under her pillow and keeps it there all the time."

This information clarified Barbara's doll play. The "daddy" wasn't Arthur, but Anthony, who had gone away. The "baby," Barbara, would find him some day. No wonder Barbara's dreams were scary; no wonder the banister and the house were falling down. Everything in this child's life seemed to be falling apart. She had now lost two fathers: she had been rejected by her natural father, and now a divorce would separate her from the man who, until recently, she had believed to be her father.

Divorce and Its Effects on Barbara

My inner reaction to Lillian when she told me about her revelations to Barbara was a mixture of shock and disbelief. Yet, as a therapist, I had to prevent Lillian from becoming aware of my disapproval. In dealing with clients, a therapist must never become judgmental. When I encounter a situation like this one, it takes all my energy to keep from exploding with outrage. In Lillian's case, I could only hope that her psychotherapist was finding it possible to deal with her egocentrism, which overshadowed any compassion she might feel for Barbara. Lillian had not experienced good mothering as a child herself, and as a result, unfortunately, she lacked some of the skills essential for raising a child, but in working with Barbara, I needed Lillian as my ally, not as an opponent.

It was very hard for me to listen to Lillian rationalize why she had had to tell Barbara about Anthony. I wondered if this revelation had been meant to alienate Barbara from Arthur. If Lillian convinced Barbara that Arthur was not her true father, did Lillian think that she would have a better chance of denying him visitation rights? These thoughts passed through my mind as I listened to Lillian justify why she had told Barbara the truth:

> ▶ Arthur has become stingy. I think Barbara should know that he's not her real daddy. Maybe one day Anthony and I will get together again.

▶ Lillian, that's a fantasy.

▶ Well, maybe not.

▶ Can it possibly help Barbara?

▶ Yes, she can think of a good father someplace waiting for her.

▶ But Arthur has been her father, and from what you've told me, he has been a good father.

▶ Not now. He's got a terrible temper. I'm worried that he'll hurt me or the kids. Look what he did with the bat.

▶ Barbara tells me you have put new locks on the doors, and chains as well.

▶ Yes, I don't want him near us. I have a court order to deny visitation and to keep him away.

▶ When will the custody decision be made?

▶ In a month, I hope. I don't want him to see Barbara. I'm not sure I can keep him away from Raymond, though.

▶ Won't this affect both children, if one child goes to Arthur for visits and one doesn't?

▶ He's a bastard. He's claiming that I starve the kids, and that I keep them up late. He told my lawyer I watch porno films with the kids. That's a lie!

▶ Look, right now, Barbara needs your support. She needs your love and should not be exposed to the bitterness you and Arthur feel.

▶ Well, tell him that!

This was a difficult session, but I could not step into the role of Lillian's therapist. She already had one. The problem was that she was obviously still thinking about Anthony, and now Barbara would join her in perpetuating that fantasy. Lillian had signed a paper allowing her therapist and me to share information if Barbara was involved, and I felt that it was necessary, for Barbara's well-being, to alert my colleague to the current situation. It certainly involved Barbara, who was now clinging to what seemed to be an impossible dream. Lillian had had no contact with Anthony for almost six years. He was a married man and an army deserter (*Had he been found? Was he in prison?*) and he had not tried to communicate with Lillian since her eighth month of pregnancy. And Lillian's unrealistic dreams were now affecting Barbara, who felt rejected by her biological father, was caught in a struggle between her mother and Arthur, and had a deep craving for a father. I was worried about the effect on Barbara of Lillian's venom. Although Barbara was gradually withdrawing her love from Arthur, I felt that this withdrawal was a result of Lillian's demands and not of Barbara's genuine feelings.

Barbara now brought repudiation to her interactions with Arthur, borrowed, it seemed, from Lillian or derived from Barbara's identification with her. In Barbara's doll play, Arthur was now portrayed as the "enemy." I speculated that, although she truly loved Arthur and missed him, she was beginning to feel anxious and guilty about her former visits to him. She may have felt disloyal to Lillian and in conflict about the time she had spent with Arthur. Her later sessions demonstrated these ambivalent feelings and supported my hypothesis. When she used the father doll in her play, it was seen both as a nurturing figure and as one not to be trusted.

Research on the effects of divorce on young children suggests that girls develop lower self-esteem as a result of feelings of guilt if they have tried to maintain a relationship with their fathers. Indeed, Barbara felt depressed, unworthy, unloved, and unwanted. She verbalized these emotions in our sessions, crying and banging her head on the table, needing my comforting and reassurance that she was not to blame for anything. Despite Arthur's lavish gifts of toys, trips to New York, and sailing on his boat, Barbara had found it difficult to accept these pleasures, knowing that Lillian was so hostile toward Arthur. Barbara was desperate to keep her mother's love, and Lillian attacked Arthur's generosity as "bribes"; it was impossible for her to match his bestowal of presents on the children. At the same time, Arthur grudgingly paid the bills, although these payments were usually late in coming.

Lillian was fighting for sole-parent custody of the children. Arthur had contested it with claims of Lillian's instability, depression, suicidal threats, promiscuity, and physical and emotional neglect of the children. However, Arthur was willing to compromise and had suggested joint legal and joint physical custody, which would include visitation rights and shared responsibility in decision making. He knew that he might lose if he demanded sole custody. At one point, Arthur's attorney had even argued for split custody, Arthur offering to take Raymond, his biological child, while Barbara remained with Lillian. Lillian had been adamant in her refusal. Thus, the Crawfords were at war, and the children were the victims.

The Dreams Continue and Change

While deliberations concerning the custody of the children proceeded, Barbara continued to see me regularly. She began to talk more openly about her dreams, most of them similar in theme. A pigeon, a monkey, a gorilla, or some "weird monster" was usually a "scary" figure in the dream that "scratched" her or "hurt" her in some way. Could the scary figures be symbols of Arthur? I offered Barbara the opportunity to talk about these animals or to draw them. She preferred to act out the dreams with puppets and generally found some relief in the repetition of one particular puppet playlet. She used the "princess" and "wolf" puppets for her story.

▸ Why does that "monster" scratch the princess?
▸ The princess is alone. No one takes care of her.
▸ Who should take care of her?
▸ The king.
▸ Well, let's get the king puppet.
▸ OK, here comes the king. But Dorothy, I need two kings.
▸ You can use the prince puppet and make believe it's a king.

Barbara took the two male puppets and held them in one hand. The "princess" was on her other hand. The princess "cried" and said, "Help, help! There's a big, big scary monster who will eat me up."
"No," said the king puppet. "I will save you."
"No," said the prince puppet. "I will save you."
Barbara dropped the princess puppet and punched the "wolf" puppet which was now on her hand, again and again. She threw it down and said:

▸ The end!
▸ Is the play over?

▶ Yes, of course. The princess is saved by two kings. The wolf is dead.

Barbara played out this same script during the next few sessions, and her dreams of monsters gradually began to subside. Who was the monster? I was puzzled. I surmised that the "kings" were her two fathers, although Barbara had not yet revealed this to me directly. But who was terrifying Barbara? Who scratched and clawed her at night in her dreams? Did the animal symbolize the custody battle, the current struggle between Lillian and Arthur? Or was the animal a person? It did not seem to be Arthur as I had once thought.

The tension in Barbara's house was mounting. According to Lillian, Arthur was demanding more time with the children, and he wanted to take them to see his mother in Chicago. Lillian tried to prevent this trip but lost. I was concerned about the trip, too, wondering if Arthur would leave the children with his mother as a means of getting them out of the state and away from Lillian before the custody decision had been made. To my surprise, the judge, ruled that the visit was appropriate and also revoked the restraining order. Plans were made for the trip, and Barbara and I talked about it during our sessions. She seemed eager to go, but somewhat apprehensive. At our last session before the trip, Barbara brought a crystal ball. She said that she could "look into the ball and see two daddies."

▶ Tell me about the two daddies.
▶ I really, really have two daddies. Raymond has only one. My daddy's name is Anthony. I never saw him. I don't know where he lives. I have his picture. I'll bring it next time I come to see you. When I grow-up—when I'm sixteen—I'll go find him.

This disclosure caught me by surprise, and I wondered why Barbara had chosen this particular time to reveal to me the true identities of the "kings." I speculated that the anticipation of the trip had made Barbara anxious and that she must have wondered, as I did, about the possibility of remaining with her grandmother. Or could it be that she thought the trip was an excursion to find her real father? Why the fantasy with the crystal ball? It was necessary to discuss the trip again, and to reassure Barbara that she would come back to Lillian and me, but I also wondered if Barbara really wanted to come back. It seemed to me that living with Lillian was a chaotic existence, whereas Arthur offered her more creature comforts and, indeed, care and love.

The playlet with the dolls and the story of the two kings who rescued the princess were the symbolic games Barbara used to express both her need to find her true father ("When the baby is all grown-up, she'll find him") and her need to have both daddies (the two kings) protect the princess and save her from harm and abandonment. Was it possible that Barbara's "scary monsters" signified her anger at her mother? Indeed, were the monsters Lillian? Perhaps Barbara was seeing Lillian as someone who had hurt her, first by losing her natural father, and now by divorcing Arthur, whom Barbara had thought for so many years was her real father.

Barbara's feelings toward Lillian needed to be clarified. I was sure that Barbara loved her mother, but she must also harbor resentment toward her. In order to deny these unpleasant feelings, Barbara had first tried to identify with Lillian and had therefore felt ambivalent toward Arthur; any love felt for him would be a betrayal of allegiance to her mother. And yet, in a sense, Lillian had betrayed Barbara twice. As a result, Barbara had little control over what was happening in her life.

Put Your Mother on the Ceiling

Barbara did come back from Chicago, and the visit had been a huge success. The airplane ride, in first-class, had been an adventure surpassed only by Grandma's huge house and her luxurious presents to the children. Barbara's previous anger toward Arthur was less in evidence. He was winning her over by material things, and Barbara now, seemed to be more overtly angry at Lillian. In her doll play, and her puppet play, she expressed this anger and seemed confused about her emotions. However, the sad, listless quality of our earlier contacts was decreasing and was being replaced by more hostile feelings. The "cruel" picture of Arthur that Lillian had painted for Barbara no longer seemed entirely valid: Barbara had experienced pleasure during her trip with him and kindness from his mother. She may have been influenced and overwhelmed by the material benefits, but she had also been temporarily removed from the tension of life with Lillian and had found some peace. As all of these feelings needed to be addressed in our sessions, I felt it was time to try some imagery exercises to help relieve some of Barbara's tension.

I started with a simple technique, using exercises from a delightful book, *Put Your Mother on the Ceiling*, by Richard de Mille. These games were designed to open up "the closed territory of the mind" by the use of vivid imagery stimulated by de Mille's phrases. De Mille argues that in a child's life, there is a time for fantasy and a time for realism. A balance is crucial. Although the Anthony fantasy was of some comfort to Barbara, I was always on guard concerning it. I was afraid that her fantasies about the reunion with Anthony would interfere with her maintaining the love she felt for Arthur— a love that was already in danger because of the divorce and Lillian's bitterness. However, completely dismissing Anthony's existence didn't seem useful either. He was Barbara's natural father, and she clung to the idea of his existence: only if her biological father was a real person could she herself exist.

I was concerned, too, about Barbara's lack of self-esteem, her self-hate, her feeling of not being effective, her depression, and her feeling of having been abandoned. Often Barbara would say, "I am ugly" or "No one loves me" or "No one wants me." Perhaps she construed the loss of two fathers to mean that she was not worthy of love. Although her drawings, her puppet play, and her doll play were all helping her to express her emotions, I felt that there were still areas of pain that we had not explored. Would the use of imagery help this wounded child?

Before each game in de Mille's book, a short introduction tells the child what it is about. The games are "imagination games," but they are also a kind of "reality training." The book starts with a simple exercise and proceeds to more complex ones, and these are direct and open-ended questions woven throughout the exercises that can be answered aloud or silently. At the end of each exercise the child is asked, "What would you like to do now? And then what? And what next?" Thus, the child has choices and can complete the exercise in several ways that feel comfortable. Some children are even inspired to make up their own exercises.

Before I began these exercises with Barbara, I wanted her to relax, and she was able to do so quite easily. I simply asked her to sit quietly in a comfortable chair, close her eyes, take deep breaths, and loosen her fingers, hands, arms, and legs. We began each exercise with this relaxation procedure. I then introduced the first exercise, "Boys and Girls." Barbara was asked to imagine a boy standing in a corner, wearing a jacket and a hat. She was then asked to change the color of his clothing; to have him lie down, roll across the floor, jump in the air, and sit in a chair; to have the boy's chair float up to the ceiling; to have the boy sing while up at the ceiling; and so on. We did this exercise with a girl as well.

Judging by her smiles and willingness to play, Barbara enjoyed this game. We did this particular exercise a few times before I introduced "Animals." Here she had to imagine, for example, a mouse, and elephant, and a dog; she had to give them colors, change their forms, change their names, and change their sizes from small to big and back again. Barbara was learning to control her imagery and found that wild fantasies could be made tame.

My goal was to work up to the exercise called "Parents." Here Barbara could follow the commands and make the parents become small, turn colors, multiply in number, stand on the ceiling, shrink, have a steam roller run over them and "flatten them like pancakes on the street," and have them grow fat and upset the steam rollers. Sharks were allowed to "eat" the parents, but the parents could then grow big, catch the shark, and eat it up. At the end, as in all previous exercises, Barbara could do anything she wanted to do with the parents in her imagination.

Barbara was delighted with this technique and later drew pictures of what she had imagined. She also playacted the exercises with dolls or puppets, and we were able to talk about her feelings during the month of these "mind games."

One session, Barbara said, after our exercises:

▸ I sometimes would like to put Daddy on the ceiling.
▸ Why?
▸ Then I'm boss!
▸ But of course you can't do that in real life can you?

▶ No, but I can think that!
▶ Does it help to think that?
▶ Yes, it helps.
▶ What about your mother? Do you want to put her on the ceiling, too?
▶ Wow! She goes under the steam roller!
▶ Sounds as if you're angry at her.
▶ No. No. No.

This was too much for Barbara. I had hit a nerve, and Barbara turned away. Obviously, she was angry at Lillian but could not tell me. Her play, however, began to change as a result of the exercises. It became more directed toward involving the mother doll, Mrs. Hart. Now Mrs. Hart was a true "villain," and Barbara directed much anger at her: "Mrs. Hart went shopping all day."

Barbara placed the doll across the room.

▶ Where's Mr. Hart?
▶ He's home baby-sitting. He's cooking, cleaning. He's exhausted (*big sigh*).
▶ When does Mrs. Hart come home?
▶ Well, she comes home late. Mr. Hart locks the door and won't let her in. She sneaks in through the window. He finds her and kicks her right out!
▶ Mr. Hart is sure angry.
▶ Oh, you bet! Get out, get out, get out!
▶ Will Mr. Hart ever let her come in?
▶ No. Never. She has to sleep in the park. The end!

Barbara was reversing roles. Now the mother was locked out of the house. She was the negligent person, whereas Arthur, the father, was the nurturer. I was somewhat mystified by the change in Barbara. Of course, the imaginative games had allowed some feelings to come out, but the anger seemed more directed at Lillian now.

My monthly visit with Lillian would soon clarify what was going on at home.

The Custody Decision

Lillian's session with me helped to explain much of what Barbara had been experiencing during that month. It seemed that Barbara had announced to Arthur during one of their visits (the judge had reinstated the visits to Arthur) that he was not her "real daddy, but a stepdaddy." Arthur had become enraged, and phoned Lillian, telling her to stop turning Barbara against him. When Lillian attempted to tell Barbara not to talk about Anthony in front of Arthur, Barbara threw a tantrum, told Lillian that she "hated" her, and "hated Arthur," and began to "beat up on herself—punching her head and punching her own arms and legs." Barbara had shouted at Lillian, accusing her of not loving her and loving only Raymond.

"I tried to comfort her," said Lillian, "and I tried to tell her I love her and that Arthur loves her. I told her none of this mess is her fault. I tried to hold her and kiss her and stroke her. Finally, she calmed down and said she loved me and loved Arthur. She wants her family to be together. She also wants Anthony to come back and live with us. My God, look at what I've done. I never should have told her about Anthony. I know now it was wrong. Maybe Arthur wouldn't have told Barbara about Anthony, but I couldn't chance it. Suppose he had told her before I did!"

Lillian was crying now, her typical tough composure shattered. She went on: "Do you know we had the final ruling about custody of the kids? I won. I have sole physical custody, with visitation rights for Arthur."

"No," I said, "I didn't know. I only suspected that something was going on. Barbara's play shifted from anger at Arthur to anger at you. I feel that she loves you both, and is terribly confused about the divorce, and her role in its occurrence, and, of course, curious about Anthony. Give her time. She expressed anger at Arthur to keep your loyalty and also because he's not her natural father. But down deep, she loves him; he has been her only father since she was born, and that love is difficult to destroy. Anthony is a fantasy figure that she holds onto now. As she gets older, you'll be able to help her understand the whole story. Right now, she seems to feel 'lucky' that she has 'two daddies.' Let's allow her to keep that idea. It would be difficult now to deny Anthony's existence."

"I did tell Barbara that Anthony will come back," Lillian said. "What should I tell her now that I have custody? Will Barbara think that's why I got divorced—to make room for Anthony? Oh, my God, my God."

"Lillian, this is a tough one. We can't tell Barbara that Anthony will come back, but we can tell her we don't know what will happen. You and Arthur can continue to give her love and security and comfort. Please try to keep your contacts with Arthur free of arguments. One of the best things you can do to ensure both Barbara's and Raymond's positive adjustment and well-being is to keep the relationship between you and Arthur amicable. We know from the many studies about divorce that children do best when their parents maintain good interactions with each other. It's also important for you to continue your therapy. The children will be sensitive to your moods and your attitudes as a single parent coping with two youngsters. Fortunately, you will be provided for financially, but I hope you can find some interest for yourself."

As we parted, Lillian reassured me that she would not attempt to undermine Arthur's attempts to "father" the children when they visited him.

I was not surprised to learn that Lillian had been granted sole physical custody despite Arthur's attempts to paint a picture of Lillian as a neglectful, selfish, egocentric mother. Both parents had been granted legal custody.

I was concerned now about Barbara's feelings of ambivalence about both of her parents, and I felt that we needed to work on the anger that she was beginning to express. It would be important for her to deal with these hostile feelings toward her parents, as well as her attempts to injure and punish herself physically. Barbara felt worthless and felt that she had been a cause of the divorce. Although her resentment toward Lillian was beginning to emerge, I believed that she loved her mother very much and needed Lillian's love in return. Lillian was indeed a person whose judgment with regard to men was poor, but she had been punished enough for her mistakes. It was time for mending. Her therapist was encouraging her to go back to school and to explore some vocational choices, and I believed that it would be possible for her to have a decent, productive life without Arthur.

I decided I would continue the imagery work to help Barbara work out her current feelings of rage toward her mother. We needed to talk about the decision concerning custody and Arthur's role in Barbara's life now that he would not be as readily available as he had been in the past.

I felt comfortable about the judge's decision to grant Lillian sole physical custody, because she had been making progress in her therapy. Studies concerning children who are in joint physical custody (children living for substantial amounts of time with each parent) have been inconclusive or have yielded mixed results. Although some reports state that children in joint physical custody demonstrate increased self-esteem and competence, a substantial proportion of the children are visibly distressed and confused. Their adjustment depends on such variables as the age and temperament of the child and, most important, the parents' psychological functioning and the quality of the parent–child relationships. Custodial parents who are anxious and depressed convey these feelings to their children, and the results often disturbed children. Barbara had not coped well with her parents' separation, not only because of Lillian's personal problems, but also because of Barbara's low threshold for anxiety.

I knew that Lillian was in treatment, but I had never met Arthur. Arthur was an enigma. He wanted no contact with either Lillian's therapist or me. The only picture I had drawn of him stemmed from Lillian's and Barbara's comments. At times, Barbara seemed to adore him, and at other times, she seemed anxious and uncomfortable about seeing him. During the separation, Lillian had tried to poison the children's minds against him. Now that things were settled, her attitude was more accepting, a shade kinder and more sympathetic.

Guided Affective Imagery

Barbara seemed comfortable playing the mind games. They evoked feelings that she attempted to express in her play, but that frightened her when she did so. She would go only so far and then would use denial of these feelings as she played. In the imagery exercises, however, she was able to unleash her anger at Lillian, get control of it, and recognize it as being related to the divorce and her fewer contacts with Arthur. Previously, she had expressed anger at Arthur. Sometimes Arthur had been the "bad daddy" in her play. After the custody decision, more anger was focused on Lillian. That reaction was understandable. Lillian had made Arthur leave the large, comfortable house. Now Arthur lived in smaller quarters, and had been left alone, deprived of house, children, and wife. In Barbara's symbolic play, she felt sorry for him, the "daddy who cooked, cleaned, and took care of the baby" while the mother spent all day at leisure, "shopping."

Barbara and Lillian now fought continuously. Whereas in the earlier stages of the separation, Barbara had visited Arthur reluctantly and had allied herself with Lillian (mainly so as not to lose her love), she now vented all of her confused, hurt, angry feelings on Lillian, both in her play and in reality. The ambiguity of her custody status had been resolved, and she felt more secure in the knowledge that she was to live with Lillian. Thus, Barbara now had the freedom to express her feelings without fear of losing her mother. My task was to help her accept *both* of her parents and their love, and to help her recognize that she had not been responsible for the dissolution of the marriage.

I was concerned, too, about some of Barbara's doll play. During one session, for example, she took a doll and said:

> ► Here's the mommy. Her face is all red. She just came back from the lawyer. She's crying . Poor Mommy.
> ► Why is she crying?
> ► The family is moving away.

At this point, Barbara took the two male puppets and put a "baby" on their laps.

> ► Here's the baby. She has two daddies. The daddies put the baby to sleep. Mommy is crying. The daddies move away.
> ► Where is the family moving to?
> ► They move out and leave the mommy. The two daddies live in the same house. Now the baby lives with the mommy. She said good-bye to the daddies. They don't talk to her.

Barbara took the baby doll and put her on a bed in the dollhouse. She put the mother doll in the kitchen and took the puppets to a box across the room.

► Here's where the daddies live. They live alone. No children, no Mommy. They won't let that mommy come to visit them. The baby is crying now. She hits the mommy. Oh, she is mad. That baby hates herself.
► I remember, Barbara, when you didn't feel good about yourself—like the baby. Can we help the baby feel better?
► Only if the mommy lets the daddy in the house.

Barbara had revealed much to me in this play: her strong desire to have the "two daddies," her awareness of the custody decision, and her anger about it: "The baby hits the mommy." And yet the tone of the play suggested to me that, despite the baby's attack, Barbara also felt sorry for her mother: "Poor Mommy."

Barbara was trying to understand the full force of the custody decision; she was also still clinging to the notion that "two daddies" were available to take care of her. I wanted to help her allow some of her fantasies about Anthony to emerge so that she could accept the fact that he was gone and that Arthur was available for her, just as he had been since her birth.

I decided to use the directed-imagery technique called Guided Affective Imagery (GAI), as described by Hanscarl Leuner and his colleagues. It is an approach more commonly used in Europe than in the United States, but one that is also respected here. As an adjunct to play therapy, this approach had worked well with other clients of mine who were about Barbara's age or a little older. Because she had responded so enthusiastically to the de Mille games, I felt this technique would also be effective.

Basically, the client "dreams, so to speak, under the direction of the therapist, who directly participates in the dream experience through his communications." Leuner found that GAI worked well with children because of their readiness to tap into material at a near-conscious level. The parent may be informed of the child's images, and the therapist can explain to the parents how the child experiences the family setting. I needed to know Barbara's covert attitudes toward Lillian and Arthur. Her willingness to express her anger was an important step forward in her therapy, but I was not convinced that her anger was genuine; it might be a cover-up for her deep longing to be loved and to love.

The use of GAI is relatively simple. I asked Barbara to sit in a comfortable chair with her eyes closed. She relaxed, as she had before the de Mille exercises. Over a period of time, I presented the standard emotional images or motifs that Leuner and his colleagues had found successful in their clinical experience with children. The eight images or motifs are a *meadow*, which is the relaxer and the starting point of each session; the *ascent of a mountain*, which encourages the child to view an imaginary landscape and helps the therapist to find out whether the child will climb the mountain by herself or himself or with help; the *pursuit of the course of a brook* to its source (the brook is an expression of vital drives that can be a place for cleansing and refreshment); a *visit to a house*, which the child enters and explores; *an encounter with relatives*, as real figures or symbolically disguised as animals (this exercise helps to reveal the child's relationships with parents, siblings, and authority figures); *observation of the edge of the woods* (the therapist learns which figures emerge from or enter the woods); a *boat*, which appears on the shore of a pond or lake (the child climbs aboard as a passenger or steers it herself or himself); and the *cave*, which is observed from a distance, and symbolic figures emerge (the child can enter the cave and stop or can explore the cave's depths).

I began the exercises with the "meadow," suggesting that Barbara picture herself in a meadow, and asking her to describe it to me. My job was to question her about what she saw in the meadow, to help her confront any frightening figures or animals she met, and to provide protection by suggesting, for example, that she placate the animal by offering food until the animal was so "stuffed" that it lay down, became completely harmless, and fell asleep. Each motif is presented several times before the therapist moves on to the next one. Thus, I offered the meadow motif at the beginning of each session, for about five minutes, and then went on to each motif in order (two sessions were devoted to each one). I then asked Barbara to draw whatever she wished from each story. In this way, we went through all eight motifs over the course of a couple of months. In addition, our play therapy continued, much affected by the images unleashed in the GAI.

The most salient features that emerged from the GAI were Barbara's use of animals in the meadow, her attempts to ascend the mountain, her use of the cave, and the subsequent striking changes that took place in her therapy as a result of these images. Barbara's meadow was filled with cows and fierce animals. When she seemed afraid to pass by one, I offered her ways to subdue it. Barbara's eyes were closed as she described what she saw in the meadow:

> ► There are birds, squirrels, deer, and some ugly animals, too. They look mean. I see a cow and an elephant. I don't like that elephant. He worries me. He scares me.
> ► Don't be afraid. Pretend you are giving him lots of food to eat. Give him so much food that he will be full and go to sleep. OK?
> ► OK, I'll feed him.
> ► Good. Now you can walk right by that sleeping elephant. Can you do that?
> ► Yes. My cow is running away, too. The cow is running away from that elephant. He's big and mean and powerful. He never lets the cow drink any water in that pond.

Barbara began to focus on two animals: the cow, which she kept throughout the GAI sessions, and the elephant. It was clear to me that the cow was the mother and the elephant was the father. In Barbara's images, the mother was gentle, and the father powerful—quite different from the way Barbara had recently portrayed the mother and father dolls in her play. Before GAI, her mother doll had been characterized as negative, and the father doll as nurturant, but Barbara's deeper fantasies invested her father with power. In reality, he had come to the house with a bat, threatening Lillian, and this was a vivid memory for Barbara.

As the GAI proceeded, Barbara used the "cave" as a place where "bad people" lived. Cavemen were "fighting" in the cave. As Barbara described them, they became quite enraged, perhaps as in the fights she had witnessed at home. The elephant and the cow finally went to the cave together. They "fight, too," and the "elephant squirts water on the cow and chases her away."

Barbara drew the elephant squirting water at the cow, making the cow a tiny figure in the corner of the page. I offered no interpretations, and let Barbara image freely and draw whatever she wished. Gradually, over several sessions, as we repeated motifs, Barbara allowed the cow and the elephant to drink from the same pond. Together, they subdued the cavemen and drove them away.

The mountain played a role in Barbara's stories as well. She struggled to climb the mountain, "falling" down, but getting up each time. She "just had to get to the top!" I felt that Barbara was struggling with her feelings about her parents and needed to gain control and master her emotions. She also wanted to be "on top of things" and "see everything below." Barbara truly wanted to be in control, and to see everything that her family was doing: in the hearings about custody, the compromises Lillian had made with Arthur, where Jackie would be, and how she and Raymond would manage. And perhaps her thoughts were about Anthony as well.

It seemed to me that, as things were settling down at home and decisions were clearer about custody, although still longing for a "family," Barbara was coming to grips with the reality of her situation. Along with Raymond, she visited Arthur about twice a month. Lillian and Arthur tried to be more polite to each other (the cow and the elephant sharing the water from the pond), and the "bad people in the cave"—symbols of her anxieties and fears of an unknown future—were under control. The hostility that Barbara had overtly expressed toward Lillian was less in evidence. The cow in Barbara's images was gentle and loving, the way Barbara wanted her mother to be. Indeed, Barbara's warmth concerning this "cow" in her imagined stories was indicative of her true feelings toward Lillian. Gradually, she shed her anger. She seemed no longer to blame Lillian for the loss of Anthony and for having evicted Arthur. Little by little, the "two daddies" theme in her doll play subsided. During one session, for example, Barbara arranged the Hart dolls in a "living room" and said:

> ► The mother is in the kitchen making supper for the children; all the family is watching TV in the living room.
> Daddy comes home—but only for a visit.
> ► Where does this daddy live?
> ► He has his own house—but not far away.

▸ What's happening in your story?
▸ Well, here's the daddy—he comes right in that door.
He's hungry. He wants his supper.

I watched and listened. Barbara was using different voices for her characters:

▸ Where's my supper? [deep, "daddy" 's voice]
▸ Here it is—potatoes, hamburgers, ice cream ["mother" 's voice]
▸ This is good—yum yum yum. [daddy's voice]
▸ Eat it all up. [mother's voice]

In Barbara's play, as in her imagery exercises, she was attempting to initiate a reconciliation between her parents. The cow and elephant in her fantasy were the mother and father in her doll play. They were able to be civil with each other and even share a meal albeit that the "daddy" lived in another house. The imagery training was powerful in effecting change. Barbara was able to get in touch with emotions that she had tried to suppress. Now she was able to translate her images into more concrete play.

Just as Barbara used one doll for the "daddy" figure, she now used one puppet for a "daddy" as well in her puppet games. Thus, just as Barbara was able to imagine one elephant who befriended the cow, she was able to relinquish the two fathers who had previously appeared in much of her family play. Perhaps she had even blended them into one: the loving, caring father she desired. Was it possible that Barbara had tucked away the notion that Anthony would reappear? She no longer mentioned him and seemed to have accepted her new life alone with Lillian and Raymond.

Barbara began to gain weight and to look more wholesome. Her self-esteem improved as well. She no longer talked about harming herself or not liking herself. She also seemed to understand that she had not been the cause of the divorce, that "Daddy and Mommy just didn't like each other so much any more." Lillian had put a lot of effort into taking better care of the children as a result of her own therapy and her growing insight into her parents' difficulties and her early childhood. It was time for me to begin the termination process with Barbara.

Lillian's Surprise

At our monthly visits during the time I had been using GAI with Barbara, Lillian had shown marked changes in both her physical appearance and her mental attitude. The brassy look began to give way to a more L. L. Bean look, as she began to wear tailored clothes ("my school clothes") and sensible shoes. She had also let her hair grow and revert to its natural light brown color. She told me that she had been trying to get her high school equivalency diploma by attending special classes, and also talked about plans to go to a community college and take business courses.

Lillian informed me that she had been in touch with her father and contemplated inviting him to move in with her and the children. She wasn't sure how this arrangement would work out, but she wanted to "think about this possibility" and was talking it over with her therapist. Eventually, Lillian carried out this plan, but after I had terminated play therapy with Barbara. As a result, I did not know how it had affected the children. At the time, I could only speculate that he would be a stabilizing force, giving the nurturing attitude he had had toward Lillian after reentering her life over six years before. They had maintained friendly contact even after he had moved out of the state. The children had no real sense of who their grandfather was, so everyone would have to become reacquainted. I asked if Lillian had discussed "Grandpa" with Barbara.

"No, not yet," she replied. "But if things look like it will happen, I sure will talk to her about it. Things with Barbara are better. We don't argue so much, especially since I don't have to force her to go to Arthur's house for sleepovers. She doesn't mind the visits for the day, but she still worries and asks if she has to sleep over. I think she's afraid she won't come back to me. I think she really loves Arthur, but she did see a side of him when he got mad that she had never seen before. Also, I guess I shocked her, too, about

Anthony. She really was a case, wondering if she could ever trust anyone."

As I listened to Lillian, I was pleased to discover that she understood Barbara's confused feelings about Arthur and her. She was proud that she could convey such positive news about herself and her future. I wasn't convinced that she had truly put Anthony out of her mind, but at least she now had some realistic plans.

We talked about the future and Barbara's own feelings about herself. Lillian felt that she had put Barbara "through the wringer" and wondered if Barbara would grow up "normal." Lillian remembered her own unhappy childhood and was afraid that Barbara might one day be destined to enter into a marriage as unfortunate as Lillian's and her mother's. I was aware of the ten-year longitudinal study of girls from divorced middle-class families. Judith Wallerstein, an expert on divorce, found that delayed reactions to divorce, which she called "sleeper" effects, had evolved over time. Many of the daughters of the divorced custodial mothers had developed close relationships with their mothers during early adolescence. When they were older, these young women identified with the divorced mother, whom they regarded as "having failed at the major developmental task, that of love and marriage." This failure made it difficult for these daughters to form close heterosexual relationships because of their concern about their own potential adequacy as wives and mothers. Wallerstein believed that, as the young women approached adulthood and contemplated leaving their mothers alone, their "normal separation process was exacerbated by guilt, anger, and anxiety, as well as by worry and compassion." Certainly, these feelings of anxiety and guilt, even now, had been manifested by Barbara, but I could not possibly predict whether Barbara would experience the "sleeper" effect described by Wallerstein. If Lillian continued to grow emotionally and intellectually, and if she and Arthur could maintain a civil relationship, I thought Barbara had a good chance of developing into a well-adjusted young woman.

I gave Lillian some information about Barbara's play and imagery stories that I thought would help her better understand Barbara's former anger and her current desire for a friendly relationship between her parents. Lillian listened and seemed to grasp this information, agreeing that Barbara still needed overt affirmations of Lillian's love. As she put it, "I'm trying to make up for all the things

I screwed up in my life. I think I can do it. With help from my therapist, and with help from you, I'm getting there."

Barbara Empties the Cave

I began to taper off my sessions with Barbara. We did continue with our traditional play therapy and, only occasionally, with the imagery methods. Barbara seemed more willing now to talk about the divorce, and in our last month together, we did just that: talk more than play. Barbara was almost six years old and was beginning to read. She printed her name for me. She liked to draw as she talked, producing numerous pictures of flowers and happy faces of people she knew, including Lillian, Arthur, and Raymond.

Barbara told me she was sorry about the divorce, and that she loved both her parents. She also referred to Arthur as "Daddy" rather than as "Arthur."

► Sometimes I was mad at Daddy 'cause he yelled at Mommy. That made me sad.
► How do you feel now?
► I can visit Daddy. That's OK. Mommy and Daddy love me—but they don't love each other anymore.
► Yes, they do love you and always will.
► When Daddy came with the bat, we went to Mommy's brother's house. My Aunt Carol let us stay there.
► Yes, I remember. Daddy was angry. But now Mommy and Daddy can talk to each other, and things are better.
► I have a sort of family.
► You have Mommy, Daddy, Raymond, and Jackie.
► Yes, I have my aunts, uncles, eight cousins, a dog, and a white mouse.
► That's a lot of family.
► Yep, a lot of family.

Barbara no longer mentioned Anthony; in fact, Lillian told me that Barbara had returned his photo to her. This was a good sign. As we drew to a close—only one more session to go—Barbara asked if she could play "imagination" again. Barbara wanted to visit the cave once more.

> ► Remember, this is where the bad men fought?
> ► Yes, Barbara, I remember. What is happening now?
> ► Well, the cavemen all came out of the cave. They get into the boat and sail away. The cave is empty. No more bad people are there. The door is open. The end!

I liked this metaphor, and I felt that Barbara had told me much in using it. Her bad feelings were gone, and the door was open to new possibilities. I could only hope that, for this child's sake, good things would enter the cave.

Our good-byes took place the following week. Barbara wore a party dress, and that sad face of almost a year before was only a dim memory. She played once more with the Hart Family, placing every-one—Mr. Hart, Mrs. Hart, and the baby—together on the couch, saying, "This is a visit—a good visit. Everyone is here, for just a little while."

She then took the father doll and, very gently, put him to sleep on the couch by himself. Mrs. Hart and the baby kissed him "good-night." Barbara drew a picture of herself, pinned it up on my wall, and said good-bye. In the waiting room, Lillian shook my hand.

"I'll keep in touch," she said.

I never heard from her again, but my colleague said things were going well for her.

A year after I terminated Barbara's therapy, Lillian remarried Arthur. Neither my colleague nor I know what has happened since.

~~~~~~~~~~~~~~~~~~~~~~~~~~~~~~~~~~

CHAPTER SIX

VICTORIA, THE BED WETTER

Sibling Rivalry and Learning to Love

Mr. and Mrs. Thornton: The Battle Begins

"We have a bright, sensitive child who doesn't feel good about herself, who tells me that she's ugly and that no one loves her." These were Paula Thornton's words to me at the beginning of our first interview. The Thorntons were a high-powered couple: she was the chief graphic designer for a large firm located in New York City; he was a senior engineer in a nationally known company in Connecticut. They had moved here from New York three months before this session.

As Paula Thornton explained, "I could not give up my job when Neil accepted his new position here. There just wasn't the same kind of opportunity available for me anywhere in Connecticut, nothing that paid as well or was as prestigious. So we decided that I would be the commuter. I get a lot of work done on the train, but I know it's hard on the kids—and maybe even on Neil."

Paula glanced at Neil; he remained quiet and averted his eyes.

The Thorntons were a handsome couple. Paula was tall, brunette, always elegantly and expensively dressed, and meticulous about her makeup and hair style. Neil was a lanky, sandy-haired man, usually wearing tweeds, button-down shirts, and horn-rimmed glasses, and looking very much like the stereotypical professor. Both were well educated and had advanced degrees.

In addition to Victoria, who was seven years old when her therapy began, the Thorntons had one other daughter, Katherine, a "sweet, friendly, outgoing four-year-old" who, according to Paula, "adores her big sister, but Victoria hates Katherine. That's the problem in a nutshell. Victoria comes to me crying and says, 'Why was I born?' This drives me crazy. I want the girls to be friends, but Victoria can be mean, even cruel, to Katherine. I have found welts on Katherine's shoulders, teeth marks on her arms, scratches on her face. I'm beside myself. What can we do? Katherine does tease Victoria—I admit that—but Victoria's behavior isn't normal, is it? I bought a book, *Siblings without Rivalry*, thinking I would read it and it would help. No, sir. It didn't help me. Victoria has even been in therapy in New York for a year. We stopped when we moved to Connecticut. The doctor said she'll outgrow her jealousy. Well, we've been here for three months, and it's worse!"

Neil interjected, "Look, Paula, maybe Vicki is reacting to our move and the new neighborhood and to your commute—"

Paula jumped in before Neil could finish his sentence: "Oh, so now it's me, is it? I was waiting for you to say it's my fault. Right, I'm not home enough. Right, I'm to blame. Right? I thought I did a pretty good job preparing the children for this move. What did you do?"

"Wait," I said. "Let's just go slowly and focus on Victoria right now. I need to know more about her if I am going to help her. We'll touch on other issues as they pertain to Victoria in future sessions, but for now, just try to tell me about your child. Mr. Thornton, can you give me your impessions of Victoria? By the way, do you call her Victoria or Vicki?"

The Thorntons simultaneously shouted their preference, Paula favoring the more formal "Victoria."

"Suppose, I let your daughter make the choice when we meet. Is that agreeable?"

They nodded their consent, and Neil picked up on the move to Connecticut: "I was nervous about this move. Vicki, as Paula said, is a sensitive child; she seems depressed now, and I'm worried. She told my sister that she wants to commit suicide. That's one of the reasons we called you. That doesn't seem like a normal idea for a seven-year-old, does it?"

Neil spoke slowly, painfully. He was guarded and uncomfortable, kept his eyes averted, and often deferred to Paula to fill in the information about school, everyday reactions, Vicki's friends, her early childhood, and even her relationship with Katherine. Although he seemed like a caring parent, it was clear that most of the day-to-day household concerns were left to Paula. Neil appeared to be preoccupied by other thoughts, somewhat distant, and yet troubled by Vicki's behavior. He pressed his question: "Suicide isn't what kids of seven talk about, is it?"

I agreed that it isn't generally a part of such young children's conversations, but that children do pick up on things that they hear or that they see on television. I added, "I won't dismiss what she said, but I need to know more about her."

Paula interrupted, "Well, that's what I thought: maybe she gets her ideas from television. You know Victoria and Katherine have a nanny, Sylvie, who's been with us since Victoria was born. I've asked her about this, and she swears she's never mentioned the word *suicide*. She also tells me that she doesn't watch the 'soaps' when the children are around. I try to believe her. I did think maybe Victoria heard about suicide on the soaps. You see, Victoria is dramatic; she has a flair for exaggeration and hyperbole. I really couldn't take the statement about suicide seriously. I do worry more about her lack of self-esteem, her anger toward Katherine—and one more thing we need to tell you about: she's a bed wetter."

Paula lowered her voice as she told me this and began to fidget with her purse, opening and closing the catch. Clearly, Paula was ashamed and uncomfortable about this revelation. Victoria was an embarrassment to her. Paula's behavior indicated that she felt she was a less-than-perfect mother: How could she, so meticulous, so organized, so good at her profession, have raised a child who caused her so much distress? I also suspected that Paula harbored guilt feelings about her role as a mother. True, she was angry that something now interfered with the smooth routine of her household but, even more, with the image she wanted to convey to the outside world: Paula could do it all—have the perfect marriage, hold the perfect job, and raise perfect children. There would be time later in our parents' meetings to explore Paula's feelings about Victoria: the disappointment in her child, her own feelings of guilt about being away from home so much, and her attitudes toward motherhood. This was not the time to examine *Paula's* feelings. I needed to know more about Victoria and the enuresis (bed-wetting), as well as this child's other problems.

The Thorntons assured me that Victoria's enuresis did not have any physical basis. The wetting had begun when Katherine was born.

"It seemed to me," said Paula, "that it was her way of taunting me—getting even, as it were. I would go into her room in the morning and find Victoria in a 'bed' on the floor, lying on her pillow or blankets. She had been completely trained at two years and three months, so I was sure this was regression, or a bid for attention. I tried to give more time to Victoria. We all did: Neil, Sylvie, my family. It was no good. She wets every night, and this has been going on since she was three. Once in a while, she's dry, but rarely. Sylvie covers up for her, I know, and strips the bed very early, but I smell the sheets. What's worse now is that Katherine is trained and she teases Victoria. No matter what I say to Victoria, or what I promise her, or how many times I try to praise her for other things, she still wets. Her therapist in New York said she would outgrow this, too. Well, we've seen no change, and if anything, the move and my commute have only exacerbated the problem. But I won't stop working. I tried that once before, and I was miserable. I really was a witch when I stayed home for that six months. I have to admit it: I'm just not the mothering type."

"Tell me more about the therapist in New York," I said. "Why was Victoria in therapy?"

"Well," Neil said, "Victoria has been depressed for a long time. Her schoolwork is suffering, too. She hasn't been reading well, not like the kids in her class. Also, she has no real friends as far as we can make out. At her birthday party when she turned seven, we had her class come over, that is, all the girls. I thought it was good, but

Vicki cried all night. She said she had no special friend and no one really liked her. I think, too, the jealousy of Katherine is out of hand. I think she's just a needy child."

"Yes, that's right," added Paula. "No matter how much time I give Victoria, it's not enough. We're both worried about her and her behavior toward Katherine. I've had Victoria examined by the best specialists in New York. The enuresis is psychological, I'm sure. She's at an age when she wants to sleep over at a friend's house, but she won't: she's so afraid she'll wet the bed. She's having a rough time adjusting to school, and she's so awkward and ungainly. The school psychologist gave me your name. Really, we're at our wits' end. But you have to know, I just can't quit my job. I just can't."

Our session was drawing to a close. I arranged a time when Sylvie would be able to drive Victoria to my office. The Thorntons seemed reluctant to leave. I felt that more than Victoria troubled them, but I had to be patient.

Just before they left, Paula blurted out, "Look, all I want you to do is help Victoria to be dry at night and to stop beating-up on Katherine. I told Victoria that she doesn't have to love Katherine, just not hit or bite her."

"Do you really mean that?" I asked. "That you don't care if Victoria loves Katherine?"

Paula looked at me surprised and then became teary-eyed: "No, no, of course not. I want them to love each other. I need them to love each other. Help me! Help Victoria!"

Paula was more "human" and more vulnerable than she would admit to, and I felt that I could work with her and Neil. I felt, too, that her "need" for the children to love each other would be proof to everyone that she was the "good" mother. Victoria's lack of self-esteem might be a reflection, perhaps, of Paula's own uncertainty about her worth as a mother, which she had managed to compensate for with her career success. It was clear, too, that Paula wanted me to know that her career was important, and that she was not going to give it up because of any therapy recommendations for Victoria. Neil's personality eluded me. It would take time before I could clearly understand his role in Victoria's life.

The Thorntons left, and I looked forward to my meeting with Victoria.

Victoria's World

> Might we not say that every
> child at play behaves like a
> creative writer, in that he creates
> a world of his own, or rather rearranges
> things of his world in a new way
> that pleases him? It would be
> wrong to think that he does not
> take the world seriously; on the
> contrary, he takes his play very
> seriously and he expends large
> amounts of emotion on it.
> —Sigmund Freud, "Creative Writers and Day-Dreaming"

Sylvie drove Victoria to her first session and agreed to remain in the waiting room with Katherine until the hour was over. I felt it was important for Victoria to know that Sylvie was close by if she needed her for reassurance. Vicki was chubby, physically unlike her slender parents. She had fiery red hair cut in short curls, reminding me of Little Orphan Annie. Her face was covered with freckles, and she had dimples when she smiled. After a few minutes with Victoria, I found her to be a child who managed to be comfortable in the presence of adults and who seemed quite self-assured.

She told me right out that the *only one*—and this was accented, the *only one*—who called her Victoria was her mother. "So," she said, "call me Vicki."

> ▸ I was so excited to come, I was also curious!
> ▸ I was curious, too, Vicki, curious about what you looked like, and about what you would like to play with.

Like the serious child Freud described, Vicki gradually invited me through her play to share a picture of her world at school and at home. She surveyed the playroom, listened very seriously to my rules and explanations about who I was and what we would do, and then asked if we could play "camping."

> ▸ First, I have to learn you a lesson—learn you all about camping. I'll show you exactly what to do.
> ▸ Do you mean you have to *teach* me about camping?
> ▸ Yes, of course. We have to pack lots of stuff and make a safe tent.

I watched Vicki take the blanket and place it over the table to make a tent. She knew just what she was about. I thought to myself, "Great, a good player, good imagination. This should be easy!"

> ▸ Now, let's see. Who goes into the tent? This doll. We'll call her Susy. And this doll. We'll call her Patty. OK, some dishes, some food. Can I make food from the Play-Doh?
> ▸ Yes, of course.
> ▸ Do you go camping with your parents?
> ▸ [*molding the clay*]: Never. Never. But I want to. OK, now you be the ranger. You come and check on us when we sleep. Make sure no wild bears are there. Use a ranger voice.

And I played the camping game with Vicki, letting her lead the way and set the theme. Her story generally followed the same pattern. Everyone ate dinner, went to sleep, and was awakened by a wild bear. The ranger (my role) came to the rescue and chased the bear away. We would then start the game all over again.

I made no interpretations this first session, although it seemed to me that Vicki was trying to master some fear of harm or danger, or perhaps she had experienced some nightmare that she wanted to work out through play. Then again, was this game just an imitation of a story she had seen on TV or had read in school? I participated in her game but was cautious, observant, and puzzled, and I wondered if I had been made the ranger to save Vicki in real life.

Vicki played "camping" for almost the entire session, and then, when told that our time was just about up, she carefully put everything away and came back to the table.

▸ That was a good game. I like it here.
▸ I'm glad you like it here. You can come back in two days, and we can play camping again if you wish.
▸ I'll see, I'll see.

Vicki wasn't so sure that she was going to follow my suggestion. "I'll see" was her way of telling me that she would determine what game she wanted to play, that she wanted to be in control. I thought about control: Was this one reason for the enuresis, a need to control her mother? Certainly, very little had been under Vicki's control, from the birth of Katherine to the current uprootedness from her home and school in New York. But for now, our time was up.

Vicki ran into the room where Sylvie and Katherine had been waiting. Katherine showed Vicki her coloring book, but Vicki ignored her, threw her arms around Sylvie, and told her that she had had "fun." Katherine told me that she was four and that she went to school. She was a dark-haired, slim, pretty child who appeared gentle and unassuming. Vicki seemed annoyed by Katherine's conversation with me.

I bid them good-bye and made a note that it would be best if Sylvie could arrange for some playtime with Katherine while Vicki had her sessions with me. It seemed important that Vicki, at this time, early in our sessions, have no rivals in my office, so that it would clearly be her special place. As it turned out, she was able to separate from Sylvie so easily that Sylvie would just drop her off for the session and return when our time was up. This arrangement pleased both Vicki and Sylvie, who told me that it gave her some time with Katherine, to read to her or color or draw. In Sylvie's words, "It is so peaceful."

Sylvie, who had been the children's "surrogate" mother for the past seven years, was from Mexico, and her English was heavily accented. She was loving, caring, and conscientious but showed little psychological insight. She spoiled the children—indulging them, as I learned—and just as she liked to eat, she allowed Vicki to eat between meals and to snack on cookies or muffins. Katherine had a poor appetite, but Vicki was usually ravenous—and her chubbiness attested to her love of food. I wondered if Vicki's need to eat was a way of seeking gratification, a substitute perhaps for the attention she craved so much from her mother, and I suspected that a chubby Victoria was an additional embarrassment to Paula, who was elegant and slender. A fat child would upset Paula's image of the "magazine family" she envisioned for herself.

The Family

Two days later, Vicki came bounding into the playroom.

- ▸ No camping today.
- ▸ Why not?
- ▸ Well, I think the tent fell down in a storm. The children died, and no one ever found them.

I worried about this and wondered about the possibility of some suicidal rumination.

- ▸ That's a sad story. Do you think we could make another tent and try another story?
- ▸ I don't think so.
- ▸ Would you like to draw today?
- ▸ OK, what?
- ▸ I'd like you to draw your family. Can you do that?
- ▸ Sure. Let's see, I need your pencils and crayons—lots of crayons.

I gave her paper, pencils, and crayons, and she began to draw. The first thing she drew was her cat.

> ▶ In my family there is a mother, a father, a sister, and a cat. My cat is Snowball 'cause she's white. I'll give my mother red hair. It's not really red, but I'll make it red. Daddy has light brown hair. I'll use the tan crayon. Katherine is four. I'll draw her over here, way over here, way by herself.
> ▶ Mm, isn't she lonely by herself, far from Mommy, Daddy, and Snowball?
> ▶ Well, that's just where she is. Right there, that's all.

And that was all. Vicki shut me out.

> ▶ Where are you in the picture?
> ▶ I'm not here.
> ▶ I see. Aren't you part of this family?

No answer from Vicki. Again she shut me out. She just continued to draw and added details to the figures: "Done! Let's tack it up. May I draw my new house and my car? We have a car now. We didn't need one in New York."

Vicki and I tacked the two drawings up on the bulletin board.

There was no Vicki in her family picture, and Katherine was drawn far away from the parents, near the top of the page. Did Vicki feel left out? And why had she colored Paula's hair bright red? Was she trying to identify with Paula, the mother she needed so much? Why had she drawn Katherine so far away from the parents? Through this drawing, Vicki was trying to tell me how she felt about her family; she was not ready to tell me in words. This was only our second session, and I would be patient.

After Vicki finished her drawings, she went over to the dollhouse

and carefully examined each figure. She then rearranged all the fur-
niture "to look like my house." I watched as she made a living room,
bedrooms, a kitchen, and a playroom. Vicki placed a doll in the
kitchen at the stove "cooking."

> ► Daddy went to work. He left early. Mommy is cooking
> breakfast, and all the children are sleeping upstairs. There
> are four little girls. The dog and cat sleep under the bed.
> Everyone smells the food, and they come downstairs to
> eat. Mommy won't let this one eat. This one is fat. Watch
> this: Mommy knocks her off the chair. Down she goes.
> She wants to eat cake. "No cake for you. You're fat!"
> ► My, how does that little girl feel?
> ► She's mad, real mad, and so she yells at Mommy, but
> Mommy says, "Go to bed, you bad, bad girl. Go upstairs
> and stay there."

Vicki put the little doll back in the bed and repeated the game with
lots of spirit and glee, making the "knockdown" scene more exag-
gerated and more dramatic each time. The mother's voice became
louder and more angry. When Vicki seemed to be losing control, I
intervened and urged her to find what else the mother and the child
could do to solve this dilemma about the cake.
  Vicki look puzzled and then said:

> ► Mommy cuts a small piece for the kid. That's all right,
> to have a treat once a week, isn't it?
> ► Yes, that's a great idea, a small piece of cake once a
> week. Do you ever have such a treat?

Vicki admitted that she "loved to eat," and that her parents tried to
control her food habits. Her mother wanted her to look "nice in a
bathing suit" so no one would call her fat or chubby.
  "I'm trying real hard, but I'm hungry so much," she said.
  Another problem of Vicki's had been uncovered. It appeared that

there was some hassle over food in the Thornton household. I made a note to bring this up in our next parents' session. There were numerous issues to deal with: Vicki's school problems, the enuresis, the sibling rivalry, her feelings of rejection and poor self-esteem, the depression, and her sense of not fitting into this perfect family, where each one was slim, attractive, and successful. Vicki was angry—at Katherine, at her mother, and at herself—and she seemed willing to talk about some of her problems.

Before our next session, I asked myself many questions. Was it possible for Vicki to live up to her mother's expectations? How could Paula and Vicki spend more time together? How much time did Neil spend with the children? How was Paula handling the rivalry between the children? Did Vicki think that she could control Paula through the enuresis? Was the enuresis an act of hostility toward Paula? I felt that I could try being more direct with Vicki. She had experienced a year of therapy before our contact, and her play seemed to be an enactment of her conflicts with her family. I was sure that the year of therapy had paved the way for what emerged in our third session.

Session Three: Vicki's Disclosure

At our next session, I decided to ask Vicki why she thought she was coming to see me. She was so forthright in her reply that for a moment I was taken aback:

I do have problems. The worst problem I ever had—and it's embarrassing. I'm doing OK, but last night I peed in my bed. I do it a tiny bit now. When I was five and six, I did it a lot. When I pee, I go on the floor to sleep, or in Katherine's bed. She lets me. One night, I went to her bed, but she played and kept me up. So I sleep on my pillow on the floor. My mom is too tired to change the sheets. Sometimes I take the sheets off and put them in the closet. I feel bad about this."

Vicki told me all this in a sad voice, and it was obvious that she was deeply troubled by her inability to stay dry all night. After she told me about making her "bed" on the floor, Vicki became very quiet and put her head down on the table.

▸ You feel bad about wetting the bed, Vicki.

▸ Yes, I feel bad and embarrassed, but I can't stop. But I want to stop. I sleep so deep that I don't even know that I have to go to the bathroom until I feel it all wet. Sometimes, I don't even get up until morning, and then I find out that I'm all wet—and smelly.

▸ Well, we can begin to work on this. I think there is a way we can help you. I'll talk to your parents about what we can do.

▸ On my birthday, last year when I was six, I went to Pamela's house for a sleepover. I slept over and had fun. I said, "God, don't let me wet," and it was like magic. I didn't wet!

▸ That's wonderful. So sometimes you can be dry.

▸ Not often, and maybe when I'm not home near Katherine.

▸ You think Katherine has something to do with your wetting?

▸ Sometimes I hate my sister so much. What I'm upset about is how my parents think I start the trouble, 'cause they think Katherine is an angel and I'm older and I should know better. But Katherine is sneaky. She teases me, takes my things, and runs away. Even Sylvie says to leave Katherine alone when she's mean to me. Sylvie makes me give my toys to Katherine. That's not fair.

▸ No, that doesn't seem fair, but maybe you can share some toys with Katherine.

▸ I hate her. She calls me "pee-pee." It makes me feel like I'm two or three years old. It makes me feel like a baby. When I wet I feel like a baby, like I can't control myself. It's not a good feeling.

Vicki started to cry as she poured her heart out. She wiped her eyes and then asked me if she could be "cured."

Vicki, I answered, "there are some things we can do to help

you. I'll see your parents next week, and we'll start a plan for you. Let me talk to them first, and then I'll share the plan with you, OK?

This seemed to comfort Vicki. She dried her tears and asked if we had any "leftover time."

> ▸ Yes, we have some time left.
> ▸ Good, I'll play camping.

Vicki rearranged the table to form her "tent" and once again put the dolls inside.

> ▸ Everyone comes to life again—Susy, Patty.
> ▸ How did they come to life again, Vicki?
> ▸ They came to life cause the ranger gave them magic.
> ▸ What kind of magic?
> ▸ He said magic words.
> ▸ Can you say them out loud?
> ▸ No, the magic words are my secret.

I watched Vicki feed the dolls and tuck them into bed. She took the toy bear and put him near the dolls.

> ▸ The bear has made friends with the girls. Look, he's sleeping, too.
> ▸ Well, it looks as if the bear isn't wild anymore. How come?
> ▸ This bear is the good one. The wild one is still out there, waiting, waiting, waiting.
> ▸ Waiting for what?
> ▸ We'll see!

Our time was up, but the session had been a revealing one. Vicki had shared her embarrassment and pain with me about the enuresis.

The relief had allowed her to play her game and revive the dolls. Were the magic words my plans to try to "cure" Vicki? Were Susy and Patty the two sisters who might possibly become friends and sleep peaceably with each other? However, all was still not safe in the tent. The "wild bear" still lurked out there, and I wondered who it could be.

Vicki was obviously greatly troubled by her inability to remain continent during the night, and it was clear that Katherine's teasing only exacerbated her humiliation.

Enuresis is characterized by repeated, involuntary discharges of urine into the bed by a child aged four or older. Most bed wetters wet several nights a week, or even every night, as Vicki did. A child who occasionally wets is not considered enuretic. Vicki was a "discontinuous bed wetter, that is, a child who had been toilet-trained, was dry for three years, and then after Katherine's birth, began bedwetting; Vicki was jealous and had regressed. She wanted her mother's attention, and bed-wetting was certainly one way to get it.

As many as one out of every four children between the ages of four and sixteen is enuretic, and more boys than girls are bed wetters. About 12 percent of children six to eight years old wet the bed, and some children wet during the day, usually when excited or busily engaged in play. Fortunately, Vicki was not a diurnal (daytime) wetter.

Discontinuous wetting such as Vicki's often appears when a child is under some external stress or is in an emotional crisis that creates anxiety, such as a physical illness, a family move, or, as in Vicki's case, the birth of a sibling. I was certain that Katherine's birth had been instrumental because of Vicki's conversation with me during this session. What puzzled me was why the enuresis continued. It is not unusual for an older sibling to regress when a new baby enters the picture, but Vicki had continued the enuresis over a long period. Were the parents favoring Katherine over Vicki? According to the Thorntons, Katherine was the "easy baby," who did "everything as the books said, right on schedule." Perhaps the Thorntons were not very subtle in their expressions of preference for Katherine. I planned to address this issue in a session with the Thorntons. Meanwhile, my task was to suggest a plan to them for controlling the enuresis. At the same time, it would be important to help Vicki deal with her angry feelings toward Katherine and Paula.

The Plan

The sessions that followed Vicki's "revelation" to me of her enuresis were a repeat of the "camping" and "food" games. She alternated between the "wild bear" that "killed" the children and the "gentle bear" that slept with them and became a "friend." The food game was a simple, repetitive story of a child who wanted to eat and was knocked off the chair by a scolding mother. Vicki was playing out her conflicts about her mother and her sister. Mother could be wild or gentle; sisters could be angry or share a bed. Death and revival seemed to be an expression both of Vicki's self-hate and of her desire to be a healthy, joyous child. There was much to share with the Thorntons, but it seemed to me that the first priority was the enuresis.

Although I was concerned about Vicki's making the statement to her aunt about suicide, it had happened only once. In general, she did not seem to fit the classic picture of a suicidal child. Some researchers have argued that children under the age of ten cannot be called suicidal because they do not appreciate the finality of death. Others have found that very young children do indeed exhibit suicidal behavior even though they do not necessarily believe that death is final. When children have some concept of death and its meaning, and when they see it as a solution to overwhelming emotional problems and a stressful existence, they may be considered suicidal, especially if they manifest certain behavior. Cynthia Pfeffer, a leading researcher in this area, stated that suicidal behavior in children is any self-destructive behavior that they *intend* to hurt themselves seriously or to cause their death. Pfeffer outlined a spectrum of severity: nonsuicidal behavior, suicidal ideas, suicidal threats, mild suicidal attempts, serious suicidal attempts, and, ultimately, suicide.

Vicki's play reflected an outsider, the "wild bear" that harmed the dolls, rather than any intention to harm herself. But I still needed to be alert for other indications that she might be harboring self-destructive thoughts. I decided first, however, to concentrate on helping her with the enuresis. This particular problem was a major cause of her discomfort, self-hate, and, of course, embarrassment with regard to Katherine, the younger sister, who was completely dry at night.

The Thorntons came for their second meeting with me eager to hear my opinions on Vicki's emotional difficulties. I told them of her frankness about the enuresis and how eager she was for a "cure." Several of the suggestions that I made the Thorntons told me they had already tried: they had kept "star charts" rewarding Vicki for dry nights; they had tried to stop all liquid intake after six o'clock in the evening; they had awakened Vicki at about eleven o'clock and taken her to the bathroom; they had required Vicki to change her own sheets in the morning: and they had tried to reduce stress before bedtime by having a quiet time before Vicki went to sleep.

"We have tried everything in the book," Paula said. "Nothing works. We think we're OK for a few days, and then bingo! she's at it again."

"I think it's just the perpetual stress in our home," added Neil. "It's just our way of life—and maybe just Vicki's own constitutional makeup. Katherine doesn't seem to be affected by our two-career family—at least not yet."

"Well," I said, "I do have a plan for you. It's different and may sound extreme. But it works in about 70 percent of cases, and I think it's worth a try. Remember your psychology classes? Well, this is a form of conditioning. It's a special apparatus: a bell-and-pad device. When it's moistened, the pad closes an electrical circuit, which rings a bell and turns on a light. There are some variations on this device. For example, there's an electric alarm that attaches to the shoulder and connects to a small sensor that snaps onto the underwear. This device has no pad and is absolutely shockproof. A drop of moisture sounds the alarm and awakens the child. Soon, Vicki will learn to inhibit urination during her sleep by recognizing her own body signals. Then you can remove the apparatus."

"God, it sounds like training a dog," Paula said. "I'm not crazy about this idea."

"Paula, it's worth a try; give it a chance. You've tried everything else, and as you and Neil said, nothing worked. You can buy this device through a catalog I have. Please think about it. If you are willing, I'll talk to Vicki and prepare her. You'll have to continue with the control of liquids and even continue to wake her up before you go to bed to allow her to urinate. Keep a record, too, of the times when the bell rings, so that you know when her bed-wetting typically occurs. I would keep up a 'star chart,' too, so that Vicki can see her rewards. Gradually, in two to three months, Vicki should be dry at night."

The Thorntons said they would try this method: they didn't need to think about it. I was pleased and gave them the information about the supplier and I told them I'd discuss the plan with Vicki at our next session.

We spent the remainder of this parents' session talking about how both Neil and Paula could offer quality time separately to Vicki and to Katherine. It was important for the Thorntons to recognize that Vicki was indeed jealous of Katherine and often felt rejected by her parents. I described the picture that Vicki had drawn of the family. They were not surprised; they had been aware of Vicki's jealousy of Katherine since her birth. What did distress them was Vicki's elimination of herself from the family picture.

Paula again asked, "Does this mean that Victoria is thinking of suicide?"

"No," I replied, "I don't think it means that, but it does suggest that she feels as if she doesn't fit in. She wants to very much, and the fact that she gives you red hair, Paula, tells me that she very much wants the two of you to be alike and close. Perhaps you can ease up on her for now about her weight. Let's just concentrate on one thing at a time. Right now, it's the enuresis. Of course, I will be alert for any signs of self-destruction, but I think that isn't the crucial issue now."

The Thorntons left. They had at least seemed receptive to the plan for the enuresis. I had also asked them to alert me if they noticed any behavior or words on Vicki's part that suggested self-destructive tendencies.

At our next meeting time, Vicki came in eating a cheese sandwich and carrying a bottle of juice. She put her food on the table and told me that she had had a "bad couple of days." Katherine had stolen her toy lipstick and dress-up kit, and Sylvie "didn't do anything about it," so Vicki had hit Katherine very hard until she cried. Sylvie had scolded Vicki and sent her to her room. Later, Sylvie believed Vicki when she "found the stuff under Katherine's bed."

▸ I guess you felt angry that you were scolded.

▸ Yes, but I'm always to blame. I hate Katherine so much. She pulls my hair when I don't look. She's a sneak.

▸ Can you tell Sylvie when Katherine is mean to you instead of hitting Katherine?

▸ That's no good. She won't believe me. Even when she does, she says Katherine is little and I'm supposed to know better.

▸ Would you like to play Sylvie and Katherine with me?

▸ What do you mean?

▸ Well, I'll be you, and you be Katherine. We'll let Katherine pull my hair. I won't hit her, but I'll call Sylvie. Then you can be Sylvie and come to find out what's wrong.

▸ Well, I'll try, but in real life Sylvie doesn't come—and when she comes, she doesn't help.

▸ But, Vicki, we can still do our play and find out what to do next if Sylvie doesn't help.

Vicki and I role-played the hair-pulling skit with many variations on what Sylvie could do. My emphasis was on using discussion, not physical attacks. Vicki liked this game and decided to act it out with the dolls. I knew that solving the problem with Katherine would take time, but at least Vicki was receptive to the role playing.

Once Vicki had settled down and seemed to have satisfied her need to vent her anger toward Katherine, I told her about our plan for the pad and bell. I described exactly how it would work.

▸ I wet last night. I think I drank too much juice, too. I also wet at Grandma's house on Saturday night. It was so embarrassing. I do want a bell. We'll pay for it!

▸ Vicki, I'm glad you want to try this plan. Mommy and Daddy have agreed to buy a pad and bell for you. I think it will work. But remember, no juice, water, or milk after six. Can you do that?

▸ I can try.

▸ Trying is important. That's a start.

Vicki's Love Boxes

A month after Vicki began using the apparatus, she still had two or three accidents a week, and she seemed discouraged. I gave her support and encouragement, explaining that it would take time. The Thorntons were cooperating by keeping a chart for Vicki, by limiting her liquid intake in the evenings, and by monitoring her bathroom habits, so that they were beginning to get a sense of when Vicki wet. It was generally toward morning—about 4:00 A.M.

Vicki told me that she felt "things were not fair." She called the pad and bell her "device" and was "ashamed" to tell her grandparents about it: "Katherine doesn't need a device, and I feel freaky wearing it." We spent some time discussing Vicki's feelings about her "shame," weighing the good feelings about the dry nights against her feelings of embarrassment and the teasings of Katherine on the wet nights. I did ask the Thorntons to discuss Katherine's teasing with her, and the teasing began to subside.

Paula also began to give Vicki some "special time." One Saturday, for example, she took Vicki to lunch and to the local museum while Neil and Katherine stayed home. This treat was extremely important to Vicki, and it seemed like such a simple thing for Paula to do that I was surprised she had never done it before.

As Paula explained over the phone, "I thought that I had to give the girls equal time, and that if I separated them for a treat, each would be jealous. I guess by giving each one a turn, it is more special. I must admit that I was enjoying myself with Victoria alone. I didn't have the bickering in the car or the teasing that I see between them when we are all together."

Paula then revealed some information about her own childhood: "I was an only child raised by my mom; my dad died when I was eight. My mom didn't care much about how our house looked, and I hated that. I knew that when I grew up, I would be different. I wanted things to look just so, like the houses on television. I guess my mom didn't teach me much either about how to raise kids. I think I do my best, but I never had a good, close mother–daughter relationship while I was a child. I think I'm a little scared by it. I read a lot, but I guess that's not the same as experiencing what it's like to have a mother who does all the mothering things. I sometimes feel as if I'm not equipped to be a mother. I'm trying so hard now, but it still doesn't feel right. My job feels right. I have no trepidation when I'm in the business world. How I wish I could do it all! Maybe in keeping a meticulous home, I've shortchanged my children."

This was an important insight for Paula, and I told her so. I encouraged her in her attempts to interact more with Vicki and also to continue to give Vicki the special times alone, without Katherine.

During our therapy sessions, Vicki enjoyed role-playing family incidents. Each squabble with Katherine was playacted and resolved. We played Vicki's favorite scenes: Katherine jumping on Vicki's bed; Katherine coming into Vicki's room and turning off Vicki's TV; Katherine "stealing" Vicki's toys, favorite candy, and jewelry. In each one of these vignettes, Katherine was the heavy, and Vicki was the victim. Vicki took Sylvie's role and doled out severe punishments for Katherine, such as "two weeks with no friends over," "Katherine's best toys thrown in the garbage," "no dessert," "no TV," "no bedtime stories," and "no 'alone time' with Mommy."

We reversed roles so that Vicki could begin to think of ways to handle Katherine other than by physical attacks. Her severe punishments were her alternatives. I wanted these to subside.

▸ Speak to my parents, Dorothy, tell them how to handle Katherine. They keep telling me to settle things myself, but they don't like how I settle things.
▸ Maybe you can think of some better ways to settle things with Katherine. Can we make a list of some ideas?
▸ I could try.
▸ Let's write some down.

We began our list of ideas. I wanted Vicki to think of less punitive remedies then the ones she used in her play. Gradually, Vicki began to think of some solutions.

▶ I can give Katherine "special time" like my mom gives me.

▶ Vicki, that's great. Maybe that's why Katherine bothers you so much. Maybe she just wants to be with you but doesn't quite know how to be with you in a nice way. Could you show her?

▶ I could, but what if she's still mean to me?

▶ That's a chance you have to take. If she's still mean, you can tell her that your special time won't take place. But remember, your special time will mean sharing some of your things with her.

▶ I hate that!

▶ I know you're not too keen on sharing with her, but look at all the fights you have trying to keep her away from you.

▶ Dorothy, you know that she is my chief botherer.

▶ I know that you feel angry at Katherine lots of times, but sometimes you do like to play with her. You told me that.

▶ I like it if she's good and doesn't tease. When she teases me, I feel sad, and when everyone takes her side, I feel sad, too, like I have no love box.

▶ What do you mean?

▶ I'll show you.

Vicki took the crayons and the drawing pad and drew her family again. Each person was drawn inside a box—a "love box." Vicki also drew herself this time. The drawing was of a tiny girl in a corner of the page. No "love box" protected her, whereas everyone else, even Snowball the cat, was safely tucked into a box. This drawing reminded me of a child I had worked with years before, who had drawn her family with large hearts and left herself heartless and empty, no "heart place." Vicki felt like that child, unloved and alone.

▶ This is a sad picture of you, Vicki.

▶ I feel like everyone laughs at me. My mom laughs, my

dad, Katherine, even Sylvie, 'cause I'm so different. I'm big and I wet and I'm fat and I'm ugly and clumsy. I hate myself. I want to be Miss Perfect.

Vicki burst into tears, and although I tried to comfort her, at first she would not listen to my words: "You feel very sad, Vicki, as if everything is wrong with you. But look at the progress you're making. You're starting to keep dry. You've had fun with your mom, and even Katherine has been nicer to you."

Vicki peeked at me from above her wads of Kleenex, and her crying began to stop. We sat quietly. Vicki asked me not to tack this picture up, but to save it. I suggested that she draw another picture—of something that made her feel good. I didn't want this session to end with so much negative feeling.

Vicki dried her tears and drew a large pink dog with one large spot on its face. She drew small lines on either side of its tail to show "wagging."

▸ This is the dog I wish I had, but with Snowball around, we can't have a dog.
▸ He's lovely. Can we hang up this dog?
▸ Yes. I'll think of a name next time.

Vicki left feeling somewhat better.

I was eager to speak to the Thorntons. Vicki had expressed a very deep feeling of rejection and a very poor self-concept. Despite the small gains so far in her therapy, there was much to do.

The Thorntons and Their Rivalry

When the Thorntons next came to see me, Paula and Neil revealed to me that they were having marital difficulties. They were willing to seek help, and I gave them the name of a marriage therapist. The main issue was Paula's job. She had just been given a promotion to the vice-presidency of her firm. This meant some additional traveling around the country, late-night meetings, and "tons of work" on weekends. Her salary had been increased significantly, she said, "More than Neil's"

Neil was visibly upset by Paula's promotion, but at first, he expressed his distress in terms of the children, who would be "deprived of Paula's time," rather than in terms of his own jealousy and resentment, which were visible despite his attempts to cover them up.

I asked how Paula's new job would affect the children. Paula was aware that she would not be able to give them the "special times" that I had recommended, and she admitted that this was a major concern. However, her solution was that Neil and his parents could "fill in" for her. Neil became furious, and a shouting match ensued, Neil claiming that this was the main problem: Vicki needed *more* of Paula, not *less*.

It was difficult during that visit to keep the Thorntons focused on Vicki. When I finally got them to talk about Vicki's reactions to Paula's new schedule, Paula told me about Vicki's rash. The urine had caused a slight rash in Vicki's genital area and on her thighs because she had stayed in damp pajamas. The doctor had given Paula some ointment, which had apparently helped. The Thorntons seemed pleased by Vicki's progress: she had had one solid week of dry nights, and the rash was disappearing. Neil, however, expressed concern that Vicki would "wet again" because of "Paula's selfishness."

Paula was enraged by Neil's comments and got up to leave, but I urged her to stay so that we could talk about how to help Vicki. Paula was adamant about keeping her job and suggested to Neil that he find "something else in New York" so that the family could have a "normal life."

Neil exploded again. His usual quiet demeanor—his "mask"—was shattered:

"Damn it, we've discussed my job situation hundreds of times. Remember, it was you who wanted to commute. You said it was going to be easy for you. We never planned on you marrying your job. You're a selfish bitch."

It was now impossible to continue this session and focus on the children. Both Thorntons were out of control, and it was obvious that their major concern that evening was their own situation, not its effect on the children. This effect would have to be addressed, but not that evening.

As I witnessed their venom, I felt helpless. When I tried to intervene and calm them, they ignored me completely and continued to accuse each other of being selfish, uncaring, neglectful of the children, and personally ambitious. It was painful to listen to two decent people unleash so much fury, especially when I knew that Vicki and Katherine would suffer from the further strain between their parents. I ended the session by urging them to seek counseling immediately.

Later that evening, Paula called and asked if she could see me alone. Neil was going to a conference the following week, and she wanted to discuss Vicki in a "calm environment." I agreed, and we made an appointment.

In the interim, Vicki's sessions were a reflection of the tension in the Thornton household. Interestingly enough, the "device" was working. Despite the tensions, Vicki was remaining dry. She told me, "There must be a lot of people who wet at night 'cause the store wouldn't have these batteries just for one person." This idea was comforting in some way just knowing that many other children shared her problem and needed an apparatus like hers was helpful to Vicki. Although the enuresis was now coming under control, Vicki's relationships with her mother and with Katherine were still major sources of distress.

Vicki now played two games in addition to "camping." Camping was still a favorite, but the "wild bear" was now more in evidence. The two children "shuddered" when the bear came. The "ranger protected" them and told the bear to "be good and go away forever," but the bear always came back to "scare the children." However, the children no longer "died"; they managed to keep "safe" inside the tent.

Vicki was less tolerant when she played "house." Here the mother (who I was now convinced was also the "wild bear") was constantly a "mean mommy" who "knocks the kids off their chairs."

► Why is Mommy so mean?
► Well, she tells the kids they can't have cake. The father

doesn't try to eat the cake—only the kids. The mother
goes to work, only she doesn't really go. She peeks
through the window to see if the children will take the
cake. When they do, here she comes: "Bad, bad girls!
Don't you dare eat this cake!" She knocks them down.

▶ Those children must feel awful when the mother knocks
them down.

▶ Yes, they do. Awful, awful. What a mother!

▶ Why won't she let them have the cake?

▶ They'll get fat. But they need that cake.

▶ Why do they need it?

▶ I don't know. They just need it.

Vicki stopped the game. She wouldn't tell me what she needed.
It was not the cake, I knew; it was more of her mother's love.
She played the game more frequently than before. Now that her
special time on Saturdays with Paula had been eliminated, Vicki
was distraught. This game alternated with a game she called
"queen."

The queen dressed up in the play clothes: a red cape, a silver
crown, a long boa, a necklace, and a blue skirt. She was very "cruel."
She kept a "sister" locked up in the castle. This sister "can't get free."
"One day, the brother came. He came to rescue the sister. He came
from a far away planet. No matter what he does, he can't get the
sister free. Then he has an idea. He tries a song. Then he tries a
magic emerald. Nothing frees her. The queen is very busy. Nothing
frees the sister. The end."

Vicki played this game during our next sessions with minor
variations. The brother offered the queen different objects, but the
queen refused to let the sister go. Although I had some hypotheses
about its symbolism, this game confused me. Perhaps the queen was
Vicki, in control of Katherine. Was the brother an aspect of Vicki,
the part of Vicki that wanted to "save" Katherine and be kind to
her? If so, that part of Vicki had still not been successful; Vicki had
not yet found a way to be truly kind to her sister and could not
yet completely eliminate her cruel thoughts and gestures toward
Katherine. But I was optimistic. During our role-playing games,
Vicki was more gentle with Katherine and less punitive. One day

she suggested to me that we make a list titled "Can Do–Can't Do."

Here are the "Can Do" items:

Put play makeup on
Watch "Duck Tales"
Watch "Flintstones"
Take Katherine's stuff if she says yes
Watch TV during dinner
Read and sing

Here are the "Can't Do" items:

Hurt Katherine
Pee in bed
Be bad
Hit Katherine
Get wet in the rain
Swim without a grown-up watching

These items were Vicki's own ideas. While writing them down, she asked for help with the spelling, and she said she would tack this list up on her door. When I told her I liked her list and was proud of her idea of making it up, Vicki beamed.

This was the first time that Vicki had spontaneously tried to deal with her problems rather than have me suggest solutions or try to elicit them from her, and it seemed tragic to me that, just as Vicki making progress in expressing her feelings and controlling her bladder at night, she would now have to deal with the Thorntons' marital discord.

Paula's Visit

"I want to apologize for both of us and the way we acted last week. The tension in our house has been awful. In a way, I'm glad Neil is away for a few days. It gives me a chance to think.

"I've been walking around with stomach pains since my promotion, and I know they're not caused by the job and its demands. It's my guilt, my terrible guilt about the girls. But you have to understand. I can be a 'mother' only if I work. When I'm home, I'm truly miserable; I think about what I'm missing out there. As a mother, I'm lousy; in my job I'm great: expert, creative, directed, sure of myself, all the things that make me feel good about myself. At home, I see my failures, my inability to control the children, and my lack of real mothering skills, because I never had a real mother myself, I suppose. Like I told you, mine was a slob, someone who couldn't have cared less about our house. All I ever thought about when I was growing up was how successful and independent I would be. I would like to give Vicki and Katherine love, but I can't stay home."

"Paula, I'm glad you can share your feelings with me, but we have to think of some ways in which you can be available to Vicki and to Katherine. They both need your love. Could you possibly work at home one afternoon? Can you begin to think about this?"

Paula told me that she would give this suggestion some thought. She also told me that she and Neil were starting marriage counseling the following week. She wanted the marriage to work and was "convinced that Neil does, too." I was pleased to hear that the Thorntons were beginning therapy, but I knew that it meant one more late evening a week for both. The sessions were timed so that Paula would come home a little earlier, eat a quick dinner, and have just about enough time to read a brief story to each child. As a special treat, Paula's in-laws had agreed to come over on therapy nights and put the children to bed, helping Sylvie. The arrangement sounded fine; I just hoped it would materialize as planned.

During the remainder of this session, I was able to discuss Vicki's progress. There were still problems with Katherine and Vicki's jealousy of her, but I wanted Paula to know that Vicki was trying to work them out through role playing and through her own games. However, she needed Paula's recognition of her attempts to do so as well. It was also important for Paula to give some suggestion about handling Katherine's incessant teasing of Vicki to Sylvie, who was reluctant to intervene, even when intervention was necessary. Paula listened and seemed appreciative and eager to do "what's right."

Obviously, the next few months would be critical in the marriage and in its effect on Vicki. Because summer was approaching and I would be ending my sessions with Vicki for the month of August, Paula and I discussed various options for her during the summer months, such as traditional day camp or attendance at a day music camp in which she had expressed interest. Paula agreed to explore these options and talk about them with Vicki. The Thorntons also planned a two-week family vacation in August, which I felt would be a wonderful opportunity for some quality time together.

When Paula left, I felt somewhat better than I had after the last session with both parents. It was evident that Paula's career was extremely important to her, but I also recognized that she truly did want her marriage to work, and that she was deeply concerned about her children's happiness. She wanted to be the Supermom, successfully handling career, marriage, and children. Given a choice, I thought, unfortunately, her career would come *before* her marriage and her children. This was te reality that I had to deal with in my work with Vicki.

The Hummingbird

It was time to prepare Vicki for the summer hiatus in our play therapy. Fortunately, Vicki would have some positive things to think about. She had opted for the music program because "I hate sports, and at regular camp, I'll have to do sports." At the camp, she planned to take piano lessons and also to join the chorus. She had a beautiful voice, and the discipline of working with a group would be excellent for her. Vicki's maternal grandmother bought her an upright piano, and Vicki was ecstatic.

Vicki had been dry for over two months, which was important because the music program had scheduled two "overnights"
during the month. Vicki brought her star chart to show me her
progress.

- ▸ Look, I'm dry all the time now.
- ▸ Yes, I see that. I'm proud of you.
- ▸ Katherine can't call me "pee-pee."
- ▸ No, I guess she can't. Does she still tease you?
- ▸ Sometimes she does, but I don't care. I just talk to her—
no hits, no hits.
- ▸ Great. You're getting to be real grown-up.
- ▸ Yes, I am!

Vicki went to the dress-up rack and put on all the frilly clothes,
glitter bows, two boas, and a pink ruffled cape. She flitted around
the room like a hummingbird, darting back and forth, dancing and
singing.

- ▸ You seem pretty happy today. I guess it feels good to
keep dry for such a long time.
- ▸ Well, that's part of it. Music camp is part of it, too. But
guess what's the best part?
- ▸ I can't guess. You tell me.
- ▸ We're going to Disney World in August. What do you
think of that?
- ▸ I think that's just grand. You'll have a lot of fun.
- ▸ I have one worry.
- ▸ What is your worry?
- ▸ I don't want to take the device. But what if I can't stay
dry?
- ▸ If you are dry now and can get up before the alarm, let's
try taking off the device to see if you can still wake your-
self up before you wet.
- ▸ I'd like to try, but I'm scared.
- ▸ I know you feel scared. If it doesn't work, we can use the

device again. You can also take it along to Florida, just in case you need it.

▶ You know what? It's hard to be grown-up. It's easier to be little. When you're little, no one cares if you wet the bed. It's allowed!

▶ Do you want to be little?

A long pause.

▶ No, I guess not, but Dorothy, it is hard to be big!

▶ I know, but you're doing a good job of being grown-up.

Vicki began to dance again. This chubby little redhead who though she was clumsy danced around the room with grace, and from the smile on her face, I knew she liked herself a little bit.

Music Camp

July was a busy time for Vicki. Because music camp involved a five-day nine-to-four schedule, I saw Vicki early Saturday mornings during that month. The Thorntons were trying to work out their problems in counseling, and I saw them only once during July, in a session that was very subdued compared to their previous "fireworks" session. Both also felt more positive about Vicki's progress.

Neil spoke first: "Vicki is like a new person. She smiles more often, practices her piano each evening, and best of all, seems to be getting along better with Katherine."

Paula added, "She's dry most of the time; we've stopped using the alarm, and she's only wet once since we stopped."

"That's all right," I said. "She's been using it for only a short time. Occasional setbacks are not unusual. Do you still keep the star chart?"

"Yes, we do. Victoria is nervous about our Florida trip. She has mentioned this to you?" asked Paula.

"Yes, I think she doesn't want to be the 'baby' on the trip. We have discussed it. Just be patient. Take the alarm along, and don't make a big thing about it. I'm curious: How is the Vicki–Katherine relationship?"

Paula said that it had its "ups and downs." Katherine was alone more with Sylvie and enjoyed the attention. She was jealous of Vicki's piano, but the Thorntons had agreed that Katherine must wait to take lessons because Vicki needed to have accomplishments that were her very own. The major issue was time. Because Vicki was at camp, Paula had not arranged for the day at home during the week to be with Vicki that we had discussed earlier, but she had been trying to spend more time with Vicki on the weekends.

"When school starts in the fall, and when Victoria is back on her routine, I'll try to get home earlier one day to be with the girls. Right now things are going smoothly—with camp, the piano practice, and her therapy on Saturday."

I told the Thorntons about Vicki's dress-up times and her dancing like a hummingbird. It was important for her parents to know that she was beginning to express some joy. I wanted them to keep this joy alive and not destroy it with their marital problems. Realistically, however I knew that the Thorntons' relationship was beyond my control, and that all I could do was support their efforts to remain in marriage counseling. We shook hands and said our good-byes, and I wished them a pleasant vacation. I had one more session with Vicki before our August break and knew that it would be a crucial one.

Vicki's Party

Vicki came bouncing into the playroom and went to the dress-up rack. She put on her many-colored capes and skirts and asked if we could play the ballet music. She enjoyed dancing to the *Nutcracker* melodies and recognized each dance, preferring the "Dance of the Sugarplum Fairy" above all. Our July sessions were reflections of music camp: Vicki danced and sang. She then began a game called "the ballerina and the squirrel."

Vicki was the ballerina and served tea to me, the squirrel. The squirrel ate "squirrel nuts" and also a "whole cake."

▸ It's OK, Squirrel. Eat the whole cake.
▸ It's too much. Can we share it?
▸ No, it's OK. Eat the whole thing.

I was told to eat it with "loud smacking noises."

▸ This is a birthday party for the ballerina. The squirrel is the only one who comes. Everyone else is in Arizona or Florida. Here's milk and sugar for the tea. After we eat, we'll play with the dolls.
▸ Isn't there anyone else besides Squirrel who can come to your party?
▸ No, there is no one but Squirrel.

I remembered Neil's description of Vicki's party. Many children had come, but Vicki had felt that none of them truly cared about her. Was Vicki telling me that she knew I cared for her? Was that why she gave me the whole cake to eat? She knew we were parting for a month. Did she want to be sure that I would be her steadfast friend and would be there for her in the fall? I mentioned that we would not see each other for four weeks. Although I had been preparing Vicki since early in July, this was now her last summer session: reality.

▸ I'll come back in September, won't I, Dorothy?
▸ Yes, you will, and you'll be able to tell me all about Disney World.
▸ I could send you a letter from Florida.
▸ What a good idea! You can certainly do that.
▸ When I come back, you know what?
▸ What?

▸ I'll be in second grade!

▸ Of course. You'll be so big.

▸ I feel good about me. Am I fat?

▸ No, Vicki, you're not fat. I'm glad you feel good about yourself. Lots of things have happened to make you feel good.

▸ I'm dry at night, I can play a little bit on the piano, and I have two friends at camp.

▸ That's a lot of good stuff.

▸ I have bad stuff, too.

▸ Can you tell me?

▸ I have Katherine, I don't see Mommy much, and I hear Mommy and Daddy fight.

▸ Parents fight sometimes.

▸ I feel scared when they fight. They could divorce like Gabriela's parents.

▸ Who is Gabriela?

▸ My friend at camp. She lives with her mother. Her daddy lives in New Jersey. I don't want my daddy to live far away.

▸ Vicki, your family is together. You're going with them on a lovely vacation. I won't see you, but you'll be with your mother and your father and Katherine. Just think about the fun you'll have. And you know what? I'll write down my phone number. You can call me anytime in August if you want to say hello.

I was feeling a little bit sad about this session. It was such a mixture of good things—the first time Vicki had openly admitted that she felt "good"—and her anxiety about her parents. She had sensed the difficulties between them, and their fighting was the validation. I said good-bye to Vicki. She knew I was her friend and that she could call me if she wanted to.

The Thorntons' vacation was scheduled for mid-August. I thought it was important to phone them and alert them to Vicki's concerns and ask that they try not to fight in the presence of the children. The Thorntons received these messages with appreciation, and all I could do now was hope for the best.

September Comes

During August, I received a postcard from Vicki. She sent a Mickey Mouse card, neatly addressed to me. Carefully, she had printed the message: "I'm having fun. I went on lots of rides. I also swimmed a lot. Love, Vicki."

We were starting our sessions again, and I was eager to see Vicki. I had received a note from Paula just before the family had left on vacation, wishing me a "wonderful vacation," but also telling me there had been some "slippage" at night due, Paula thought, to the "excitement" about the Disney World trip. She also mentioned that part of the "device was lost," but she would try to replace it before they left for Florida. I heard no more and assumed that they had found the replacement.

Vicki resumed her therapy by mid-September. She told me that she had "had a great summer." She was bubbly about Florida and delighted with her new teacher.

▶ In school, my teacher said if kids call me silly to ignore them, or to tell them I'm not silly. I could do that—I could really do that, in front of them. I could do that.
▶ That's good. I think that's better than yelling at them, or crying. I'm proud of you.
▶ And you know what? I only wet twice the whole vacation. What do you think of that?
▶ I think that's just wonderful.
▶ But I have to tell you something bad. I called Mommy a dummy. I really didn't mean it. It's like it came out, like a big raindrop came to me and said "dummy."
▶ Did you apologize?
▶ I did, but she didn't listen the way you do.
▶ Maybe you can tell me why you called her dummy.
▶ Well, she was brushing my hair, and it hurt, so this raindrop made me say "dummy."
▶ Sounds as if you were angry. You can tell her when it hurts. Can you do that?

▸ I could.

▸ We can role-play that if you like.

We role-played the hair-combing game. Then Vicki told me other things that angered her, such as Paula's emphasis on diet, her working so hard, and her commuting to New York. Now Vicki was able to *talk* about her worries, rather than use her "camping," "queen," or "house" games. She seemed more mature and more willing to discuss her problems concerning Paula.

Our sessions began to change tone over the next two months. On occasion, Vicki would revert to her game of "house" and the "mommy" who "beat up" the children for eating cake, but when she played this game, it was different. Her new version seemed to be a parody of the earlier game, in which more angry feelings had been expressed. Now Vicki seemed to be laughing at the idea of the "mommy" depriving the children of cake. Vicki told me that she saw her mother as "perfect," but that she, Vicki, didn't want to be "Miss Perfect."

Vicki's relationship with Katherine was much improved. She teasingly told me it was "perfect" with Katherine. What had helped, of course, was Katherine's enrollment in kindergarten. Now Katherine felt important, less like a baby, and did not feel compelled to intrude on Vicki's space.

The one piece in the Thornton puzzle that was still missing was the relationship between Paula and Neil. I tried to schedule a meeting with them early in October, but they canceled it. We didn't meet until the beginning of November, although Paula and I talked briefly on the phone several times. She seemed reluctant to discuss anything over the phone, so I was apprehensive about the November appointment. I wondered what was happening in the marriage, in Paula's job, and, of course, concerning their attitude toward Vicki.

The Thorntons came late for their appointment. Paula had missed her train, so Neil picked her up at the station, and they came directly to the session. She had had no dinner, felt bad about not having seen the girls that evening, and seemed utterly exhausted.

Paula spoke first: "We've been seeing the counselor again since September. I've been giving my life some serious scrutiny, and I think we've decided on a new plan. We're moving back to New

York. Neil will commute now, and I'll have more time with the girls. I know this means an uprooting again for the kids, but we will wait until June to do it. By then, Victoria will adjust to our plans, won't she? It's a trade-off: She'll have more of me. Isn't that what she wants? And we all keep our jobs. That's what I want. Neil says he'll commute."

"How do you feel?" I asked Neil.

"It's for the best. We can't go on like this. It's a strain. Look, I wanted to commute in the first place. Paula was the martyr. I also have more regular hours. I can drive to Connecticut and be home by six or six-thirty. God, we should have stayed in New York. We should have done this in the first place."

"Maybe you needed to try this arrangement in Connecticut to convince yourselves that New York was where you belonged," I said.

"But Dorothy," Paula interrupted, "Victoria had her problems in New York, too. She bed-wet there every night."

"Yes, I know that. I know that some of her problems were not related to the move. I know that she felt unloved and had a poor self-image. She feels better now. She's accomplished so much. I think she'll handle the move back rather easily. We have time to discuss this in our play sessions, and we can all prepare her for the change."

Neil added that this move would be at a good time for Katherine because she would start first grade in her new school. The Thorntons were applying to a private school for the girls, one of the best in New York, and I felt that the girls would do well and thrive there.

But now, I would have to work with Vicki. Changes were always difficult for her, and her attachment to her second-grade teacher in Connecticut was a strong one. I suggested that the whole family visit the new school in the spring if the girls were accepted. I also gave the Thorntons the name of an excellent psychologist for Vicki in New York, in case she had any setbacks.

Paula and Neil appeared to be relieved. I think they'd been afraid that I wouldn't approve of their decision. They were planning to remain in marriage counseling through early spring. As their marriage seemed to be on firmer footing than before, I was optimistic about its continued improvement.

Vicki's Last Months in Therapy

Vicki continued to make great strides in her therapy over November and December. The piano lessons had continued after camp ended, and her plate was full. Vicki's therapy sessions were reduced to once a week so that she could take the music lessons. It was important for her to keep them up because of her pride in her accomplishment.

Reducing the number of sessions with Vicki had no ill effects. She began to make friends, and she began writing out long lists of the children she would invite to her eighth birthday party. Her standing joke about her relationship with Katherine was "perfect, perfect, perfect," always accompanied by a twinkle in her eye. We both knew what this meant. It was our "secret signal," according to Vicki.

Vicki's one major concern now was whether she could "stay dry" on a sleepover. All the girls in her class were going to pajama parties, replete with pizzas, sodas, and rock records. Vicki was invited to these parties but had been reluctant to go. Even though she had had only one accident since September, she was still fearful about her bed-wetting. A particular friend, Amy, had invited Vicki and Gabriela to sleep over. Vicki was worried about drinking soda all evening and how it would affect her.

> ► I'll die if I wet the bed. I'll die.
> ► You can drink only little sips and be sure to go to the bathroom before you go to sleep.
> ► I know, but what if my body doesn't listen when I have to go?
> ► Your body will listen. It's been listening for a long time.
> ► I'm worried, too, about my birthday party.
> ► What are your worries?
> ► What if no one comes?
> ► Everyone worries about that. But you know what? They do come.
> ► Sometimes, Dorothy, I don't know how to feel. I'm

happy, but I don't know if I'm happy. I feel like a love box is coming to me, but I worry.
► You worry about staying happy?
► Yes, yes. What if I don't stay happy?
► Vicki, everyone feels happy sometimes and sad sometimes.
► Is that OK?
► Yes, it's OK. Can you tell me what some of the sad things are?
► Will I have good friends in my new school? It's so hard to make friends. I have some now. What if no one likes me in that school?
► Vicki, I think they'll like you. You're very different from the girl you were before. You like *yourself*, and that's important.
► I do like myself. My love box is private.
► You don't want anyone to know you care for yourself?
► Dorothy, I'll tell everyone when I want to!
► That's all right. You can do just that.

The Love Box

Vicki was enthusiastic about her visit to the private school in New York, and "best of all," the apartment that the Thorntons had purchased was within walking distance of the school. Vicki felt sad about leaving her friends but planned to have sleepovers for them. Her sleepover at Amy's had been a success and had given Vicki the confidence she needed. Her schoolwork was going well. She did need some extra help in arithmetic, but even that was coming along. We agreed that we would say good-bye right after her birthday party. I had been gradually phasing out Vicki's therapy. seeing her in alternate weeks.

As her birthday approached, Vicki did have one setback. She wet a week before her party. Her tears during our session were nonstop, but she managed to get control and explained that she had had a "bad" day in school, that she had fought with Katherine, and that

Mommy hadn't keep her "reading date" with Vicki that night—but had "read to Katherine."

> ▸ So you felt a little bit unloved and jealous again.
> ▸ Yes.
> ▸ When you feel bad and sad, you become like a little baby, I think, and wet.
> ▸ Yes. I think that's why I wet. I was angry at Mommy and Katherine, and I just didn't care.
> ▸ You can control your wetting when you want to.
> ▸ Yes, I really can. You know what? I can do something else when I'm angry.
> ▸ I hope you can. Tell me.
> ▸ I can talk about it the way we do here.
> ▸ That's important, Vicki. Can you truly remember that? Can you talk about your feelings with your mom and dad the way you can in this room?
> ▸ I can. I think I can.
> ▸ If I know you can, we can say good-bye to each other.
> ▸ Do I have to?
> ▸ You're able to help yourself now. Let's try it out for a while. If you need me, I'm here. We've been talking about our last time together for a few weeks now, and after your party, we'll have it.
> ▸ Dorothy, can I draw a picture for you?
> ▸ I'd like that.

Vicki came to the table, chose a red crayon, and drew a girl. On her chest, she drew a box and, inside it, drew a heart, saying, "I have a love box now." She printed the word *love* on the heart. She also drew a "love box" around the girl. Perhaps Vicki felt that she was now enfolded in an atmosphere of love and was also able to love. On the top of the page Vicki printed, "For Dorothy. MY LOVE BOX IS HERE."

Vicki's party was a huge success. She saved me a piece of cake and brought it to our last session.

"Here" she said, "remember when you were the squirrel? This

time I shared the cake with lots of kids. I have lots of friends now."

Indeed, Vicki did have friends now. I was no longer the only one who would receive her friendship, and that was good.

The Thorntons came for their last session with me, too. Paula looked more like her old self—less harried and more composed than she had seemed over the summer and early fall months, when the stress was at its high point. Neil actually seemed excited about the move back to New York. They thanked me for my help and said they would keep in touch.

They did. I heard from the Thorntons a year after they had moved. A brief note from Paula said all was well. She enclosed a picture of Vicki, who was beaming. Paula still called her daughter Victoria—and I think she always will. On the back of the photo, Vicki had printed, "My love box is still here."

EPILOGUE

I often ask myself: How is Lois? Has she finally worked through her grieving for Jean? Is Perry able to maintain control of his aggression? Will Tom be a whole young man—or only half a person like the figure he once drew for me? And Barbara—does she still want to search for Anthony, the father she never saw? Is Marty able to learn in school? Will Vicki maintain her "love box"?

Part of the work I do has a down side: the loss of contact with the children after the therapy is over. Sometimes I have called a former client, and sometimes a parent has called me months or even years later either to give me some good news or to ask for another appointment. This is rare. Usually, when a case is completed, I no longer hear from the parents. I like to think the reason is that all is well, and that if there is a problem, the children have learned to face situations on their own. From both research and my own experience, I know that after psychotherapy, children generally do function better. Sometimes, too, parents' reluctance to initiate therapy again may be based on their unwillingness to face their own problems and how these problems are affecting their children.

I often reflect on the relationships of the spouses in the six families I have discussed in this book. I especially think about the fathers. Generally, they were more distant and less informative than their wives; and I had more contact with the mothers because they usually brought the children to my office, enabling me to talk more to them and to get more of their day-to-day input. Of course, there were the exceptions. Perry's father was the more stable, giving parent, whereas his mother remained cold and aloof.

In thinking about these six children, I find that I am hard on myself. I look back at my notes and see places where I could have said more—or could have said less. Writing this book was a heart-wrenching process for me. I relived each case, and many memories of these children and their suffering flooded me. I found that I thought about them continuously as I tried to put their feelings on paper. In reviewing my notes, I also found significant benefits in working with the children I am currently seeing. For these benefits, I am grateful. Each of the six children helped me sharpen my skills so that part of their growth process has led, in some way, to the healing of another child. That perhaps is their legacy: out of their pain, I learned more about my own strengths—and weaknesses. I learned to listen with a keener ear, to observe with a clearer eye, and to enlarge my capacity for empathy. I have recognized, too, how important it is for parents to establish what Erik Erikson called "basic trust" for their children. The early years are critical in a child's life. If a child is afforded the love, consistent care, and respect in her or his first few years, the child will find it immeasurably easier to cope with adversity later on.

In my work, a key theme is helping a wounded child learn how to trust an adult. Through that trust comes a willingness to interact more positively with others and gains in the children's sense of themselves. Once each child has learned self-respect and self-esteem, I know it's time to begin our good-byes.

There is a temptation to play God when one is a psychotherapist, a feeling that one can have a sustained influence over the lives of others. But life for these children will be long and complicated, fraught with new challenges and perhaps even further losses or tragedies. What I have seen, however, is that when they emerge from the therapy, children have a greater trust in their capacity to face problems head-on.

SUGGESTED READINGS

INTRODUCTION

O'Connor, K. J. (1991). *The play therapy primer.* New York: Wiley.

Piaget, Jean. (1962). *Play, dreams and imitation in childhood.* New York: W. W. Norton.

Schaefer, C. E., Gitlin, K., and Sandgrund, A. (Eds.). (1991). *Play diagnoses and assessment.* New York: Wiley.

Singer, D. G., and Singer, J. L. (1990). *The house of make believe.* Cambridge: Harvard University Press.

CHAPTER 1

Altschul, S. (Ed.). (1988). *Childhood bereavement and its aftermath.* Madison, CT: International Universities Press.

Freud, S. (1917). *Mourning and melancholia: Vol. 14. Standard Edition.* London: Hogarth.

Gesell, A., and Ilg, F. (1946). *The child from five to ten*. New York: Harper.

Kane, Barbara. (1978). A Piagetian discussion of the development of children's concepts of death. In R. Weizman, R. Brown, P. J. Levinson, and P. A. Taylor (Eds.). *Piagetian theory and the helping professions*. (pp. 65–72). Los Angeles: Children's Hospital of Los Angeles and the University of Southern California Schools of Social Work and Education.

Kübler-Ross, E. (1964). *On death and dying*. New York: Macmillan.

Nagy, Maria. (1948). The child's theories concerning death. *Journal of Genetics and Psychology, 73*, 3–27.

Osterweis, M., and Townsend, J. (1988). *Helping bereaved children: A booklet for school personnel*. DHHS Publication No. (ADM) 88–1553. Rockville, MD: U.S. Department of Health and Human Services.

Piaget, Jean. (1962). *Play, dreams and imitation in childhood*. New York: W. W. Norton.

Piaget, Jean. (1976). *The child's conception of the world*. Totowa, NJ: Littlefield, Adams.

Shibles, Warren. (1974). *Death: An interdisciplinary analysis*. White Water, WI: Language Press.

CHAPTER 2

Bandura, A. (1973). *Aggression: A social learning analysis*. Englewood Cliffs, NJ: Prentice-Hall.

Barker, R. G., Dembo, T., and Lewin, K. (1941). Frustration and regression: An experiment with young children. *University of Iowa Studies in Child Welfare, 18*, 1–314.

Baron, R. A. (1977). *Human aggression*. New York: Plenum Press.

Buss, Arnold. (1971). Aggression pays. In J. L. Singer (Ed.), *The control of aggression and violence* (pp. 7–18). New York: Academic Press.

Dollard, J., Doob, L. W., Miller, N. E., Mowrer, O. H., and Sears, R. R. (1939). *Frustration and aggression*. New York: McGraw-Hill.

Frey, D. E. (1986). Communication board games with children. In

Charles E. Schaefer and Steven Reid (Eds.), *Game play* (pp. 21–39). New York: Wiley.

Gardner, R. A. (1969). The game of checkers as a diagnostic and therapeutic tool in child psychotherapy. *Acta Paedopsychiatrica*, *38*, 140–153.

Geiger, L. E. (1991, March 26). A group treatment model for child reactions of violence. Paper presented at American Orthopsychiatric Conference, Toronto, Canada.

Gorer, Geoffrey. (1941). Mimeographed paper, Institute of Human Relations, Yale University. Reproduced in Martha Wolfenstein, (1955). *Childhood in contemporary cultures* (p. 31). Chicago: University of Chicago Press.

Huesmann, L. R., and Malamuth, N. M. (Eds.). (1986). Media violence and antisocial behavior. *Journal of Social Issues*, *42*(3).

Kramer, E. (1971). *Art as therapy with children*. New York: Schocken.

Kramer, E. (1979). *Childhood and art therapy*. New York: Schocken.

Lusebrink, V. B. (1990). *Imagery and visual expression in therapy*. New York: Plenum.

Nickerson, E. T., and O'Laughlin, K. S. (1983). The therapeutic use of games. In Charles Schaefer and Kevin J. O'Connor (Eds.), *Handbook of play therapy* (pp. 174–187). New York: Wiley.

Olweus, Dan. (1980). Familial and temperamental detriments of aggressive behavior in adolescent boys: A causal analysis. *Developmental Psychology*, *16*, 644–60.

Piaget, Jean. (1976). *The child's conception of the world*. Totowa, NJ: Littlefield, Adams.

Straus, Murray A. (1980). A sociological perspective on the causes of family violence. In Maurice R. Green (Ed.), *Violence and the family* (pp. 7–31).

CHAPTER 3

Blumberg, Marvin L. (1984, October). Sexual abuse of children. *Pediatric Annals*, *13*(10) 753–758.

Child victims of exploitation: A fact sheet. (1985, October 31). Washington, DC: U.S. House of Representatives, Select Committee on Children, Youth and Families,

Finkelhor, David. (1986). *A source book on child sexual abuse.* Beverly Hills, CA: Sage.

Finkelhor, D., and Browne, A. (1985, October). The traumatic impact of child sexual abuse: A conceptualization. *American Journal of Orthopsychiatry, 55*(4), 530, 541

Goodman, G. S., and Aman, C. (1990). Children's use of anatomically-detailed dolls to recount an event. *Child Development, 61,* 1859–1871.

Kolko, D. J. (1988). Educational programs to promote awareness and prevention of child sexual victimization: A review and methodological critique. *Clinical Psychology Review, 8,* 195–209.

Magnuson, E., Grant, M., and Wilde, J. (1983, September 5). Child abuse: The ultimate betrayal. *Time,* pp. 20–22.

Psychiatric News. (1989, January 20), Dolls often misused in dealing with suspected sex abuse victims, p. 4.

Saunders, B. E., Kilpatrick, D. G., Lipovsky, J. A., Resnick, H. I., Best, C. L., and Sturges, E. T. (1991, March 25). Prevalence, case characteristics, and long-term psychological effects of child sexual assault: A national survey. Paper presented at a meeting of the American Orthopsychiatric Association, Toronto, Canada.

Sgroi, S. M. (1982) *Handbook of clinical intervention in child sexual abuse.* Lexington, MA: Lexington Books.

Watson, R., Lubenow, G. C., Greenberg, N. F., King, P., and Junken, D. (1984, May 14). A hidden epidemic—Special report. *Newsweek,* pp. 30–36.

CHAPTER 4

Kazdin, A. (1975). *Behavior modification in applied settings.* Homewood, IL: Dorsey.

Piaget, Jean. (1976). *The child's conception of the world.* Totowa, NJ: Littlefield, Adams.

Rothstein, A., Benjamin, L., Crosby, M., and Eisenstadt, K. (1988). *Learning disorders: An integration of neuropsychological and psychoanalytic considerations.* Madison, CT: International Universities Press.

Schaefer, C. E., and Millman, H. L. (1981). *How to help children with common problems*. New York: Van Nostrand Reinhold.

Sherman, W. M. (1990). *Behavior modification*. New York: Harper & Row.

Singer, D. G., and Revenson, T. A. (1978). *A Piaget primer: How a child thinks*. New York: New American Library.

Slovenly Peter. Quoted in G. Weiss (1991), Attention deficit hyperactivity disorder. In M. Lewis (Ed.), *Child and adolescent psychiatry: A comprehensive textbook* (pp. 544–561). Baltimore: Williams & Wilkins.

Tyron, A. S., Kane, S. P. (1986). Promoting imitative play through generalized observational learning in autistic-like children. *Journal of Abnormal Child Psychology, 14(4)*, 537–549.

Van Berckelaer-Onnes, I. (1986). Different play in different children: Implications for treatment. In R. van der Kooij and J. Hellendoorn (Eds.), *Play–play therapy–play research* (pp. 133–143). The Netherlands: Swets & Zeitlinger.

Vitulano, L. A., and Tebes, J. K. (1991). Child and adolescent behavior therapy. In M. Lewis (Ed.), *Child and adolescent psychiatry: A comprehensive textbook* (pp. 812–831). Baltimore: Williams & Wilkins.

CHAPTER 5

Bloom, B. L. (1988). *University of Colorado separation and divorce program: A program manual*. DHHS Publication No. (ADM) 88-1556. Rockville, MD: U.S. Department of Health and Human Services.

Camara, K. A., and Resnick, G. (1989). Styles of conflict resolution and cooperation between divorced parents: Effects on child behavior and adjustment. *American Journal of Orthopsychiatry, 59*(4) 560–575.

de Mille, Richard. (1973). *Put your mother on the ceiling*. New York: Viking Press.

Healy, J. M., Jr., Malley, J. E., and Stewart, A. J. (1989). Children and their fathers after parental separation. *American Journal of Orthopsychiatry, 60*(4), 531–543.

Johnson, E., Sechels, E., and Sayres, F. (1970). *Anthology of children's literature*. Boston: Houghton Mifflin.

Johnston, J. R., Kline, M., and Tschann, J. M. (1989). Ongoing post-divorce conflict: Effects on children of joint custody and frequent access. *American Journal of Orthopsychiatry, 59*(4), 576–592.

Kalter, N., Kloner, A., Schreier, S., and Okla, K. (1989). Predictions of children's postdivorce adjustment. *American Journal of Orthopsychiatry, 59*(4), 605–618.

Leuner, H., Horn, G., and Klessman, E. (1983). *Guided affective imagery with children and adolescents*. New York: Plenum Press.

National Institute of Public Health. (1981). *Caring about kids: When parents divorce*. DHHS Publication No. (ADM) 81-1120. Rockville, MD: U.S. Department of Health and Human Services.

Pfeffer, Cynthia R. (1986). *The suicidal child*. New York: Guilford Press.

Wallerstein, J. S., and Corbin, S. B. (1989). Daughters of divorce: Report from a ten-year follow-up. *American Journal of Orthopsychiatry, 59*(4), 593–604.

CHAPTER 6

Freud, Sigmund. (1908). Creative writers and day-dreaming. In *The Standard Edition of the complete psychological works of Sigmund Freud*, Vol. 9, (pp. 143–144). London: Hogarth.

Pfeffer, Cynthia R. (1986). *The suicidal child*. New York: Guilford Press.

Schaefer, Charles E., and Millman, Howard L. (1981). *How to help children with common problems*. New York: Von Nostrand Reinhold.

EPILOGUE

Erikson, E. H. (1963). *Childhood and society*. New York: W. W. Norton.

INDEX